Rising *to the* Challenge

100 Years of the
Ladies Scottish Climbing Club

1908 – 2008

HELEN STEVEN

SCOTTISH MOUNTAINEERING TRUST

Dedication

In memory of my father, Campbell Steven, who introduced me to the hills and Christina Macnair who introduced me to the LSCC.

ISBN 978-1-907233-12-8
A catalogue record for this book is available from the British Library

This book is published by the Scottish Mountaineering Trust, a charitable trust registered in Scotland. Revenue from books published by the Trust is used for the continuation of its publishing programme and for charitable purposes associated with Scottish mountains and mountaineering. Visit <www.smc.org.uk/trust/trust.htm> for more information

Front cover:
Main picture, Beinn a' Bheithir; Sgòrr Dhònuill from Sgòrr Dhearg
Richard Wood
Below from left, Founder members Mabel and Jane Inglis Clark, 1905 *LSCC Archives*; Anne Murray climbing in Glen Coe *Anne Murray Collection*; Helen Geddes climbing Ardverikie Wall, Binnein Shuas *Mary Lothian*; Eilidh Nisbet and Helen Steven climbing Ardverek, Greenland *Mora McCallum*

Produced and co-designed by Tom Prentice for Scottish Mountaineering Trust (Publications) Ltd
Typesetting and co-design: Ken Crocket
Printed and bound in India at Replika Press Pvt Ltd

Distributed by Cordee Ltd,
(t) 01455 611185, (w) www.cordee.co.uk

Contents

Foreword
& Acknowledgements

The idea of writing a history of the LSCC had its origins about ten years ago when I was staying at the Club hut at Kincraig. We were ambling down Glen Feshie after a pleasant day on the tops, and as the discussion rambled on it gradually became apparent that I seemed to have been nominated as the happy author.

In some ways I seemed an obvious choice. I was a historian by training. As far as the hills were concerned my father, Campbell Steven, was a member of the SMC and had taken me up my first Munro at the age of six (some might say I didn't stand a chance). I joined the LSCC at the plump and rosy-cheeked age of 17, when some of the original members were still alive.

Founder, Mabel Jeffrey, taught me how to use an ice-axe, Christina Macnair introduced me and encouraged me into the Club, Barbara Macfarlane gave me her tweed knickerbockers (!), May Green taught me how to be rebellious, and A.E.Robertson's wife, Winifred, taught me manners. I owe a great debt of gratitude to these intrepid early pioneers of women climbing.

As it progressed I discovered what a privilege it was to be writing the history. The more I researched and read and wrote, the more memories of good days and grand companions came flooding back. Of Anne Littlejohn, Mora McCallum, Eilidh Nisbet and Alison Dinwoodie who shared so many epic adventures with me in Scotland, Norway and Greenland; on rock climbs, snow pitches, bog-trotting and kayaking. To all those friends of the days before the knees stiffened, thank-you.

And the more I read, the more I admired all these women in our Club who pushed the boundaries for women climbers. The first woman Munroist, first women's expedition to the Himalayas, first women's expedition to Greenland, and so on and on, an unfolding story of bravery, imagination and sheer good fun.

As far as the actual writing is concerned many people have helped me and I can only name but a few. Thank you to all those who lent me their diaries and memoirs and sent me stories – Eilidh Nisbet, Suilven Strachan, Rhona Weir, Pat Brown, Mary Lothian, Kate Ross, Alison McLure, Marion Boyle. A special thank you to Eilidh Nisbet and Diana Preston who combed through the text for errors.

The book would be a mere shadow of itself without the wonderful photos from our archives, and for that a huge thanks must go to Alison Higham and John who worked endless hours digitising photos. Thank you too to our archivists Margaret Jones and Marion Boyle and our former librarian Janet King, and also to the Club through the years for keeping such good records.

It is especially good in view of our long-standing links with the Scottish Mountaineering Club to have the book published by the

Scottish Mountaineering Trust, and thanks are due to Tom Prentice for his encouragement.

Any author has moments (hopefully few) of being hard to live with and so, many thanks to Ellen Moxley who lived through the chaos of papers, and took lots of time to read my text critically and carefully.

Most of all my thanks go to all the members of the LSCC past and present who are still making history.

Helen Steven
Raffin, Lochinver 2010

*Mabel and Jane Inglis
Clark, right, founder
members, 1905*

LSCC Archives

1: Stepping Out Boldly

NOT FAR FROM THE JUNCTION between the A85 and the A827, the
road between Lix Toll and Killin, there is a large boulder with a ledge
running up one side enabling the energetic to scramble up to the top.
It is presently hidden deep in forestry planting, but to some it is a boulder of great significance and has already been the scene of more than
one anniversary celebration. In the lee of this mighty boulder on April
18th 1908 the Ladies Scottish Climbing Club was founded.

History no longer relates exactly why three women were sheltering
there; maybe they were waiting for their husbands to return after a big
day in the hills; maybe they were simply taking shelter themselves from
a blatter of April sleet; maybe they were waiting for a horse and trap
to take them to the railway station at Killin. We can picture them
huddled there, turning tweed-clad shoulders against the icy wind, holding onto their wide hats, perhaps muttering about the late arrival of
their men-folk. Whatever the reason, these women were hatching great
ideas.

Jane Inglis Clark, her daughter Mabel, and Lucy Smith had all three gained considerable climbing experience in both Scotland and the Alps in company with their husbands and brothers, who were members of the Scottish Mountaineering Club, which had been founded in 1889. Jane Inglis Clark was the wife of William Inglis Clark, President of the SMC from 1913 – 1919. Both her son Charles and her daughter Mabel were keen climbers, and at this particular time they had joined up with Lucy Smith, daughter of William Smith, also a former President of the SMC, for a climbing holiday in Killin.

This is how the SMC Journal for September 1908 records the event.

Lucy Smith, the third founder member

LSCC Archives

> The Ladies Scottish Climbing Club. The Victorian Era has seen the rise of many things, and the lot of man, collectively, has improved beyond conception. Sport in its many aspects has advanced with rapid stride, and woman, making up the leeway of centuries, has jostled to the front to take her place alongside man in the many active pursuits so long considered to be alone suited for the masculine persuasion. But although women had shared in the joys of mountaineering with their husbands, brothers, or guides, it has been left to the present gracious reign to find lady climbers banding themselves into Clubs with the same aims as those of the various male Climbing Clubs. Last year the Ladies Alpine Club came into existence, and now the Ladies' Scottish Climbing Club has not only been formed, but has carried out several highly successful meets. Perhaps a few lines may be spared to tell of its inception, organisation and aims. In its origin it has been so much bound up in its relation with the SMC that I imagine my fellow-members will wish to know more about it, and to wish it a successful career. During the month of April, the daughter of our former President, Mr W.C.Smith, (Lucy Smith) was spending a short holiday with my wife (Jane Inglis Clark) and daughter (Mabel Inglis Clark) at Killin, the special object of which was to carry out climbing expeditions in the neighbourhood. Some were accomplished guideless, others in company with members of the SMC The idea of a Ladies' Climbing Club has often been mooted before, and this now soon became an accomplished fact, the actual date of its birth being April 18th.

Interesting to note that the men of the SMC cast themselves in the role of 'guides' for their errant sisters!

Perceptions differ, and Jane Inglis Clark's account in the LSCC Journal of the founding of the Club is rather gentler and more matter of fact than her husband's description of woman 'jostling to the front to take her place'.

> Personally I have found it an extraordinary privilege to have been one of the pioneers of this sport and one of the founders of the LSCC.
>
> I have no doubt that members of the Club will be interested to hear how this came about.
>
> Our daughter and son had climbed with us from their earliest years, and when the former had begun to gather climbing friends around her, the idea, long in my mind, of forming a Ladies' Climbing Club took shape. At Killin on April 18th, 1908, when Lucy Smith was spending an Easter holiday with us, we three – Lucy, Mabel and I – formed the resolution that we would there and then found the Ladies' Scottish Climbing Club. A boulder above Lix Toll, Glen Dochart, marks the spot where this momentous decision was made.

It is hard to imagine nowadays with hindsight the amount of 'resolution', determination and energy required by these essentially conventional middle-class ladies to assert their right to be different and climb independently of their menfolk. The Ladies Alpine Club, the first women's climbing club in Britain, had been founded only the year before. These Scottish women were experienced alpine climbers with the additional advantage of the growing discovery of Scotland as a serious climbing playground, as Jane Inglis Clark so eloquently describes.

> When I made the astounding discovery that I was a rock climber, I took 'climbing fever' rather badly. Thanks to my husband, I had eleven years of wonderful climbing experience with him. Each summer season saw us either in Switzerland or Tyrol; a long list of giants of the Alps and 'blue-ribbon' climbs of the Dolomites stand to our credit, some of them being first ascents. In winter it was no uncommon thing to take the 4am train to Crianlarich or Tyndrum and climb the Highland hills in snow, returning the same night. We also had the privilege of making first ascents in Scotland under the brilliant leadership of Mr Harold Raeburn and other members of the Scottish Mountaineering Club.

From its small beginnings behind a boulder, the Club grew rapidly. By 1911 an article published in *Madame Magazine*, entitled 'Madame at Sport' shows how rapidly the Club was growing in confidence .

> The Ladies Scottish Climbing Club is a society rapidly growing in members and repute. It has now been established some four or five years, and during that time, many useful and interesting climbs have been accomplished by parties and individuals...The Club had a most successful meet in Glencoe during Easter this year. Very trying conditions were experienced, as the weather was most stormy and unsettled; snow lay deep on the hills, and a fearful gale prevailed for three days. Each party encountered blizzards on the summits, and the new snow made the ascents most difficult. However, in spite of all, several good climbs were made. Bidean nam Bian (the highest of the Argyllshire peaks) was climbed by a snow gully – with an icy pitch in it – on a terrible day, and on the ridge several of the party were blown down by the terrific force of the wind. Another party had a fine rock climb on a buttress of rock on Sron na Creise, a peak overlooking Kingshouse Inn.

To go back to its beginnings, the first meeting was held in Edinburgh on May 27th 1908, a committee appointed and a constitution agreed. The stated aim of the Club was –

> ...to bring together Ladies who are lovers of mountain-climbing, and to encourage mountaineering in Scotland, in winter as well as in summer.

It is worth noting here perhaps that the Club has had subsequent moves to amend our Constitution to become politically correct 'women' rather than 'ladies', but to date a rather affectionate nostalgia for our historical roots always wins the day. Hats, however, are no longer required!

Right from the start there was no doubt but that these were 'Ladies' in every sense of the word. In 1908 only the wealthy could afford annual trips to the Alps and the use of alpine guides, and only the wealthy had the leisure to spend long weekends in the highlands, often staying in

hotels. These were well-off middle-class ladies, often married to professional men, such as doctors or ministers, in a pre-First World War society
of fairly stratified class division. The Inglis Clarks owned the first auto-
mobile in Edinburgh, and along with the car came not only the driver,
but also hampers of food brought by the housekeeper. Many long days
on the hill in those early days were made possible by the driver taking
the car to a distant rendezvous and waiting. One account of a day's walking near Moffat concluded.

> The steep side of Saddle Yoke was descended to Blackhope Burn, and from
> there some of the party walked back to Moffat by the high road, while those
> who preferred to drive returned by carriage, having ordered the conveyance
> to await them at Blackhope Farm.

Of course they were dressed like ladies as well. These women set off
for their climbs – and even rock climbed – in long skirts and hats. Jane
Inglis Clark writes in retrospect.

> There were no sports clothes for women in those days. It was almost impos-
> sible to get suitable strong boots, and for a long time I had to wear either
> boys' boots or buy them in Tyrol. The whole tyranny of clothes has disap-
> peared since then. Clothing for women is now practical and hygienic. Perhaps
> mountaineering for women has had an appreciable influence for good upon

*May Meet, Arrochar,
1908. The First Meet
of the Club. From
left: I.McBride, Kitty
Stuart, Daisy Gillies,
Jane Inglis Clark,
Lucy Smith*

LSCC Archives

OUTFIT for WINTER CLIMBING IN SCOTLAND.
(ADVISED BY THE LADIES SCOTTISH CLIMBING CLUB—OCTOBER 1908).

CLOTHES.

*STRONG BOOTS, with Low Heels and Mountain Nails.
*THICK STOCKINGS.
PUTTEES OR GAITERS, to keep out Snow.
TWEED KNICKERS.
*SHORT SKIRT.
*WOOLLEN UNDERWEAR.
*WOOLLEN BLOUSE.
SLOUCH FELT HAT.   2/6 at Jenner's, Princes Street, Edinburgh.
*WOOLLEN CAP (or Shetland Helmet) 1/6 at Jaeger's, Princes Street, Edinburgh.
1 PAIR WOOLLEN GLOVES with Fingers.
*SNOW GLOVES—this Pattern 🖑 at Jaeger's, Princes Street, Edinburgh.
SHETLAND JERSEY.
*JACKET, GOLF JERSEY, OR SWEATER.
SHETLAND MUFFLER.
WATERPROOF CAPE, or a "Wettermantel."

IMPLEMENTS.   ACCESSORIES.
*ICE-AXE and Sling for Axe.   *RUCKSACK.
ROPE.   LANTERN AND CANDLES.
*COMPASS.   SPIRIT FLASK.
*MAPS.   POCKET KNIFE.
                               MATCHES.
                               STRING.

* Those with "Stars" are absolutely essential.

Any inquiries regarding Purchases should be made to the Honorary Secretary.

LSCC leaflet issued to members listing suitable winter climbing outfit, 1909

LSCC Archives

Dame Fashion! Let us hope that gone for ever are skirts that trailed in dust or mud, the hats that did not fit but had to be held on firmly – sometimes with both hands!

How awkward that must have been for hard rock routes! However breeches were often worn underneath the skirts, and the tiresome skirts hidden behind some convenient boulder. There is a delightful tale of two women returning from a day on the hills to collect their skirts from where they had been hidden, only to find a shepherd standing guard with his dog. Looking the ladies up and down somewhat severely, he removed his pipe to comment dryly, 'Aye, ye'll have come back for your wee bits o'decency'!

In its early days the Club issued newly aspiring members with an illustrated leaflet showing suitable mountain gear. Headed 'Outfit for Winter Climbing in Scotland. (Advised by the Ladies Scottish Climbing Club – October 1908)' it lists the following.

Strong Boots, with Low Heels and Mountain Nails
Thick Stockings.
Puttees or Gaiters, to keep out Snow.
Tweed Knickers.
Short Skirt.
Woollen Underwear.
Woollen Blouse.
Slouch Felt Hat. 2/6 at Jenner's, Princes Street, Edinburgh
Woollen Cap (or Shetland Helmet) 1/6 at Jaeger's, Princes St., Edinburgh
1 Pair Woollen Gloves with Fingers
Snow Gloves (pattern enclosed) at Jaeger's, Princes Street, Edinburgh
Shetland Jersey.
Jacket, Golf Jersey or Sweater
Shetland Muffler.
Waterproof Cape, or a 'Wettermantel'

Implements	Accessories
Ice-Axe and sling for Axe	Rucksack
Rope	Lantern and Candles
Compass	Spirit Flask
Maps	Pocket Knife
	Matches and String

Contrast that outfit with an advertisement for a Walking-Gown for the Summer published in *The Woman at Home* in the same year.

Smart walking-gown of striped alpaca in shades of chestnut and white, the coat and bands on skirt being of plain alpaca. Waistcoat and rosettes of black satin. Hat of white Leghorn, draped with chestnut-brown silk and brown roses.

One of the great joys of mountaineering gear (until recently, that is) is that fashion has never been the arbiter. Indeed one might almost say that climbers competed for the ultimate in scruffiness. Molly Johnstone, who joined the Club in 1948 reminisces about changing styles of clothing and the spirit of make-and-mend.

A well-dressed woman climber in the late twenties had a tailored jacket with belt, with breeches to match. I inherited Winifred Robertson's suit and wore them in Chamonix in 1954. My first rope was 60ft of full weight hemp – devilish to coil and a heavy pull when leading and wet.

During the Second World War, reasonably priced clothing was rationed by coupons and climbing equipment was available in some sports shops. At first school jersey, reversible golf blouse and my school trench coat with the bottom cut off to make a hood sufficed. In winter I wore a leather motorcycle helmet with a fur lining inherited from my step-grandmother. I had two pairs of baggy ski trousers and ex-land army corduroy breeches. My father-in-law made me an ice-axe from a mattock head and wheel shaft. This did me for several years until I got an ex-War Department Danny axe.

What a difference from the present day where climbing shops abound, hung around with glistening gear, and it is possible to acquire a jacket much reduced in price in the end-of-season sales because it is 'last year's colours, madam'!

To return to our enthusiasts of 1908, the Club also set up a library of books and maps, which has continued to grow and be enlarged right up to the present day, and they also purchased a 'Club Climbing Outfit, consisting of rope, lantern and compass, to be had from the Hon. Treasurer on application' and to be returned within a week.

Qualifications necessary for membership were also laid out at the first committee meeting. They decided on a minimum of:

> Four peaks over 3000 feet in Scotland
> Two climbs in snow (not included in the above)
> Two rock climbs of sufficient difficulty
> These climbs not to have taken place in one season, but over a period of three years.
> More qualifications might usually be necessary, and in some cases exception might be made.

As can be seen these qualifications were somewhat vague. Applications were made in writing and scrutinised by the committee, which had the 'power of judging unquestioned the qualifications of candidates for election', after which the whole club held a postal ballot on whether or not to accept the candidate. All somewhat arbitrary and exclusive by today's standards, as it is clear that there was ample scope for blackballing.

A year later these rules were revised to include a hillwalking category and names in the record of membership are listed as 'climbing' or 'hillwalking'. As standards and attitudes change over the years, so membership qualifications remain a live issue, frequently being revived and amended and always providing lively fodder for debate at Annual General Meetings. At present the Club has two categories, graduating and full membership, depending on the amount of experience on the Scottish hills, and also how much climbing the aspiring member has done with the Club. Whereas climbing standards have become increasingly regulated over the years, the LSCC puts the emphasis not so much on the number of routes accomplished to a certain grade as on general all-round competence on rock and snow in all kinds of weather conditions.

The first New Year Meet, Crianlarich, 1908/09. From left: Lucy Smith, Kitty Stuart, Ruth Raeburn, Jane Inglis Clark, M.Eckhardt, I.McBride, Pauline Ranken

LSCC Archives

Inevitably Club membership fluctuates, going through energetic, pioneering times, when new climbers are attracted, and then entering a period of doldrums, when members age and membership falls off. During the Second World War the Club went through such a phase, partly due to the curtailment of activities caused by the war and petrol rationing. One Meet immediately post-war attracted only four members. In a bid to attract younger blood, the Club began actively recruiting from both Edinburgh and Glasgow University Mountaineering Clubs, and this quickly bore fruit during the '50s and '60s with keen young hill-walkers and good rock climbers such as Elma Wrench, Molly Johnstone, Cynthia Marr and Rhona Weir joining the Club. To these keen young, devil-may-care students, the older founding members must have seemed formidably daunting throw-backs to another era. Rhona Weir's comment was that the old seemed *very* old and *very* experienced. Fortunately, however, every new generation of climbers has received a warm welcome, and these older stalwarts have always been generous in sharing their experience.

The pattern of weekend outings was soon developed and, with some minor amendments, the basic outline has remained virtually unchanged. Four Meets a year were held at New Year, Easter, the Edinburgh or Glasgow holiday weekend in May and the September holiday weekend. These were usually held in hotels, and early records and photographs show Crianlarich, Inveroran and Kingshouse in Glencoe as favourites. Gradually as membership of the Club grew and social conditions changed, the tradition of hotels changed to become one of camping, bothying or hostelling, with a handy B&B nearby for the more sybaritic or the less agile. However, even as late as the 1960s, the author (then an impoverished student!) recalls raising the question of a camping alternative, and being told that 'any member of *this* club can afford a hotel'. Fortunately such days are long past.

Of more recent years with the advent of flexible working hours, and the dates of Meets no longer bound by set holidays at Christmas, Easter, the Glasgow Fair, Victoria Day, or the Queen's Birthday, the pattern of Meets has changed. Nowadays a Club outing is arranged almost every weekend of the year, often with an Alpine Meet in the summer. Also Island Meets in the summer have proved very popular.

Another change has been in the whole concept of 'leadership' of a Meet. For many years the accepted arrangement was that one person was designated the 'Leader' of the walk. She would choose the venue and often a preferred route, and those who came were more or less expected to follow this route. Often 'less' rather than 'more' as when Mabel Jeffrey led a 'crocodile' of 36 members up Cruach Ardrain, and soon they had all disappeared into the mist in small groups, all to reappear safe and sound, having found an infinite variety of routes off the mountain.

Often graduating members aspiring to full membership were expected to lead a walk with older members on hand to see how they acquitted themselves. And a nerve-racking experience it was too, as compass bearings were meticulously worked out in advance, wind direction taken into account (it invariably changed on The Day!), times calculated according to formula, and every last detail well organised. And how on earth could a nervous young novice call the august, independent-minded veterans to order?

Sometimes the problem was the other way round, as the Club attracted young highly experienced members who understandably chafed at the bit with older, slower members, and needed the freedom to go off in smaller groups, go at different speeds, climb to higher grades, and generally enjoy the feeling of competent independence. This positive aspect has been greatly encouraged of late. The title of 'leader' has been replaced by 'co-ordinator', partly to reflect their change of function, but also because of the responsibilities implied in the title in an ever more litigious society. One cannot conceive of the Club's founder members, whose whole character was one of carefree adventure, pausing to consider the implications of Club members suing each other in the event of an accident. How times change!

Early on a pattern of one 'Highland Meet' a year was established in places as far-flung as Dundonnell, Skye and Inchnadamph. Bearing in mind the state of single track roads, with ferry crossings at Ballachulish, Dornie, Kylesku and over to Skye, such journeys were of epic proportion and the destinations considered primitive and very remote.

Long skirts trailing in the snow with Lucy Smith (top) and Pauline Ranken. Arrochar, April 1909

LSCC Archives

On the other hand public transport was in many ways more extensive, with rail links between Edinburgh and Oban, all the small stations still in use and branch lines to places like Killin. Early Meets make frequent mention of dog carts and charabancs and staying in convenient shepherds' cottages.

At its inception the Club invited the Marchioness of Breadalbane to become its Honorary President. She was an obvious choice as her acceptance showed a deep love and knowledge of the Scottish hills, but her support of the Club was expressed in rather more practical ways, as early New Year meets recorded amazing gifts of gourmet hampers of American wild turkey and pheasant. We no longer appoint Honorary Presidents, hence the lack of New Year hampers – alas for modernity. It was the Marchioness who suggested that the Club's annual social gatherings, usually following the AGM, be called ceilidhs in the Gaelic tradition, and such they have remained.

One of the McBride sisters has a witty account in the 1938 Journal of her first ever Meet with the LSCC

It's too good to be true! I am really going to my first Meet. Novices must be a nuisance. Is it difficult to use an ice-axe? Roping up. Hitches. Middleman's knot. All rather frightening, but of course *she* knows everything and I am actually to share her room!

Glorious, beloved hills, sparkling with snow. How enormous my feet look under my long skirt! I hope I won't feel shy when I remove it. Following up steep snow is quite easy after all. How kind everyone is and how jolly! My breeks, made in Paris, and 'won' by an enterprising batman from the quarters of a short but rotund colonel, are not very successful. They must be replaced.

So this is a pitch. How wonderful Mr Raeburn is! He appears to float up. Supposing I stick for ever at that slab! A tiny crack. Will my nail hold? It does. Can life possibly hold anything more glorious!

How terribly steep the descent looks. My knees are shaking. I shall never keep my balance. No, I thought not. How do these marvellous people keep upright? My clothes are crammed with snow. Why won't my ice-axe behave like other people's?

How pleasant is the long tramp back to the hotel. Dry clothes. Cosy fires. Cheery and friendly companions. Oh that this Meet might last for ever!

Long hard winter days on the hill were followed by cheerful evenings of warmth and comfort, and social entertainment. The April Meet of 1911 is remembered as being particularly musical, with duets on the penny-whistle and Elizabeth Ranken playing the bagpipes in the kitchen in the evening. (One hopes any serious cooking was finished. Perhaps it speeded along the dish-washers). For many years there was a tradition in the Club (loved by some, abhorred by others) of performing charades at New Year. One particularly memorable performance was when the Meet was held at Fortingal in Perthshire. There is a legend that Pontius Pilate was born there, so of course the charade included a suitably classical theme. A rather stately club member, Grizel Paterson, reclining on a couch, suitably toga-ed, called imperiously for a drink. When it arrived, she drank it down, only to spit it out spectacularly, as the drink turned out to be methylated spirits!

In between these quarterly Meets, Club members met regularly for more local walks. Being Edinburgh based initially, these were usually in the Pentlands, and there are many accounts of long and enjoyable walks in all weathers, making ingenious use of buses, trains and helpful husbands with cars. Soon they became more adventurous and developed an intimate knowledge of the lower ranges of hills so often overlooked today; the Lammermuirs, Moorfoots, Kilpatrick Hills, Campsies and the Ochils.

Dorothy Crerar sings the praises of 'The Little Hills' in the first Journal.

> No survey of Club activities would be complete without some attention being given to those frequent excursions made from Edinburgh to the Pentland Hills, the Moorfoots, and the Lammermuirs.
>
> Familiarity makes it possible to visualise most of the chosen walk beforehand, but in this case familiarity breeds only affection; and no matter how familiar are those hills of home, such is the effect of our changing atmosphere and climate that views and landscapes are never the same, but always present different and varying charms.
>
> And yet among these hills one can capture many of the sensations of bigger days, for here are to be found, in miniature, most of the features of Highland bens and glens. Those who are not able to take part often in serious expeditions and official Meets of the LSCC, find in these day walks much to recall to them the experiences of more strenuous days. The wind blows at times on the narrow top of West Kip as cuttingly and fiercely as on the edge of Ben Cruachan; the snow lies as soft and deep on the side of Scald Law as on the lower slopes of Ben Laoigh on a winter's day; you may wander in grey mist on the top of Lammer Law with as bewildering a sense of remoteness as though you were lost in the Cairngorms; the music of Logan Burn falls as sweetly on the ear as that of any peaty Highland burn; the heather is as bonny and the air as bitter-sweet as that of the far-away high places of the west and north.

One thing that emerges clearly from the early records is an unquenchable spirit of exploration and adventure. Climbing as a popular sport was still in its infancy, so these hills would be relatively untrampled apart from the occasional shepherd and keeper. Not only did these women pioneer new terrain, they took an obvious perverse delight in finding original, untried routes up almost everything. Not for them the easy way or the tourist route. The question was always 'would it go?' and a considerable amount of vertiginous scrambling up muddy grassy gullies took place as an alternative to the obvious route.

To what extent, then, was the LSCC the 'daughter of the SMC'? It is true that many members were in fact daughters of SMC members (as is the author herself). Obviously the Inglis Clarks were connected to the SMC by marriage, as was Winifred Hutchison, married to Rev A.E.Robertson, the first Munroist; Ruth Raeburn was Harold Raeburn's sister, Lucy Smith's father was a President of the SMC and many other links continue to the present day. These husband and wife climbing teams carried out some remarkable pioneering routes. One of the annoyances of early records is that they do not convey the extent to which women took the lead on those epic climbs. When a first ascent is

*Easter Meet,
Inveroran, 1909.
Sitting: I.McBride,
Kitty Stuart, Jane
Inglis Clark, M.Hood,
Margaret Urquhart
and Anna Ranken.
Standing: Mabel
Inglis Clark, Joan
Smith, Ruth Raeburn,
Pauline Ranken,
Lucy Smith and
Daisy Gillies*

LSCC Archives

recorded it is customary to attribute the climb to the person in the lead
– on the 'front end' of the rope. But many long climbs are done by 'leading through'; that is the person coming second on the rope will follow
the leader up to a safe stance, where the leader will be tied on firmly.
Then the second may continue on up the next pitch as leader, and so
on turn about until the end of the climb. The hardest pitch on the route,
the 'crux', by which the climb is graded according to standard of difficulty, is often done by the leader, but who knows from those early
records what part these women played in getting their partners over
the crux, or indeed, whether they led it themselves.

One thing is sure; the women of the LSCC were never simply hauled
up these climbs like a sack of potatoes. It was for this very reason that
they formed their own club, so that they could explore and pioneer
routes in their own right, and develop their own climbing skills to the
full.

Certainly these fathers, brothers and partners have given enormous
support and encouragement to the Club, often in the most practical
ways. At the end of a walk in the Pentlands one record delightfully
mentioned –

A surprise awaited all but one of the party, when Mr Sang was discovered making tea in a corner of the field. This unexpected picnic was much appreciated by all, and Mr and Mrs Sang further added to their kindness by motoring the whole party back to their respective homes.

Ruth Raeburn's brother Harold was a well-known pioneer of some of the classic routes in Scotland, and his name appears frequently in connection with the LSCC. It is obvious that he and others were enormously supportive of the budding LSCC and he accompanied them often on their walks and Meets. On his death in 1926, the LSCC President, Mrs Sang, paid him this tribute.

> The Club has been bereft of one of its best friends by the death of Mr Harold Raeburn. Without his kindly and practical help, it is safe to say that the foundations of the Club would not have been so surely laid. He grounded some of the early members in the craft of mountaineering, displaying the greatest patience with beginners, and his fearlessness and self-reliance imparted a wonderful confidence to those who were fortunate enough to have him as their guide and teacher. We think of his wonderful climbing record with admiration; we marvel at the spirit which carried him through so many dangers and difficulties; but above all, we remember with gratitude the brotherly helping hand he always held out to the Club.

The outbreak of World War I dramatically changed this happy, leisured, carefree lifestyle for ever. As usual in the summer of 1914, many Club members were on the Continent climbing and exploring, and some had epic journeys home. This is Margaret Murray's account of her return from Austria;

> The first part of the journey (24 hours) was made by diligence, the people crowding in at every station until the coach was nearly upset. In 33 hours Hamburg was reached in time for the last train that went through before mobilisation. Great enthusiasm over the gathering of the troops prevailed everywhere. At Hamburg, Miss Murray got on board a British steamer bound for Grimsby, but the German naval authorities played with the vessel a game of cat and mouse, sending it up and down the river for three days, until war was declared with England (sic), when they seized it and disembarked the passengers at Hamburg.

Eleven days later they eventually made it to Newcastle, but without any of their luggage. Another Club member had an exciting time of it making her way back from the Dolomites, at one point making it as far as Basle.

> Three melancholy days were spent at Basle, filled even at that early date with rumours of disaster. It was impossible to obtain any information, and the British Consul confined his efforts at assistance to requesting the stranded tourists to go away, as he did not wish to have people about the Consulate! He apparently found it impossible to realise that that was the one thing the tourists were anxious to do.

An immediate response to the announcement of hostilities was for the Club to curtail its activities drastically.

> In accordance with the general wish of the Club no New Year Meet took place in 1915. The President voiced the thought of the members in her allusion to the shadow of the great war which had fallen so suddenly and unexpectedly

on us all, making it seem inappropriate that we should hold our annual festival of rejoicing.

However, there was also a valiant 'life must go on' attitude, and it is clear that amidst the pain and bereavement their modest outings on the Scottish hills offered comfort and strength.

War affects everyone and the women of the LSCC were soon deeply engaged. Not only were they voting money from their coffers for warm gloves for the men at the Front (to be conveyed by Mabel Inglis Clark's brother Captain Charles Inglis Clark), but many were engaged in active war work, Jane Inglis Clark was Commandant of the Red Cross VAD, Mrs Douglas was a member of an emergency committee to look after the families of interned Austrian and German civilians, another member worked as matron at the hospital at Craigleith. Perhaps the most adventurous were Lucy Smith who travelled to Serbia to work with the Scottish Women's Hospital for Foreign Service, and Florence McLeod who related her adventures in the Club record.

> In November 1915, I sailed for Archangel with the Anglo-Russian Hospital, which started work in the Dmitri Palace in Petrograd early in 1916. The patients were Russian wounded – very delightful men, who seemed very content in a British Hospital....The winter was exceptionally cold, the thermometer falling to 37 degrees Fahrenheit below zero on one or two occasions.
>
> In July, I left Petrograd with the Millicent Fawcett Hospitals to work among refugees. As it happened, there was little to be done in that direction, and the Units undertook work in Zemstvo Hospitals in the Government of Kazan. After three weeks in Kazan itself, I was sent into the country, east of the Middle Volga, about 100 miles from Simbirsk, and 30 miles from a railway, to a very primitive place indeed...We had a variety of peoples to deal with – Tartars, Tchuvash, Mordva, a few stray Poles, and, of course, many Russian peasants in their sheep-skin coats.

A recent book, *Corsets and Camouflage, Women and War*, by Kate Adie, the war correspondent, has vivid descriptions from records in the Imperial War Museum, which describe the kind of conditions faced by these Edinburgh women who travelled out to Serbia with Dr Elsie Inglis, founder of the Scottish Women's Hospitals. One woman working in a Serb hospital wrote.

> Patients were sent to us in batches until the wards were full, and we still get them at intervals when we discharge convalescents...They come to us in a terrible condition, having had absolutely no nursing. You can imagine, perhaps, from this what the hospitals are like. It is really not the Serbians' fault. The whole country is one immense hospital – doctors, Serbs, and prisoners alike work all day merely to get the dressing done and the drugs given.

Much of the work at the Scottish hospital was a constant battle with hygiene, sanitation and drains. A sister in the fever hospital wrote.

> Our costume in the wards was hardly that of the stereotyped English nurse, with cap and apron and stiff collar, and our friends would not have recognised us. Instead of the usual uniform and apron, we wore a white cotton combination garment, with the ends tucked into high leather riding boots. Over this, for the sake of appearance, an overall was worn, and our hair was

entirely covered with a tight-fitting cap. Round neck and arms we wore bandages soaked in camphor oil, and our boots were smeared with the same, so that no encouragement was given to the little insect by which typhus is spread.

One can't help wondering how the gently reared Edinburgh ladies fared. Perhaps they were well prepared by being accustomed to hobnailed climbing boots and resisting the depradations of Scottish midges. At all events, Lucy and Florence returned alive and well to be welcomed back by the Club.

By 1919 the Club was emerging from the war, still alive but sadly battered. The Meet at Blair Atholl for that year records only three members attending and for some years the membership remained static. Many had lost family members, including the Inglis Clarks, with the loss of Charles Inglis Clark, son of Jane and brother of Mabel, two founder members. The well-known and well-frequented Charles Inglis Clark (CIC) Memorial Hut in the northern corries of Ben Nevis became the scene of many epic adventures for climbers in later years and was a fitting memorial to a keen climber.

Gone for ever, however, were the days of charabancs, chauffeurs and food hampers. In many ways the Club became more open and ready for growth with the passing of the days of exclusive class affluence. Two

Easter Meet, Tyndrum, 1920. From left: Harold Raeburn, Mr Paton, Mabel Jeffrey, Mr Menzies, Miss Murray, Miss Finlayson, Ruth Raeburn

LSCC Archives

May Meet, Kingshouse Hotel, Glencoe, 1928. Twenty years on, a growing club and faster transport. From left: William Inglis Clark, Grace Stark, Ann Foster, Betty Burt, M.Wilson, Mabel Jeffrey, Byles (guest), I.Menzies, Florence Sang, Margaret Murray, E.Milne, D.Sang, M.Brown, Barbara MacFarlane

LSCC Archives

members joined from Glasgow in 1924, but the Glasgow membership was still deemed 'not strong enough' to be a separate branch. Horizons were broadening beyond Edinburgh, and weekend walks were held in the Campsies and the Kilpatricks as well as some exciting rock climbing on the Cobbler near Arrochar. However expansion came somewhat reluctantly, and a proposal to hold the Annual Business Meeting alternately between Glasgow and Edinburgh was turned down in 1925 and not approved until 1930. By 1951, however, Glasgow members were so well established that they even called themselves the 'Glasgow Section' and produced a couple of witty newsletters. A regular pattern of evening lectures was established and they were very proud of themselves, as this editorial by Riona Barclay illustrates.

> Humility is an emotion commonly enough experienced by climbers among the hills. So surely in the city, on occasion and without too much concern, we may indulge in one a little less lauditory. Let's give ourselves a pat on the back!
>
> Our Glasgow section was inaugurated a year ago and has flourished ever since by the preaching of the climbing word. We have had a good many talks from our own members and from others.

Such monthly evening meetings have continued up to the present day, and proliferated from their inception in Edinburgh, to Glasgow, Perth and the Inverness area. Of their regular summer rock climbing excursions, more will be told later.

In 1925 the committee proposed that Meets could be held 'furth of Scotland', although this too aroused opposition with Mabel Inglis Clark (now Jeffrey after her marriage) stoutly opposing the motion arguing that it contradicted the original aims of the Club However, the Club was ready to look beyond Scotland and the first official meet outside Scotland was held in Borrowdale in the Lake District, establishing a tradition of regular autumn meets in the Lakes or Northumberland. Links with other Clubs were also established and joint meets and huts shared.

The Fell and Rock Climbing Club, based in the Lake District was only two years older than the LSCC. In 1921 the Pinnacle Club, a climbing club for women in England, was founded, and a joint Meet held in 1926. The Club even received a letter from the Japanese Alpine Club in 1918. Addressed 'Dear Sir' it proposes;

> With a view to increase our knowledge and information towards our common aim and further to cement our friendship, I beg to propose you to interchange our journals and other publications.
>
> This Club will be happy to offer necessary information and facilities to any of your members visiting this country with the view of climbing our mountains.

Sadly there is no record of the Club taking up this opportunity. One wonders if the invitation still stands. At any rate by the 1920s the fame of the Club was indeed spreading.

By its coming of age in 1929 the Club was well-established with a total of 70 members, a good number of new members joining annually, and the 1927 Meet at Killin described as 'the largest and merriest Meet on record'. The anniversary was celebrated with the publication of the first Club Journal and other lively festivities.

The Journal attracted widespread press coverage with editorials reflecting the enthusiasm and liveliness of the Club. This is how *The Scotsman* described it.

> The pages are alive with the spirit of fun and adventure that lured the pioneers out in those early days of trailing skirts and heavy ulsters to brave the mountains in summer and winter. That it really was possible to do rock climbing in that amazing kit the camera gives proof in a striking photograph of two who wore it scaling Salisbury Crags. I doubt if many modern madams would attempt the feat in the latest knickerbocker outfit. Nevertheless some 65 such women do exist in Scotland, for that is the present membership of the Club. They should have some stirring tales to tell us.

The President's remarks in 1929 sum up the position of the Club.

> The past year must always be a memorable one in the history of the Ladies Scottish Climbing Club, for it marked the coming of age of the Club, an occasion which was celebrated by two outstanding events, firstly by the issue of the LSCC Journal, a publication of which the Club is justly proud, and, secondly, by the Anniversary Dinner held at Easter at Ballachulish. There, within reach of the hills that set the seal upon good fellowship, 62 members and their friends toasted the Founding of the Club, recapitulated early triumphs and achievements, and lived over again happy days in rain and sunshine.
>
> The Club has other special events to its credit. The membership of the Club stands at the record number of seventy, and it is good to welcome new members, and to feel the stimulation of fresh vigour and enthusiasms...The need for ability to lead expeditions was faced, and the readiness of members to realise the importance of being able and willing to take responsibility is an excellent sign.

Climbing for women was firmly on the map, and the Ladies Scottish Climbing Club was poised for adventure.

2: Pioneering Women

IN THE 21ST ANNIVERSARY Journal of the Club, Founder Jane Inglis Clark wrote.

> Mountaineering for women is the very best of sports, for here there is no rivalry, no seeking applause, no possibility of heart-sickening sense of defeat. We leave our differences behind, and when climbing there is time to feel, to think, to be oneself. Mountaineering for women seems to have come as part of their emancipation, especially from the old conventional restraints. Indeed it is almost impossible for the girl of today to realise the great difficulties and prejudices that had to be overcome in those early days of climbing for women.

It is indeed hard today, in these times of at least nominal equality when we celebrate the achievements of such world class women as Catherine Destivelle, the late Alison Hargreaves, and circumnavigator Ellen McArthur, to imagine the amount of prejudice experienced by the founding mothers of our Club.

In her book *A Woman's Reach*, Nea Morin, an outstanding member of the Pinnacle Club, cites the following alarmingly chauvinist attitudes from Samivel's Amateurs d'Abimes:

> Well do we know them...lonely crows who, aping men, haunt the huts and great mountain faces and ply the harsh tools of the mountains, baring their faces to the winds in ecstasy and straining to their bosoms the unfeeling rock with the ardour of lovers.
>
> No! True women are too tender for the rigours of the mountains, and men will not accept that they should penetrate their domain.

It must be remembered, perhaps in mitigation of such attitudes, that immediately pre and post First World War a spirit of chivalric protection may have prevailed and it was in the face of such sentiments that women had to struggle free. Nea Morin again quotes a certain C.E.Benson in *British Mountaineering* written in 1909, only one year after our Club was formed, giving salutary advice to men climbing with women;

> They must ever keep a watchful eye on the ladies and see to it that they are
> never in danger of being hurried or overtired, for the woman who has once
> over-walked herself seems doomed to be more or less of an invalid for life.
> Doctors in this age of feminine athletics are constantly having girls on their
> hands who have once overdone it and will never be quite the same again.

Obviously neither our valiant three under the boulder at Lix Toll nor their husbands can have read such sage advice!

One of the pioneers of women's alpine climbing, Mrs Aubrey le Blond, brought out her first edition of *True Tales of Mountain Adventure* in 1902. It was an instant success and within three months was in its third reprint. In the introduction her husband writes.

> There is no manlier sport in the world than mountaineering.(*sic*)
>   It is true that all the sports Englishmen take part in are manly, but moun-
> taineering is different from the others, because it is sport purely for the sake
> of sport. There is no question of beating anyone else, as in a race or a game,
> or of killing an animal or a bird as in hunting or shooting. A mountaineer
> sets his skill and his strength against the difficulty of getting to the top of a
> steep peak. Either he conquers the mountain, or it conquers him.

It is worth noting that Mrs Aubrey le Blond while recounting such prejudices was herself an accomplished alpinist.

The early 1900s was the era of climbing clubs. The Fell and Rock Climbing Club for climbing in the Lake District peaks was founded in 1906, and in 1907, just a year ahead of the LSCC, the Ladies Alpine Club was formed. The event is recorded in a magazine of the time, *The Woman at Home* in an article entitled *Women Mountaineers* and it is interesting to note how egalitarian it is in tone.

> The formation this season of the Lyceum Alpine Club for women marks a new
> departure in the annals of mountaineering, and serves to draw attention to
> the position which women have attained in this healthy and invigorating
> pastime, and sometimes hazardous sport. In no other region of enterprise is
> a woman placed so completely on an equality with a man as in mountaineer-
> ing. Both tread the same way to the peaks and passes they would conquer,
> and share the same fatigue, peril, and exposure. Rocks, avalanches, glaciers
> and crevasses are no respecters of sex. That women can climb the highest alti-
> tudes has been demonstrated by Mrs Bullock Workman, who in 1906 made
> the first ascent of a peak in the Himalayas of 23,300 feet, which gives her the
> world record for mountaineering with men.

The account goes on to enumerate many dramatic and thrilling ascents by women and concludes with a recommendation for the Lyceum Alpine Club, pointing out that it is the only alpine club in the world exclusively for women.

The formation of a women's club in Scotland was a natural develop-ment, not only of a passion for climbing, but also of the growing confidence of women. The campaign for women's suffrage was alive and well and vociferous by 1908, and although there is no reference to polit-ical activity in the annals of the Club, some early members are rumoured to have been active suffragettes. There are clear indications that the founders of the Club were well aware of their pioneering role, and that they were conscious of a mountaineering ethos that was significantly different from that of the men.

This is shown in the enthusiastically noble aspirations expressed in the founding records of the Club, and is still reflected in the Constitution.

Referring to this, somewhat tongue in cheek, the SMC Journal of the time points out: 'The rules of the Club are avowedly based on those of the SMC, and are therefore perfect'! However the article concludes with this somewhat condescending acknowledgement;

> In one respect the Ladies Scottish Climbing Club has gone one step in advance of our own. At the conclusion of the rules are found the following wise precepts, which might not even be found unworthy of adoption by ourselves:-
>
> > The spirit of rivalry should never enter into mountaineering expeditions.
> >
> > Always climb deliberately, slowly, and carefully; a slip, even when harmless is something to be ashamed of.
> >
> > Remember above all that *each member* has the reputation of the Club to make and to uphold, and that even the slightest mishap would immediately bring the Club into disrepute.

Although today there are many women who do climb competitively, it could also be argued that there is a strong survival instinct among women and, may it be said, a sense of responsibility that often precludes highly competitive climbing. Regrettably too, when women do make it to the top, and obviously expose themselves to high risk, they almost inevitably come in for a storm of criticism from the media, claiming that they are irresponsible, neglectful of their families, and unnatural. Such criticism, however, is not directed in such measure against the men, who are depicted as heroic, struggling against the odds. It is in great measure due to the efforts and enterprise of women like these founding members who have changed such attitudes and made it possible for women today to develop their skills to a high degree and enjoy the mountains in their own right.

Alas, however, such male chauvinist attitudes cannot be relegated to a bygone era. Even as late as 1989 an article in *The Scotsman* was able to quote a well-known Scottish climber who should have known better saying; 'Glencoe is quite a technical area for rescuers and not very amenable to women climbers' This in a decade when women climbers had pioneered over one hundred 'Extreme' routes and even broken the record of an 'E5' route, then the highest grade.

That same article was celebrating the publication by our sisters in the Pinnacle Club of a *History of Women Climbing* and it shows a fine photograph of Pinnacle Club member, Sheila Cormack, with the caption 'The hardest, the fittest; Sheila Cormack taking the Pinnacle Club to the top of women's climbing.' The LSCC is proud to own Sheila as one of its members also.

To a certain extent even today women climbers have still to overcome that dreaded, inhibiting concept of what is 'ladylike'. Sleeping out in bothies, burning up the miles on a motorbike, arriving back at the end of a long day hot, sweaty and dishevelled often earned them comments like; 'The Ladies are becoming nothing more that a bunch of tinkers' or 'Do you always have to make yourself so ugly to go climbing?'

So do women indeed climb differently from men? Let us return to Nea Morin, who became one of the best known woman mountaineers in Britain. She had a career spanning over forty years, beginning in the 1920s, with a fine record of first ascents in the Alps and being the only woman member of an ill-fated expedition to Ama Dablam. She gave this surprisingly modest assessment of women climbers:

> The average athletic, well-balanced girl is fully capable of leading hard climbs, and enjoying it; in due course she should be as safe leading up to Severe standard as seconding some tiger on much harder climbs...No doubt this sense of satisfaction can be obtained by women at a considerably lower standard of difficulty than for men, but the weaker – and shorter – sex must have some advantages. Their many disadvantages include problems of marriage and motherhood, which cut right across a woman's climbing ambitions. With motherhood there are obviously immense changes, and it almost inevitably entails a gap of at least a year during which any serious climbing is impracticable....
>
> Generally speaking most women climbers are handicapped by lack of muscular strength...So for women, achieving a high standard of climbing depends largely on attitude of mind. At the same time a woman must use her head, study the more delicate techniques and in particular rely on balance in order to make up for lack of brute strength.

One only has to watch an elegant climber like Catherine Destivelle swinging delicately to place her feet somewhere on a level with her head to question some of these assumptions. And pregnancy didn't seem to hamper her ascent of the Old Man of Hoy.

It is probably true that women have less attitude of conquest. Of course women do pit themselves against each other and against the mountain, but far more important is to develop the kind of relationship and balance with the mountain that enables one to survive competently in all weathers; to feel that tingle of danger when the blizzard is stinging one's eyes to blindness and yet to know that one has the skill and confidence to live with such risk and survive happily to tell the tale. The LSCC quite deliberately has resisted setting a specifically high grade of achievement as an entry qualification, putting the emphasis rather on the ability to travel safely and competently in the Scottish mountains in all weathers.

This love of the mountains in all aspects has encouraged a wide range of interests within the Club, quite apart from making first ascents or ticking off the tops. Throughout its history the Club has produced its share of highly accomplished botanists, ornithologists, geologists, artists and photographers, and many of these members have led some of our most fascinating days on the hills sharing their knowledge.

Of necessity a women's club has to accept that there will be times when some members are less fit to go on the hills due to childcare and family responsibilities. The important thing is that women are still welcomed and encouraged to participate in Meets and helped to regain their fitness. Perhaps this acceptance is why the LSCC is a good club

Pam Cain, prusiking near Ballachulish in 1969. 'Should you be doing this at your age?'

Photo: Eilidh Nisbet

to grow old in. Older members are not abandoned when, as one member put it 'she needs four hands for rock climbing – two to hold onto the rock, and two to push her knees straight!' Winifred Robertson made her first ascent of Ben Nevis at the age of 70; Pam Cain, who recently celebrated her 90th birthday, has regularly attended the Club's alpine meets, and members look forward to returning to camp after gruelling epics in the mountains, to be greeted by Pam, crawling out of her little mountain tent with welcoming glasses of sherry in her hands. It should also be noted that not so many years previously this same Pam Cain was an active member of the East Greenland Expedition. On one occasion she had just completed the first pitch of the Douglas Boulder on Ben Nevis, when a young man shinned up beside her. 'Should you be doing this at your age?' he was rash enough to say!

Our Club therefore does not have a great list of dramatic first ascents to its name. Having said that however, our Club has played a significant part in leading the way in Scotland for women climbing. It is time to look at who these pioneering women were and find out a little more about their achievements. Molly Johnstone remembers meeting some of these founding members.

> Ruth Raeburn came occasionally to Edinburgh evening meetings in the late '40s and '50s. She was dressed in dark clothes as I remember most elderly ladies of the '20s. She was slim with long dark hair and a bun and she had a black velvet ribbon high on her long neck. Margaret Murray was short, white-haired and wore bright modern clothes and had opal and diamond rings on her hands. I don't remember much about Mrs Inglis Clark except that she sat at the back of our AGM wearing a large wide-brimmed black hat.

Elegant they may have been, but one has only to look at the photograph of Jane Inglis Clark to appreciate that this was indeed a formidable lady, with all the energy and determination needed to found a climbing club for women in an unfavourable climate of opinion. Quoting from her obituary in 1950.

> Filled with indomitable courage and unwavering faith, Mrs Clark was able to inspire others with her enthusiasm and high ideals. Herself a keen mountaineer and lover of nature, it had long been her wish to see established a climbing club for women on somewhat similar lines to that of the Scottish Mountaineering Club. The idea at that time was almost revolutionary, and as we know, opposition and disapproval were not lacking. But our Founder was unmoved by these considerations, and believing that the time was ripe for action, took the first step towards the formation of the Club.

Described as having 'tireless energy' there is ample evidence in the long list of climbs and ski tours accomplished year by year. She and her husband, Dr William Inglis Clark, often accompanied by her daughter Mabel and son Charles, went sometimes many times a year to the Alps, carrying out long and difficult high-level ski tours, and in the summer exploring around Chamonix, where they pioneered some new routes on the Aiguilles du Midi, or on the fine rock of the Dolomites.

She was the ideal person to lead the infant Club during its early years. Obviously an organiser, as is evident in the many civic duties she took on, she was filled with enthusiasm and was able to inspire others with this same love of the mountains.

> With an unusually full, active and busy life, Mrs Clark never lost interest in the Club. Having started it on the right lines, she saw it develop and expand from year to year, bringing happiness and wellbeing and a fresh zest for life to many women. This was what she wanted; to share with others the joy and exhilaration which climbing can give and in this she ably succeeded.

Her knowledge of the Scottish mountains was extensive, and that in all weathers. Records tell of a 12 mile ski tour near Ballater, of long traverses of mountain ridges, of the first summer ascent of South Castle Gully on Ben Nevis, and a casual mention of an early ascent of North East Buttress on Ben Nevis. This is a long classic rock climb, about 1200 feet high, and has one notorious move near the top, known as the Man Trap, precisely because it is a long reach to the vital hold for a six foot man. Vertically challenged females simply have to use their ingenuity!

An equally able colleague in setting up the LSCC was Jane Inglis Clark's daughter, Mabel, who married Robert Jeffrey, another keen mountaineer. There is an apt description of a first encounter with Mabel.

> Then the door opened: like a burst of sunshine Mabel Jeffrey came in. She simply radiated enthusiasm, energy and friendliness.

Mabel was always eager to initiate newcomers into the joys of mountaineering. Many a novice can recall the care with which Mabel Jeffrey would show, often by example, how to use an ice-axe to arrest a slide, or how to cut steps up a steep snow slope rhythmically and efficiently with an economic two swipes with the axe. Not all these lessons were as thrilling or as devil-may-care as Mabel Jeffrey's own account of Florence MacLeod's first alarming lesson in glissading.

> I see Florence MacLeod gripping her ice axe in despair and determination when, at the top of Stob Coire an Lochan, I decided that the party should glissade down the central gully, not knowing that she had never glissaded before and was terror-stricken. There was a vertical pitch in the middle which I did not realise until I went over it, and I am told I laughed loudly and heartlessly as the members of the party appeared out of the spraying snow, turning innumerable somersaults, some without axes, but Florence, the novice, proudly clutching hers.

One wonders what 'risk assessment' would make of such antics nowadays!

The author, when a fresh-faced eager new member, recalls the sometimes whimsical demands of a venerated founder member. On returning footsore and weary to Muir of Inverey after a long day in the Cairngorms, she could see the cottage tantalisingly close on the other side of the River Dee, but was faced with a frustrating two mile detour to cross the river at Linn of Dee. Mabel Jeffrey welcoming the travellers back, affirmed with a bright smile; 'Of course in *my* day we forded the Dee.' Nothing daunted the next day, when faced with the same problem, our two intrepid explorers forded the Dee up to their waists. Looking the two dripping youngsters up and down, our honourable founder shook her head sadly, 'Young people today have no sense!'

The sheer energy of Mabel Jeffrey leaves one breathless. In 1910 alone,

Mabel Inglis Clark, June 1914

LSCC Archives

Mabel Inglis Clark facing the blizzard. Kinlochleven Meet, April 1914. 'The weather was quite as bad as usual, if not a little worse!'

LSCC Archives

Easter 1913, Stob Coire nan Lochan, Glencoe. Lucy Smith and Freda White negotiate 'a sensational and steep exit over a cornice'

LSCC Archives

only two years after the founding of the Club the records recount that Mabel led Castle Ridge on Ben Nevis, kept fit in between times on Salisbury Crags in Edinburgh, then had a strenuous summer in the Dolomites, reaching all her peaks without guides – a rare achievement in those days. The following year sees her doing two 18 mile ski tours from Newtonmore, including several tops. When one takes into account the amount of travelling time simply to reach some of these places, they rate as major achievements.

1929 was perhaps the peak of Mabel's climbing career.

In 1929 the Jeffreys returned to Scotland. Mabel was welcomed back with open arms and immediately elected President. This was particularly appropriate as it was the year of the Club's coming of age, so Mabel presided at the celebration dinner at Ballachulish and was present at the opening on Ben Nevis of the Charles Inglis Clark Memorial Hut, dedicated to her brother who was killed in the First World War. For Mabel, the year also provided one of the most dazzling rock climbing seasons of her career. It included the traverse of the Aiguille des Petits Charmoz and the Aiguille du Midi; the Dent du Requin; the Aiguille de Grepon, and the Grand Dru and the Petit Dru.

Mabel's own *Mountain Memories* written for the Jubilee Journal speak not only of her unfailing spirit of adventure, but particularly of the importance of friendships.

The first time I planned to go off on my own was previous to the Easter Meet of 1909 at Inveroran. I contacted Daisy Gillies, caught the early morning train to Crianlarich and we climbed the Y Gully on Cruach Ardrain in perfect weather and Alpine conditions. A slight slip by Daisy on an exposed ice-step proved the belay to be sound, and our climbing partnership was sealed from that moment.

At the Laggan Meet of 1912, Margaret Murray, Hoodles (Mrs McLaren) and I were driven in the 'machine' (a wagonette with usually two horses) to the north end of Loch Pattack, from where we had an arduous experience walking to Ben Alder Cottage on Loch Ericht. We found the Allt Cam and Allt Bealach Dubh in full spate and had to ford them waist high and roped together. In crossing the latter, Hoodles slipped on a rock in midstream and would have been swept away but for the rope. We encountered a violent gale and blizzard when crossing over the Bealach Bheidhe and arrived at the Cottage just as darkness was falling, with our clothes frozen and chilled to the bone. The keeper, Mr McCook, and the Postmaster from Dalwhinnie made us most welcome, gave us blankets to wrap ourselves in, served us with a hot meal, then sat up all night drying our clothes.

Mabel's energy was unflagging right up to her later years. In 1955 when Mabel Jeffrey was 70 her exploits for the year are recorded as follows:

February – ski-runs from Saanenmoser, Switzerland. **March** – six days ski-ing on the Ochils from Sheriffmuir. **April** – five days ski-ing on Cairngorm. **June** – Ben Attow. Sgurr nan Gillean from Sligachan, Skye. **August** – from Zinal, Switzerland, Roc de la Vache, descent to Zinal Glacier; Col de la Lex; to Upper Zinal Glacier by Petit Mountet; Sparrhorn from Belalp. **September** – from Pontresina, Segantini Hut from Muottas Muraigl, descent by Upper Schafberg; Diavollezza Hut from Bernina Hauser; Lago di Cavloccia and Val Forno from Maloja; from Bernina Pass by Lago Bianco to Restaurant del Sassal Mason, descent to Alp Grun.

Easter 1913, Stob Coire nan Lochan. Lucy Smith and Freda White post cornice

LSCC Archives

Elspet Mackay was an active member for 71 years, May 1981

Photo: Eleanor Lloyd
(LSCC Collection)

At least there is the comfort of knowing that she stopped at least once at a restaurant!

When she died at the age of 82 she was in the process of writing about a trip to the Dolomites for the Club Journal. Her obituary sums it up beautifully;

> Her keenness was the keenness of youth when the hills were new and it seemed as if they always would be.

Continuing active climbing long into old age seems to be a feature of the Club. In 1995 a party was held to celebrate Elspet Mackay's 90th birthday. She had been a member of the Club for 71 years. Janet Smith, who with her sister Annette had been a member of the Club since 1930, set off on her own over fairly rough ground up the highest hill on Colonsay. On her return she remarked fairly sheepishly

> I suppose it was rather stupid of me going up on my own, but I just couldn't resist it.

At 87 years of age that was rather typical of an LSCC member. It was this same pair, Janet and Annette, who had a magnificent garden in their house outside Ratho near Edinburgh. Part of it was a very steep rock garden and the obvious way of weeding it was to abseil down the rock-face!

It should by now be fairly obvious that these early members of the Club were all fascinating individualists, strongly independent women and often amusing characters. Lucy Smith, one of the original trio at the Boulder was a frequent climbing companion of Mabel Jeffrey, who described her thus.

> On looking back, I find that climbs are connected in my memory with my companions, as I never wished to climb alone. Vividly I see Lucy hacking her way through the cornice at the top of the gully of Stob Coire an Lochan, or scaling the cliffs of Buachaille Etive, Nevis and Skye. At a time when women had never climbed alone, Lucy was outstanding. A splendid leader, tireless, optimistic and enthusiastic – any route she planned was sure to 'go', and I was lucky to have her as a contemporary companion on the hills.

Another of the original members of the Club was Ruth Raeburn, sister of SMC member, Harold Raeburn. Ruth was one of the pillars of the Club, serving on the Committee for over 19 years, and instituting and editing the Club annual Record, which was so suitable that it has changed little in format until the present day. She was described as 'devil-may-care Ruth' and it is certainly true that she roamed the mountains of Scotland with a kind of gay abandon. However this was tempered by a careful competence. Mabel Jeffrey again.

> We also learned from Miss Ruth Raeburn who had wide experience on snow and rock. She gave us good advice, restraining us from attempting too much until we had learned our own powers and improved our technique.

Ruth's climbing experience was impressive. She was a member of the second ascent of Crowberry Ridge in 1909 and also did a second ascent of Pinnacle Ridge on Garbh Bheinn of Ardgour. In addition between 1909 and 1916 she climbed almost all the classic routes in Skye, Arran and the Lake District, including the impressive Bhasteir Tooth and some new routes on Pillar in the Lakes. She also climbed Number Two Gully on Ben Nevis in very severe winter conditions – all this with hemp ropes and nailed boots.

However it is fairly typical of the LSCC members that Ruth was far more than a gifted mountaineer. Her friends and climbing companions described her as -

> always such a kind and helpful person on the hills, we have had many happy days together and she knew and loved the hills. Her sweet and affectionate nature endeared her to all, while her tact and courtesy made her a popular official…She was an affectionate and staunch friend and she will always remain a bright star in my circle of memories.

Then there was May Green who joined the Club in 1922, sending in her list of climbs in the Lakes for that year. Napes Needle, Kern Knott's Chimney, Kern Knott's West Chimney, Needle Ridge, Eagle West Ridge (ordinary route), Arrowhead Ridge, descent by Arrowhead Arete, Pillar Rock, Slab and Notch…and so on and on…a fine list for a novice. May was tall and lean, with a long thick pigtail wrapped around her head. She was reputed to have been an active suffragette, had a penchant for black coffee and strong French cigars. Annie May Pirie summed up her free spirit.

> May Green kept cropping up – evergreen – along the route of the years like a diving sea-bird, appearing, disappearing, re-appearing, escaping from over-turned cars and entering hotel windows at blood-curdlingly early hours.

Her obituary conveys some of the essence of May's originality.

> With the death of May Green on July 26th, 1975 the Club lost a pungent and controversial personality. From the first she was something of a legend, but few of the stories told round the fire about a member with the hair of a Godiva and the tongue of a bargee were apocryphal. Younger members who saw only the gaunt ageing figure setting forth reluctantly on the hills with many colour-ful imprecations must find it difficult to picture the vivid dare-devil who strode the hills in her youth with reckless but masterful abandon.
>
> May's love of the hills though seldom expressed was deep, enduring and real. In her case however it was impossible to give the conventional summary of her outstanding climbs. She climbed as she herself would have said 'for the hell of it'.

The 1930s saw a blossoming of good rock climbers in the Club. Pat Bell was described as the most outstanding woman climber of her day. She was a colourful, controversial character, and for many years Club AGMs were enlivened by the combative vociferous style of her partic-ipation. She was married to the legendary J.H.B.Bell and they formed an exceptional climbing partnership, putting up many exciting new routes and climbing classic routes up to Very Severe which was an excep-tionally high standard for the 1930s. Some of the rock climbing exploits will be described later in this book. Of all the Scottish mountains, Pat's great love was the Cairngorms.

> Were I told that in future all my climbing in Scotland must be confined to one group of mountains, it would be the Cairngorms I should choose. They

The redoubtable Barbara Macfarlane (always known as 'Miss Macfarlane'), climbed in most of the mountain ranges in Europe

LSCC Archives

offer such a wide variety of climbing, both in summer and in winter, that one can never tire of them. I should cast a glance of regret at the Black Cuillin, and a very regretful one at the cliffs of Ben Nevis, then go back to the Cairngorms year after year, confident that in their rocky corries, deep glens and high rolling plateaux I should ever be finding something new and satisfying.

It was typical of Pat's individuality that she was the first woman to carry out a solo traverse of all the 4000 foot tops in the Cairngorms; a distance of 19 miles with 6869 feet climbed. Nor was it easy going.

> The mist was very thick. This was the tricky part. I had never been over the route to the Dhondail track, or indeed on the track itself, so I had nothing to rely on but that memorised compass bearing. It should, I knew, be a little north of west, very little north. But I was haunted by the fear of going too far westward and getting on to the huge moss on the plateau at the head of Glen Einich. The result was that I went northwest, and, instead of contouring, soon found myself labouring uphill again on to the Braeriach plateau. At last a huge cairn loomed up in the mist. I had had the luck to strike the southmost of the two Einich cairns, with a visibility of less than thirty yards. It was 7.10 p.m. I set off due west and, after a while, came to a burn. This must be the Dhondail burn I thought, and followed it. At last I began to emerge from the mist and could see a shoulder below me, and far below it to the right the Dhondail Track.

A superb example of good common sense and competence in a very tricky situation.

Another stalwart of the Club, who joined in the 1930s, was Winifred Robertson. She was not a rock climber, but being married to Rev A.E.Robertson, the first Munroist, she had an incomparable knowledge of every aspect of the remote places of Scotland. In many ways her wide-ranging appreciation of the Scottish hills epitomises the nature of the LSCC. On the one hand were the hard rock skills of a person like Pat Bell, but Winifred could recount stories from Scottish history, write knowledgably about the early surveyors and map-makers, recognise birds, and give the botanical names of the tiny alpine plants found on the high tops. A day out with Winifred was an education not to be missed.

The Club may have been reared in the drawing rooms of Edinburgh, but it wasn't long before there was a shift westwards, with a keen and active group of climbers from Glasgow joining the Club. Of these, the most outstanding in the early days, was Barbara Macfarlane, who joined the Club in 1922. Barbara taught English and Geography at Shawlands Academy in Glasgow, or as one pupil commented, 'She taught English via the mountains!' So many of her colleagues and pupils were inspired by her enthusiasm, that Shawlands Academy proved a fine recruiting ground for new members. She took many of her pupils out on the hills and even to the Alps. To them, even when toiling uphill, she was always 'Miss Macfarlane', and she was a conspicuous figure in her tailor-made tweed jacket and breeches. Even in old age her climbing memories were relived with younger members of the Club, and one only had to look at Miss Macfarlane's mantelpiece of Christmas cards to realise that there was hardly a mountain range in Europe that she had not visited, and that she had retained the friendship of those with whom she had

Cordee Ltd 11 Jacknell Road, Hinckley, Leicester LE10 3BS
Tel 01455 611185 **Fax** 01455 635687 **Email** info@cordee.co.uk
www.cordee.co.uk

With Compliments

Sent on behalf of Scottish Mountaineering Club

Anne Murray climbing in Glencoe 1966

Below: Margaret Parker on the Aonach Eagach Ridge, Glencoe

Above: Alison Higham on a perfect winter afternoon, Braeriach, Cairngorms

Below: Evening at Blackrock, Glencoe. The cottage has been occupied by the LSCC since 1947

climbed. She travelled abroad every summer and climbed in Switzerland, the Tyrol, Corsica, Czechoslovakia, the Caucasus, the Tatra, Germany, Austria and Norway.

It is hardly surprising that she was elected a Fellow of the Royal Scottish Geographical Society, reflecting her great enthusiasm for exploration. But above all was her love of the high tops which is expressed in her own description of her first Alpine summit, the Zermatt Breithorn, beginning by lantern light and watching the glorious colours of sunrise creep over the snow.

> As I stood on the summit and saw the splendid company of peaks around, I knew they were claiming my allegiance.

It might be true to say that the main objective for going to the mountains pre-World War II was exploration, and that post-War there was a subtle shift to ticking off the tops. A later chapter describes the origins and addictions of 'Munro-bagging'. Suffice it to say here that the LSCC was not lagging behind in getting their names onto the famous list of those who had completed all 283 hills in Scotland over a height of 3000 feet.

Annie Hirst, an LSCC member, was the first woman to complete all the Munros, but it wasn't until some years later, in 1960, that Anne Littlejohn and Nan Rae completed their Munros, being the forerunners of a trend in the Club. Soon other members were following in their bootprints. In 1964 Anne Littlejohn became the first woman to complete all the Munros and Corbetts (mountains over 2500 feet in height), and in 1967 Mora McCallum became the youngest woman, at 26, to finish all the Munros and all the tops. Kathy Murgatroyd, in 1982, was the first woman to do all the Munros in one expedition using only her feet and a bicycle, apart from the ferries to the island Munros – a trip which lasted from 1st May to 11th September.

This spirit of adventurous exploration was ably continued by Esme Speakman, who joined the Club in 1939. Esme was a superb alpinist and rock climber as well as having been trained in photography in Switzerland. In August 1957 she made the first ascent of the south face of the Grand Cornier in the Alps in the company of a guide. Always somehow managing to appear as the last word in elegance, she travelled all over the world, bringing back fascinating stories – mostly of the sheer hell of being an explorer – and illustrated with breathtakingly beautiful slides. Her account in the Club Journal of an expedition to Turkey in 1966 has a thrilling account of a typical Esme adventure when she was captured by bandits.

> In the early afternoon we were again on our way, travelling through a narrow, rocky glen, Ferec leading the horses, I, riding, and the other members of the party strung out behind. Suddenly, there were shouts, and two men with rifles pointed at us bounded down the hillside. One seized Ferec, while the other pulled me from my horse, and, before we could realise what had happened, we were all being pushed and pulled up the rocky hillside, while a third brigand watched from a point of vantage and kept us covered with his rifle. At length we arrived at a real 'Robbers' Den', hidden behind a spur of the hill. Here we were pushed down behind a large rock and the unfortunate Ferec

was cruelly bound with ropes. The whole thing happened so quickly that it was indeed hard to realise that this was not a stage melodrama, but real life, and that robbery and very possibly murder awaited us.

Once one has left behind the age of disobedience, and can no longer be picked up, a screaming, angry child, and smacked or put to bed, it very seldom falls to one's lot to be forced, physically, to do the bidding of another, and our reaction was one of shocked fury. We were, however, unarmed and in no position to argue with the bandits. Our every movement was watched, and twice, when Peter and Ferec showed signs of resistance, one of the men made a violent movement to bring the butt of his rifle crashing down on his victim's head. Mercifully, however, at our screams of anger the chief of the bandits stopped this.

Money was, naturally, the brigands' first demand, but we had very little with us, a fact they were, of course, quite unable to believe…They searched us thoroughly, thrusting their hands into our pockets in an effort to get at our wallets, then snatching watches from our wrists, and cameras and field glasses from our shoulders, while one, finger on the trigger, watched the operation. Next they took our rucksacks and settled down to sort out the contents, and while this went on we were able to study our captors. All three were young and very dark…all wore cartridge belts and bandoliers stuffed with ammunition and carried British rifles.

While we were being searched , the horses, still tied together, had strayed and were in difficulties on the rocky hillside, and eventually Henri and Peter were sent to fetch them. My first thought was that the bandits might well decide to shoot us all and make a quick getaway with the horses and all our belongings, however, either our mountains of baggage discouraged them – it would not have been easy to hide – or they felt perhaps that five bodies would take some explaining, for when the horses appeared we were ordered to go quickly…up to Bay Gol, there to carry out our planned programme. We needed no urging, and, conscious of the watchful gaze and the rifles of our captors, we hastened to put as much ground between us as possible.

Her laconic entry in the 1971 Club Record, describing an expedition to the Andes, typically underplays her achievement.

August. Andes, 17,200 feet approx. (Peru) Padre Huerca, First Ascent; Quolque Cruz 17,150 feet approx. First Ascent. Traverse up SW face (snow/ice; severe) descent easy. NE glaciers; Pico di Condor. First Ascent, entirely rock, 16,000 feet approx.

However the account written for the Club Journal conveys some of the danger and exhilaration of the ascent of Quolque Cruz.

Here no steps could be cut, no piton placed to safeguard the leader – delicacy of movement and of balance was our only protection. Very gently Faye edged up the ridge till she was below the final wall at a place where there was a gap in the cornice, and there I joined her. With two ice screws planted as firmly as possible at the base of the wall we had the illusion of a belay, but Faye's words 'If I come off, mind you fall down the opposite side of the ridge' were not spoken entirely as a joke.

The wait seemed interminable as I paid out the heavy, sodden rope, while Faye cut and clawed her way up the wall. When I came to follow her I marvelled, for I had the impression of climbing on soap suds, so fast did this powdery substance melt in my hands. Faye's shout of relief, however, had put an end to the tension. She was safely installed on solid ground, so that almost swimming in the frothy snow, ignoring the niceties of technique, I emerged at last, sprawling and panting at her feet. We almost ran up the final slopes and soon were standing, laughing and triumphant, on the summit of Quolque Cruz.

Esme was dogged by ill-health which prevented her from being on the first women's expedition to the Himalaya, recounted later in this book. However Betty Stark and Evelyn McNicol, both members of that expedition, also went to the Andes in 1964, the only women members of the Scottish Peruvian Expedition. What Evelyn describes as a 'most successful nine weeks climbing' included a first ascent of Sirijuani (18,400 feet), and four other first ascents of peaks which they named and described as giving 'interesting climbing of considerable difficulty'. It sounds as if they had fun!

Esme was an all-round internationalist in every sense of the word. In 1945 she headed up an international team for the Red Cross, arriving at one of the concentration camps in Holland just 24 hours after it had been liberated. Her team fed between 3000 to 5000 people, all suffering from extreme starvation. She then went on to evacuate children from the rubble of Berlin, became Commandant of a large hospital in Poland, and was then put in charge of 150,000 refugees in northwest Germany. After the war, in connection with the Girl Guide movement, she travelled to South Africa, the (then) Belgian Congo, Rhodesia and Angola. No wonder she took Turkish bandits in her stride!

All in all the Club 'firsts' were interesting and varied. As long ago as 1919 Mary Lumsden spent three years in China exploring Yunan Province; Jane Inglis Clark made a pioneer traverse of over 400 miles of the Sahara, Eleanor Lloyd went botanising on her own in Tibet long before that country was in any way open to the West. In 1926 Helene Greiner, a Club member initially based in Switzerland and later moving to Manchester, was one of the first three western women to penetrate into the High Atlas region of Morocco – an area where later members of the Club have followed. In the company of the French Alpine Club, Helene Greiner made a first ascent of Djebel (Mount) Tachdirt, continuing on her own to the summit at 3900 metres.

As the obscure corners of our planet become increasingly open to tourism it becomes harder for the present-day would-be explorer to find a truly pioneering adventure, but even here our Club has not lost its cutting edge. The first two women's expeditions to Greenland in 1968 and 1970; Kate Ross's ascent of Ama Dablam in 1996, and of Khan Tengri in Tien Shan; Kate Charles as one of the first women to overwinter with the British Antarctic Survey – all these are thrilling tales to be told in later chapters.

The Club has always avoided climbing as a competitive sport, but it could be true to say that on the whole the women of the Club rarely set out to be 'first'; being first almost crept up on them unawares. It was the product of their enthusiasm, willingness for adventure, and competence that made their achievements possible. The peaks had indeed claimed their allegiance.

Esme Speakman led the first ascent of January Jigsaw, Glencoe, and was also on the FA of the Grand Cornier in the Alps. Pictured here on a Scottish summit in 1967

Photo: Lyndsey Urquhart (LSCC Collection)

*Blackrock Cottage,
Glencoe. Date
unknown*

LSCC Archives

3: A Home of Our Own

IT MUST BE ONE of the most photographed cottages in Scotland. A typical Highland 'but and ben', trimly whitewashed, galvanised roof held down by boulders, it nestles snugly against the dramatic backdrop of the Great Shepherd of Etive, Buachaille Etive Mòr. Blackrock Cottage is timeless and when its welcoming light is seen on a dark stormy night across the bleakness of Rannoch Moor, it is the very essence of warmth, shelter and comfort.

Nor does the interior disappoint. Coming in from the rain, hanging dripping clothes above the stove in the stone-floored kitchen, one is welcomed by a cheery blaze into the woodlined sitting room, greeted by friendly faces, songs, stories, maybe a dram or two, before climbing the steep wooden stairs to sleep in warm comfort, listening to the chatter of voices below as plans are made for the hill the next day.

The LSCC has leased Blackrock from the Flemings, owners of Blackmount Estate, since 1947. It is good to know that before that it was a thriving family home. On August 30th 2005, the ashes of Colina Cameron were scattered outside the cottage in which she had spent her childhood, and members of the Club were privileged to be present at the simple ceremony and hear something of the history of their much-loved Club Hut.

Colina's parents were Colin and Janet Cameron and her father worked as a deerstalker for Blackmount Estate. Colina was the youngest of eight children – four boys and four girls – and one can picture the children giggling and laughing in the two crowded rooms upstairs. Their Aunt Mary was their teacher – possibly with some training, as she also taught pupils at Dalness in Glen Etive. Lessons were in Gaelic, of course, and took place in the sitting room in front of the fire. On occasions another four children would come across from Black Corries near Kingshouse on the other side of the glen, and if there was a blizzard, all would have to stay at Blackrock. It must have been some crowd.

It is good to picture the ceilidhs round the fire in the evening. Colin Cameron was a keen piper, and it is told that on Sundays, after the service of worship in Glencoe, the Church of Scotland minister and the Catholic priest would come up to Blackrock bringing their chanters with them and have a grand evening of music making on the bagpipes. A great example of ecumenism in action!

Colin Cameron died very suddenly of a heart attack while out on the hill. He was only 55 and it must have come as a disastrous blow for the family. As Blackrock was a tied house, the family would have to move, and they went to live with an uncle in a railway cottage near Tyndrum. One wonders how the whole family managed to fit into one of these tiny railway cottages one sees by the West Highland Line. By 1947 Blackmount Estate was ready to let the cottage go for lease.

And so we come to the LSCC. Just before World War II many ski-ing and climbing clubs were acquiring club huts as a base for their activities. The LSCC had spent a most enjoyable Meet at a club hut in Wales, and, inspired by this, had decided to look for a home of their own. A sub-committee was set up, and various options were considered, ranging from disused railway carriages to roadmender's huts and caravans. In 1940 there were indications that Lagangarbh, further down Glencoe at Alltnafeidh near the foot of the Devil's Staircase, was about to become available.

The LSCC was definitely interested, and indeed began 'nest-building' almost at once, collecting pieces of equipment and furniture that 'might be useful for our Club Hut'.

Alas, the best laid schemes of mice, and particularly men..! This is the account of how events turned out in the Club Journal.

> We were told that the cottage Lagangarbh would be available at the end of the War, and that, though the Scottish Mountaineering Club had 'first refusal' of it, it was unlikely they would avail themselves of this option. So for a time we counted our unhatched chickens, until, immediately Peace returned, our basket of eggs was firmly squashed under the big hobnailers of our respected husbands and brothers who claimed Lagangarbh in no uncertain voice.

One hesitates to picture some of the scenes of domestic discord over the morning toast and marmalade of some LSCC wives!

For the LSCC it was rather disconsolately back to the drawing board, and the sub-committee was again reduced to looking at roadmen's huts. Then in 1947 Blackmount Estate put Blackrock Cottage up for lease, and the LSCC was poised and ready for action. Riona Barclay was elected first hut custodian and there followed a frenzy of enthusiastic domesticity.

The Club was somewhat optimistic about the physical state of their new abode.

> We had believed at first that only minor repairs would be necessary, but in these first weeks, before it really knew us, Blackrock was very shy and retiring – in fact it nearly retired into the bog altogether.
>
> Grizel (then our President) was in Glencoe and made a bee-line to see our precious newly-leased cottage, and to her horror, found a goodish chunk of the coal-house wall coming unstuck and bulging outwards, which disaster she immediately and very generously offered to repair for the Club. Only a few weeks later Winifred went to meet the Building Contractor re the specification and, to her dismay, found the back kitchen wall caving inwards. These two Masonic subsidences came to be known for the purposes of reference as Grizel's bulge and Winifred's bulge.

Indeed these walls were to remain a continuous problem and on one occasion they were repaired by using plaster and bandages courtesy, it is said, of Philipshill hospital in Glasgow!

At last the great day of the opening of Blackrock arrived. The opening party lasted for two, maybe even three days, from May 24th to 25th 1947, and is enthusiastically described in the Club Record for that year.

> The day was fine and sunny at first, but a cold wind sent everyone hurrying indoors after Mrs Inglis Clark (Founder and first President of the Club) had declared the hut open by untying the tartan ribbon at the doorway. Crowding into the sitting room, the party found a table laden with dainties which made them long to sample them…(speeches ensued)…And then TEA! and what a tea! The fascinating birthday cake – a replica of Blackrock Cottage, designed and decorated by Winifred Robertson – was cut by the Founder with a Highland Dirk and thereafter enjoyed by everyone
>
> The cosy wood-lined sitting room, and the whitewashed kitchen with its open chimney and old-fashioned grate, evoked admiration, and although the steep stairway and low-raftered ceilings required care, nothing deterred those anxious to explore each neuk and cranny, and all expressed their satisfaction at the comfort and equipment of the Hut.

There was even a special Hut Song written in honour of the occasion, sung to the tune of Bonny Strathyre, of which these verses are a sample.

> There are hostels at Nevis and clachans in Skye,
> There are huts and hotels and there's camping forbye,
> But the seemliest shelter for me and for you
> Is our canty wee cottage of bonny Craig Dhu*
> There were leaks in the roof, there were holes in the wall,
> But repairs are all done and we've mended them all;
> Now there's warmth and there's cheer and there's comradeship true,
> In our cosy wee cottage of bonny Craig Dhu

*Gaelic for Black Rock

Perhaps not award-winning verse, but it certainly conveys the affection of Club members toward their new cottage.

A pleasant evening of songs and the drinking of toasts followed and the party didn't break up until 11pm. However, as the record shows, partying was not the only purpose of the Hut, and the Club remembered that its main priority was climbing.

> Dr Bell and Pat returned at midnight, having climbed pitch 10 of the Chasm of Buachaille Etive and then the Ladies' Pinnacle, and it didn't take much persuasion to make Dr Bell forsake the excitements of camping for the comfort of Black Rock.
>
> Sunday dawned wet and misty, but in spite of the weather three parties spent the day on the Buachaille. Dr Bell took Betty Stanton up the Central Buttress by the left-hand direct route and down the Curved Ridge. Pat and Betty Stark ascended Collie's Route and had an exciting descent of the Crowberry Ridge, which, owing to the mist, was mistaken for the Curved Ridge, while Esme, Ilse and Rhona climbed up and down Collie's Route.
>
> On Monday the remaining members of the party, Riona, Esme and Betty Stanton made a strenuous crossing of the bucket bridge in Glen Etive, and then climbed Sron na Creise.
>
> Riona's trials and efforts were not yet finished, however, as a wheel came off her car en route for home, and she didn't get her well-earned rest until 3am on Tuesday morning. Let us hope her dreams and memories of the momentous weekend were as happy as those of us who did little work, but enjoyed the results of her labours.

Blackrock was ideally situated for the post-war burgeoning of excellent Glencoe rock routes. In his classic book *Undiscovered Scotland* Bill Murray evokes the enthusiasm and sheer wonder of a young climber on seeing the Buachaille for the first time.

> I think that for me the most vivid experience was my first view of Buachaille Etive Mor. In the clear morning air every detail of the enormous, pointed cliffs stood out sharp. But the most striking moment was turning a corner of the road and seeing the great shape, black and intimidating, suddenly spring up in the moor. To me it was just unclimbable. I had never seen a hill like it before and my breath was taken away from me.

But later after years of exploring every nook and cranny, every weakness in the rock, every line of a good climb, and, for Bill, after five years in a prisoner of war camp, he is able to recapture the magic and delight of climbing a familiar friend.

> Now was the test. I looked at the rock, light-grey, crystalline, very rough – and so very steep. I stood back and chose my holds. What would happen? Was the old skill lost? – rock climbing a thing of the past? I gave myself, as it were, a prod, and climbed.
>
> At the very instant my hands and feet came on the rock six years rolled away in a flash. The rock was not strange, but familiar. At each move I was taking the right holds at the right time – but no, I did not 'take' the holds – of their own accord they came to me. Hand, foot, and eye – nerve and muscle – they were co-ordinating and my climbing was effortless. I reached the top feeling trust in rock and, what in the circumstances was far more wonderful, trust in myself.

This ably describes the thrill so many LSCC members experienced on the fine rocks of Glencoe and soon the Club records are full of accounts of climbs on the Buachaille, Aonach Dubh, and many many

Early Skiing. From left: Maureen Waddell (Brocklehurst), ANO, Joan Tebbutt, Nora McIntosh, Margaret Camrass (Jones)

Photo: Margaret Jones Collection

traverses of the Aonach Eagach, that wonderful long ridge stretching the whole north side of Glencoe with pleasant scrambling along its entire length.

During this time there was an interesting, if somewhat ambiguous, relationship with both the Edinburgh University Mountaineering Club and Glasgow University Mountaineering Club. On the one hand the Club was actively recruiting younger members from the universities, but at the same time, students were falling foul of the houseproud tendencies of the Ladies, and one reads of both clubs being banned periodically. After all baked beans and bootmarks on the mattresses were not always appreciated!

There has always been a tension between establishing Blackrock as club territory and the growth of other, slightly more anarchic clubs. Howffs became rather a perennial problem. On one occasion it was noted that seven howffs and a multiplicity of tents had been removed from the premises. Constant reference is made to new padlocks, gates, bars on the windows and other protection. The author remembers arriving at Blackrock at about mid-day in the company of Christina Macnair, then Hut Custodian, to find a tent pitched right across the front door, barring all access. An irate Custodian marched up to the offending tent, kicking out all the guy ropes, and was greatly surprised when a tousled head emerged from the cocoon of a sleeping bag. With the development of the West Highland Way, which goes right past the door of Blackrock, this could potentially become more of a problem. However, the owners,

Blackmount Estate, are quite firm in their refusal to allow camping around the cottage.

Ski-ing was also a growing sport, developing from a makeshift rope tow in the corrie of Ben Lawers, to a mechanised tow on Meall a' Bhuiridh, and eventually a chair-lift just behind Blackrock. Many Club members became expert in the new sport and made full use of the facilities. Mabel Jeffrey had been one of the pioneers of ski-ing in Scotland and adapted rapidly to the latest developments. Another Club member, Janie Cameron, was a keen skier and was a great encourager of others to take to the boards, as this account tells.

> Blackrock Ski-ing Weekend, February 11th and 12th 1956. Saturday afternoon Janie skied on Meall a' Bhuiridh and Cynthia, Elma and Margaret, who arrived later walked to Black Corries. Sunday, Janie, Christina, Irene and Joyce had an exciting first trip (free) on the new ski-tow, still in the experimental stage, and skied on Meall a' Bhuiridh, but found much ice on the summit slopes.

However, these developments brought their own problems. In 1954 the building of the chairlift and a new ski-road, which went right past the door, caused concern about access from the road, and eventually even gave rise to a challenge for the tenancy of the cottage from the Scottish Ski Club, who offered to pay more than the 'peppercorn' rent the Ladies were paying. After a flurry of Extra-ordinary General Meetings and correspondence to and fro, the lease was extended to the Club in return for an increased rent. Sighs of relief all round.

Tenancy secured, Blackrock soon became a base for numerous exploits and adventures. Step out of the door, climb resolutely past all the metal detritus of ski tows, chairlifts and mechanical uplift, and one is already launched on one of the classic routes over the tops. The summit of Meall a' Bhuiridh is easily reached, but thereafter more interesting territory immediately reveals itself. There is a pleasant rocky ridge leading down from Meall a' Bhuiridh with a final steep section onto the plateau of Clachlet, which can be quite exciting when plastered with snow and ice. A cairn of stones marks the spot where the ridge joins the plateau, but this can be buried under snow, and many an adventure has been had searching for this elusive cairn in thick mist or a blizzard. Some have even been known to dig themselves in for an uncomfortable night on the plateau rather than attempt to find the ridge in the dark.

A pleasant tramp across the top of Clachlet brings one to a steep descent to the col above Coire Ba, and then another tricky little bit of route-finding leads up a ridge to the summit of Stob Ghabhar. This fine top gives superb views of all the Blackmount hills and right across the desolate Moor of Rannoch to the far-distant cone of Schiehallion. Many a time climbers have left Blackrock for a short day on Meall a' Bhuiridh and been lured ever onwards by these tempting ridges, often totally oblivious to the inevitable onset of darkness, causing interesting late descents into Coire Ba and a long tramp home. Even a tedious night tramp, however, can be transformed. The author has vivid memories of an iron hard winter descent where the glimmer of stars reflected brilliantly in the frozen lochans, and of another time when crampons were worn from start to finish on crisp ringing ice.

Often the route is done in reverse, starting from Stob Ghabhar and

finishing with the warm welcome of the hut. One such Club outing on an October day started out dreich and drizzly on Stob Ghabhar, but as they neared the summit the cloud thinned and the party emerged into full sunlight with all the high tops raising their heads above a sea of cotton clouds. As they descended from this magnificence to the col between the next two mountains, the rain closed in again, but this wonderful experience was repeated three times, ending with a golden sunset above the clouds on Meall a' Bhuiridh.

Not that the weather in Glencoe is always so kind. Kinlochleven, just down the glen, is reckoned to have the highest rainfall in Scotland – one of the reasons why an aluminium smelter was situated there. Blackrock can be quite spectacularly wet, with the river bursting its banks, a regular torrent flowing past the front door, and the fire almost obscured by dripping clothes.

Storms and blizzards too can lash the cottage. Long ago there was a substantial lean-to shed at the eastern end of the cottage. During one particularly severe gale this blew away completely. The tale is told that the hut was full at the time with a party from the Junior Mountaineering Club of Scotland, but they were so busy having a gambling session in the sitting room that they never heard a thing!

Burns night has often been celebrated in fine style, with a rendition of Tam O' Shanter particularly eerie in the Blackrock candlelight. One memorable Burns Supper in 1993 contrasts the 'storm withoot' to the cosy scene in the cottage.

> As it had been snowing or sleeting all day, the main road was now getting dangerous. So with slight apprehension we headed north towards Blackrock. On arrival we lit both fires and soon got the place cosy. Outside the wind howled and the sleet continued, so we settled down for a quiet evening. Surely nobody would venture out unless their journey was essential.
>
> Then about 6 o'clock the door rattled more vigorously than normal. This was Jean and Moira arriving from Glasgow. They were somewhat shattered as they had had an epic journey braving the hurricane, and would have turned back but they thought the Loch Lomond road would be blocked with floods.

Then a few minutes later Fionna arrived from Skye. Blackrock certainly has a magnetic appeal!

Shortly after their arrival somebody glanced out of the window and noticed flashing blue and orange lights on the main road. In the morning it was revealed that a large lorry had been blown off the road into the bog. It was a wild night!

Other kinds of drama have occurred as well. One member suffered a perforated ulcer while staying at Blackrock, and had to stagger with her children an agonising three kilometres to Kingshouse Hotel for help. Another had acute stomach pain and ended up in an ambulance being taken to Belford Hospital in Fort William. Perhaps the strangest incident was when a young Belgian woman camping nearby stood on a crochet hook which became anchored around a tendon in her foot and had to be driven down the glen to the district nurse.

Then there was the memorable New Year when Olive Osborne describes her first ever visit to Blackrock. She arrived on a night of snow and stars, but no moon, to find the cottage in darkness and the lock frozen.

The shapes of the unfamiliar mountains loomed, first on one side, then on the other, giving an eerie feel to it all. The front door had several key holes. I tried them all – with both keys. I pushed and pulled, but no way would the door yield. By now it was nearly 11 o'clock. Should I return to Kingshouse, or...? I thought of all I had read about being benighted in snow. I shone my torch into the shack. The floor was dry. There were a few handfuls of heather. I decided to stay.

I took out my spare clothing, put on everything I could under my top clothing, arranged the bits of heather as best I could, took off my boots and put on my spare socks, then put my feet in the rucksack (it didn't prove as warm as I had hoped!), made my day sack into a rather uncomfortable pillow and relaxed hoping for sleep.

As the snow showers came and went, snow crystals filtered through the holes in the corrugated iron onto my face. I reached out for my large aluminium plate and propped it at a suitable angle to protect my face. Thoughtfully, I had a half-pound bag of glacier mints with me – they were all gone by morning!

Fortunately her resourcefulness was rewarded by a reunion with key-holding Club members the next morning, and a good New Year was had by all.

It was on one such memorably wet weekend that the idea of the West End Bothy was born. Rain had battered the windows of the cottage all day, and any suggestions of intrepid deeds were quickly overruled by more cups of coffee or tempting offers of cake. The fire was burning brightly and no-one wanted to set foot out of doors. However, although lazy in body, the minds were active, and a suggestion was mooted that the coal shed at the west end of the Hut could be converted into an excellent bothy for the use of members when the hut was let out to other clubs. Enthusiasm ran high. It would have bunk beds, the walls would be wood-lined, there could be a stove for heating. It was at this point that Pam Cain, one of the more practical members of the Club, popped her head round the door. The idea was put to her. She too was enthused, but, practical soul that she was, she said; 'Yes, but have you measured it up?' 'It's too wet to go out' was the rather lame response. On venturing forth with measuring tapes it was discovered that in fact the sun was shining!

A core group of four Club members spent the next year working hard at weekends making the dream become reality, and Blackrock now has a very comfortable West End Bothy for the use of the members.

Once a year a maintenance weekend is organised and this can be as much sport (and often as fraught with danger) as a climbing weekend. On one occasion while fixing the roof in a gale, Molly Johnstone's husband, Scott, just happened to open his mouth to shout a remark, when his false teeth were whipped away in the wind! With the roof requiring regular painting, drains to be dug, chimneys to be re-pointed, walls whitewashed, rafters scrubbed , mattresses taken out and beaten, and all the countless cleaning jobs that even the most reluctant of housewives can find, there is plenty of scope for willing hands and good fun while they're at it. Countless photographs have been taken at maintenance weekends and the gourmet food has become a tradition even rivalling the early hampers of the Marchioness.

However, even on these work weekends, the hills are not forgotten, and on at least one occasion hills have been climbed by moonlight so as not to waste any precious time. One has to wonder whether the moonlight climbers were as enthusiastic about the daylight chores. The Records show a typical post-cleaning day on the hills.

> On Sunday the party split into two groups. Nan waited for some Perth friends to arrive, with whom she climbed the Chasm. Irene and Heather did the Aonach Eagach Ridge. Louise and Ken set off home via Cruachan; Hazel, who was going on the afternoon bus, went for a walk; and the rest of us went to the East Face of Aonach Dubh. 'Ikes' (Isobel Dickson) and Joyce went to the top and from there on to Stob Coire nan Lochan, returning by the Hidden Valley. The others climbed Lower Bow and Quiver, collected their packs and wandered wearily up Barn Wall...Joyce and Elma made the fatal mistake of sitting down to admire the shadows on Rannoch Moor. *(Only fatal in the sense that they might have stayed there lolling at ease for ever, Ed.)*

Partly because of uncertainty regarding the lease of Blackrock, a decision was taken in 1960 to look for a property that the Club could actually own itself. After a two year search and some abortive attempts, a cottage came on the market.

Milehouse is a small cottage close to the shores of Loch Insh, exactly a mile from Kincraig and a mile from Feshiebridge – hence, possibly, the name. There is some uncertainty about its original name, the granddaughter of the previous inhabitant remembering it as 'The Gatehouse', although it appears on the earliest available map in 1899 as Milehouse. From its position on what was the main highway through Strathspey to Grantown, and situated almost exactly a mile from Feshiebridge, it might well have been a toll house. Mrs Rosa Grant who is descended from the family who last occupied it said that her great-grandfather, Alexander MacPherson, who lived in the cottage, worked as a cobbler, and may have used the lean-to shed at the back as his workshop. As

Opening of Milehouse Cottage, near Kincraig, October 1963. The LSCC bought the cottage at auction for £690

LSCC Archives

with Blackrock, a large family was crammed into the two rooms – one son and five daughters – and there is a grand old sepia photograph showing a charabanc piled high with family members arriving at the front door of Milehouse.

The actual purchase of Milehouse happened amidst great drama. It came up for sale at public auction when most of the committee members just happened to be in the Alps attending a Meet at Saas Fee. In the days before e-mails and mobile phones, urgent telegrams and phonecalls were flying back and forth to empower Club member 'Ikes', to act on behalf of the Club and bid up to a limit of £700. She was successful and the cottage was bought for the grand total of £690. Nan Rae became the first custodian of Milehouse.

> Then came the fun (and it was fun) of renovating it. In view of what the Sanitary Inspector had said about the order (he had condemned it) all that was possible was done to improve the building. The walls and ceilings, which had been covered with paper (newspapers, magazines, and even brown wrapping paper – with the postage stamps still adhering) and painted over, were stripped bare and repainted. By sacrificing a cupboard in the large bedroom and making the small bedroom slightly smaller, space was provided to form the toilet. This alteration was suggested by the plumber and has proved so handy that I have long since forgiven him his remark, 'It would be better if the toilet were inside the house so that if any of the ladies weren't well during the night it would save them a long trek down the garden'.

In the process of examining and repairing the roof, it was discovered that underneath the usual corrugated iron, there was a heather thatch. This was left intact and greatly added to the warmth.

Milehouse was officially opened on October 26th 1963, and this of course afforded the occasion for another party. A big crowd of Club members and many guests from other clubs and local folks gathered outside on the road. Mr Hutchison, the local minister blessed the cottage, and then Mabel Jeffrey cut the tartan ribbon across the front door.

> Shortly after the departure of the guests, something resembling a witches' orgy

erupted amongst the LSCC. This, being in the nature of 'private business', was rather less formal than the afternoon session. A meal in the village hall (next door) (champit tatties with real silver threepennies – and champagne) was followed by the kindling by Mrs Jeffrey of a bonfire in the grounds. The bonfire so far exceeded expectations that a stirrup-pump squad was called into action to restrain its exuberance. A treacle-scone competition (advisedly held outdoors), dooking for aipples (inadvisedly held indoors), and a session of Mrs Jeffrey's tales of mystery and imagination occupied the remainder of the evening. Especially memorable were the many handsome neep lanterns and the magnificent Milehouse cake devised by Mrs Jeffrey's cook.

And inevitably such festivities had to be recorded in lyrical song;

The Milehouse Song (sung to the tune of The River Clyde)

I sing of a cottage I'm happy inside
Of Milehouse that hut by the bonny lochside
Of all Scottish huts it's the dearest to me
For it belongs to the L.S.C.C.
It's strategic, hygienic, electric as well
Now painted and polished it looks simply swell
For the work of Nan Miller could not be surpassed
Through her efforts we now have two club huts at last.

The purchase of Milehouse opened up the playground of the Cairngorms, and many happy expeditions were planned and executed using Milehouse as a base. Snow and ice climbs in Coire an Lochan, moonlit ascents of the Glen Feshie hills, winter training weekends, navigation exercises on the Cairngorm Plateau, high level camping, walks through the passes of Feshie, Minnigaig and Gaick, all began and ended by the fireside at Milehouse to be the subject of epic tales.

Nothing is more guaranteed to arouse passionate debate at a Club AGM than any alteration to our club huts. Cats, dogs, children and even men in huts can cause controversy, but try to instal a new fireplace and the arguments can rage for years. Fortunately Blackrock has maintained its unique character as an old-fashioned Highland bothy, but over the years as demands for home comforts have grown, changes have slowly been made. The old kitchen range (which must have used up an inordinate amount of space in a small kitchen) was replaced by a stove; in 1955 calor gas replaced primus stoves, oil lamps and candles in the downstairs rooms. In 1959 there was a proposal to instal piped water, but that was turned down, and part of the routine on arrival is still to go down to the nearby burn and draw buckets of water to fill up the old 'wash-day' boiler in the kitchen. There are occasions when an ice-axe is necessary to break through to the water below, but that is all part of the mystique, so they say. It was 1994 before a water pump was installed in the toilet and a septic tank dug in, but the only showers available at Blackrock to this day are those provided free by standing outside.

The biggest change was the installation of electricity. In 1981 the lease was secured for a further 25 years, and this coincided with an offer from the hydro-electric to instal power at a reduced rate right down Glen Etive. Inevitably there was a luddite faction arguing vociferously to retain the romance of gas light and candles, fearing the advent of such decadence

Milehouse, with Sarah Mackay on high. A hut maintenance weekend is held annually

Sarah Mackay Collection

as tvs, microwaves and saunas. However, when it became apparent that the Club's refusal of the offer would have prevented the permanent households of Glen Etive from the use of the modern appliances taken for granted by most of us, romance had to give way to common sense. Strangely enough these opponents of the 'electric' didn't show any reluctance to turn on the heater first thing on arrival on a cold winter's night!

However, while the charm of Blackrock lies in its old-world primitive comfort, Milehouse was a different story. Other clubs renting the cottage of a weekend were beginning to demand higher standards. The

Blackrock Cottage.
Marion Boyle wields
a paintbrush
LSCC Archives

time had come to upgrade the Hut, installing showers, a drying room and a more modern kitchen. The Club decided to build on a whole new extension at the back of the cottage to provide more accommodation and to incorporate these modernisations. Obviously this required energetic fund-raising and applications for grants, but after a huge output of effort, the target was reached and a beautiful new extension built, with the interior thoroughly modernised, yet with enough of the old character retained to make us all feel thoroughly at home. The process of building the extension involved opening up part of the roof, and it was discovered that pipistrelle bats were roosting in the rafters. This held up proceedings somewhat, as the builders had to wait until the bats had moved off to their winter roosts thus allowing access to the roof.

Of course the opening of the extension gave an excuse for yet another party. Both our huts are ideal venues for parties and by now it must be pretty obvious to the reader that any history of the LSCC would be incomplete without some reference to memorable parties. New Year is often celebrated in one or other of the huts. In spite of Blackrock sometimes being unspeakably wet, it is possible to shut the door, light the fires and have a roaringly good time. Sometimes too the weather at New Year can be sparklingly bright, as is described in 1979/80.

> This was a very select Meet, due (it is suspected) to the defection of certain members to The Other Place (Milehouse). It was none the less memorable in many ways – for conviviality and hilarity; for fabulous weather, with bright sunlight and bright moonlight and the glitter of powder snow; for a highly addictive brew of Green Ginger; for an exceptional amount of broken glass in the kitchen....
>
> Pamela and Stella, the first arrivals, spent part of Sunday at Fort William and walked up to Lochan Meall an t' Siudhe, enjoying fine weather but not enjoying the soft powder snow. Later in the night everyone took a moonlight stroll, Helen and Stella going about half-way up Meall a' Bhuiridh.
>
> On Monday...an unpromising morning gave way to a 'peerless' day. Helen, Stella, Eilidh and Christina reached Stob Dubh just as the sun set and the moon rose simultaneously. Everything was sheer beauty except for the tedious going in dry powdery snow. The arrival of 1980 was duly celebrated with sundry potations, music-making and dances.

Milehouse, situated further east, tends to be even colder than Blackrock, and there have been many occasions when cars have failed to start as the frost lingers long in the shady pockets amongst the pine trees. Some hardy types have even been known to camp in the garden of Milehouse when the temperature has plunged well below zero. Going to bed then involves not undressing, but muffling up in pullovers, down jackets, bedsocks, longjohns, even gloves and balaclava, not to mention the furtive sneaking of a decadent hot water bottle into the sleeping bag. The cosy inmates of the cottage will merrily shake the hoar frost off the tent in the morning to wish one a Happy New Year with a mug of rapidly cooling morning tea.

Both Huts have come of age and 21st birthday parties were the order of the day, However, Blackrock's 50th anniversary in 1997 involved some interesting retrospective activity, as it was decided to emulate the example of our foremothers 50 years before.

Saturday dawned fine and at least 12 members and guests set out for the East Face of Aonach Dubh, where we were intending to climb some of the rock routes which had been put up in 1947, the year we signed the first lease for Black Rock. LSCC teams were climbing routes all over the crag, much to the amusement of other parties. There was one ascent of Barn Wall in nailed boots, and a climber wearing tweed jacket, flat cap and nails was also spotted.

Some LSCC members walked over Stob Ghabhar and Meall a' Bhuiridh to arrive at Black Rock on foot as members had done 50 years ago; Stella Crampton even started from Bridge of Orchy Station.

There is a fine long bench along the west wall of the cottage, put there in memory of Riona Barclay, the first Custodian. When the midges allow, there can be nothing finer than to sit watching the sun set behind the Buachaille casting long shadows over a golden moor. There is a feeling of timelessness, of being part of a long line of folk who have known and loved these mountains. In an article about the fiftieth anniversary of Blackrock written in *The Scotsman* by well-known climber and writer Rennie McOwan the spirit of Blackrock is brilliantly brought alive.

The old cottage has seen and heard so much, flickering candles and dim lamps, winter storms howling round the roof, songs and laughter, the Buachaille lost in mist or glistening in sun or snow, the 'feel' of a base that looks as a mountaineering howff should.

Some buildings take on the character of their owners. Many faces have now gone forever and a chapter in mountaineering history is perhaps ending. Gear has been modernised, but Blackrock is steeped in the club's love of the mountain world. Here's to the next 50.

Milehouse, on the other hand, is changing. The little south facing window seat looks out over tall gently swaying silver birches; but not for much longer, as the land around has been bought and will be developed for housing. Nothing, however, can take away its location amidst the ancient Caledonian pine forests of Rothiemurchus, the silver loops of the Spey, and the subtle vastness of the Cairngorm plateau looming remote over all. May we and others enjoy our Huts for many years to come. Perhaps the Club's affection for their huts is best summed up in another verse of the Milehouse Song.

Imagine you've left smokey cities behind
And northwards with spirits uprising you wind
Through Perth and Pitlochry, Dalwhinnie you go
Turn right at Kincraig for the cottage you know.

Next morning on rising the sun's shining so
Through birches and pines to Braeriach you go
From Einich to Feshie the way is so long
But the miles shrink to Inshes when singing this song.

Oh the climbing hut, that hut on Speyside
The thought of it thrills me and fills me with pride
And I'm satisfied whate'er may betide
I'll sing of Milehouse by the bonny lochside.

Lucy Smith and Pauline Ranken, Salisbury Crags, Edinburgh June 1908. The route is possibly 'The Long Stride'

LSCC Archives

4: Rock Bound

FROM ITS OUTSET, the Ladies Scottish was a climbing club – that is to say, they did not only wander the tops and explore remote corners of Scotland, they took to the rocks with ropes and gear. It was only at the latter end of the nineteenth century that climbers realised that it was not necessary to go abroad to the Alps to find good sport and there was a boundless rock playground waiting on their doorstep in Scotland.

Nowadays when planning a rock climb one studies the guide book and follows a graded climb and it is increasingly hard to find a new route that does not involve spider-woman techniques clinging to impossible-looking walls. It is hard to imagine the excitement of having the whole of Scotland lying open waiting for the routes to be discovered. In 1908 when the Club was founded many of the rock routes were still to find and there was a lively spirit of exploration which must have been most exhilarating. Indeed from the early accounts it would seem that these women deliberately sought out the hardest ways up the mountains, as for example when the redoubtable Mabel Jeffrey led a group up the Pinnacle Ridge of Garbh Bheinn of Ardgour looking for 'the most difficult rocks we could find'!

*Easter 1939
Inchnadamph Meet.
West Face of Caisteal
Liath, Suilven ,
Nancy Ridyard (top),
Nancy Forsyth
(bottom left) and May
Green, (bottom right)*

Photo: Ilse Bell

Anyone who has seen the dramatic 'sugar-loaf' outline of the steep west face of Suilven in Sutherland would not readily contemplate going up that way unless they were looking for a really hard climb. However, in 1939 the Club record has this account.

Nancy Ridyard and Nancy Forsyth led Ilse Bell and May Green up the centre of the west face of Caisteal Liath. Their accounts of the climb were guarded, and we gathered that, though rich in verdure, it could not be called an easy day for a lady.

I.Keay (known as 'Ikes') on Crowberry Ridge, Buachaille Etive Mòr, Glencoe, May 1933

LSCC Archives

During these early years many of the classic routes were being pioneered, most of them 1000 foot to 1200 foot lines up long ridges leading to the summit of the mountain. The Cuillin of Skye, Ben Nevis and Glencoe became magnets for climbers and the names of the routes became as familiar as toast and marmalade. The four long ridges of Ben Nevis; North East Buttress, Observatory Ridge, Tower Ridge and Castle Ridge; and in Glencoe, Crowberry Ridge and Curved Ridge on Buachaille Etive Mòr; and of course the Great Ridge of the Cuillin in Skye all became familiar classics.

The founders of the Club led the way in pioneering some of the hard routes of their day. This is Jane Inglis Clark's account of the second ascent of that Glencoe classic, Abraham's Route on Crowberry Ridge in 1905.

Our climb of Crowberry Ridge (Abraham's Route) was so difficult and so exciting that the memory of every bit of it stands out today clear and distinct.

The LSCC was yet but a dream of mine that was fulfilled three years later. I was truly a pioneer of rock climbing for women in Scotland...We travelled luxuriously in our car the two miles from Kingshouse Inn to the base of Buachaille Etive, where we met Mr Harold Raeburn who was to lead us up Crowberry Ridge. In May, 1900, three years before, Abraham's party, after carefully reconnoitring the route, finally accomplished the climb and pronounced it the most difficult climb in Britain.

My husband writes thus in the *SMC Journal*: 'The ascent of the appalling cliffs at the bottom of the Crowberry Ridge by the Messrs. Abraham and party seemed something quite beyond the powers of my wife or myself...Little wonder that, as we wound our way up the steep hillside amid rock scenery, impressive and beautiful, we felt possible misgivings as to the advisability of our being of the second party to attack this formidable climb. When our fingers gripped the splendid rough rock and the boots felt the excellent footholds, we were reassured.'

The climb begins at the bottom with 80 feet of steep rock; the abundance of holds makes this part comparatively easy. After this a somewhat broad ledge is reached, and the next sixty or seventy feet from here is the crux of the climb. 'To the left the ridge fell in an appalling vertical cliff for about a hundred to a hundred and fifty feet. To our right the deep-cleft gully was walled in by precipitous cliffs...' We turned to the left and braved the dangers of that appalling precipice. 'Stepping off the edge, the left foot seeks for a two-inch foothold round the corner.

This consists of a narrowing ledge sloping steeply upwards and outwards. The right hand retains a rough grip, while the left is rested on a slender pinnacle projecting some half-inch from the face. Having fairly balanced on these slender supports, the body is taken round the corner.' The nearest available hold was some distance from Mr Raeburn's reach, and he 'had to forego the little pinnacle and trust to mere hollows for support.' An anxious and silent interval was only broken by the slow movement of the rope, but soon it moved more rapidly, 'and after thirty-five feet were out, the second climber followed and then the third....'

I have accomplished some very difficult rock climbs such as the Kleine Zinne and the Winkler Thurm in Tirol, but it was the absence of holds, the trusting to mere hollows for support, the squirming and wriggling up that rock face of Buachaille Etive that I can never forget.

Inevitably in the early days of the Club excursions to the now familiar rock playgrounds were restricted by transport. Few but the very rich could afford a car and as already mentioned the Inglis Clarks owned the first car in Edinburgh. Glencoe, now reached in an easy one and a half hours drive at most from Glasgow, was then considered difficult of access, and the occasional glimpse of the narrow twisting 'old road' tells why. Ben Nevis, conveniently near Fort William, and the Arrochar hills were much easier because of nearby railways. Every year there was a 'Highland Meet' often near such places as Crianlarich, Bridge of Orchy, Killin, or even in the far North West, but for the rest of the year rock climbing had to be accessible to Edinburgh.

Second only to Castle Rock itself, the most significant feature of the Edinburgh skyline is the crouching lion of Arthur's Seat, thrusting upwards behind Holyrood Palace. And all along its west face is an impressive rock escarpment known as Salisbury Crags. Right on their back doorstep this was an irresistible playground for rock climbers and many weekends, and even week nights, were spent there by the Ladies. However, the very proximity of the Crags to the entire populace of Edinburgh – eager schoolboys and rash adventurers alike – soon made them liable to restrictions. Even as early as 1908 'health and safety' was making its presence felt. Perhaps the all too frequent ignominious rescue by fireman's ladder gave rise to the rule that all climbers had to be off the rock by 9am. The reason given was that it was to avoid too many curious spectators putting themselves in the way of falling rocks, however, as Hester White's account in *Climbs Before Breakfast* pointed out;

> This rule certainly attains its object as our audience has been limited to three Old Age Pensioners (slightly interested), a large number of rabbits (mostly petrified), and a flock of sheep (wholly indifferent).

The Club still possesses a meticulously hand-drawn map of the crags belonging to Lucy Smith, one of the founders of the Club, and she has also left a notebook as a guide to some of the routes on Salisbury Crags. A classic photograph shows her making an incredibly long stride on the rocks attired in her long skirts, boots and elegant wide-brimmed hat. She must surely have been on the climb entitled the Long Stride, a climb described in the SMC Journal of 1900 by Inglis Clark himself;

> Quite close to this (Ordinary Quarry Climb) is the 'Long Stride Quarry Climb', the most difficult of the three. Keeping into the angle of the rock, it is easy to get up the first 6 or 7 feet. The direct ascent of the angle can be accomplished, but is beyond the powers of most climbers, the holds being small, the rocks nearly vertical, and the slabs slippery. The usual route is by means of a long stride to a narrow ledge on the left, where the left hand finds a convenient hold at arm's length. Thence, standing on a needle of rock, another narrow ledge must be reached by a straight up pull and careful balance, and after that the climb is nearly at an end. For those of short stride, like the writer, the step to the ledge is risky if not impossible, and should not be undertaken without a rope from above. To others of weak arm power and defective balance, the next move may prove still more unsafe.

No mention is made of the added difficulties of long skirts and hats!

In her 1938 article Hester White describes the joys of climbing on Salisbury Crags before breakfast.

The Cuillin Ridge and Inaccessible Pinnacle

Rab Anderson

The climb to the west of the Long Stride is the Blowhole Climb, whose first pitch can also be attacked direct by utilising the blasting hole. The start to the left is much easier. The only awkward pitch is circumventing a bulge, or, for the tall, getting over it.

One morning we started up what appeared to be a route on the West Buttress. In all modesty I must confess we worked with a rope from above, and anyone who wishes to try to lead this route and claim a first ascent is at liberty to do so. We are not ambitious for the honour. Between the Easterly and Middle Corner Climbs, above the First Platform, we found nail marks, which came to an abrupt finish at a bulging wall. The only foothold to the right was so awkward that we found it easier to descend a few feet and try farther to the right, and attack the angle of the rock, which we were aiming to gain, from the foot. The holds here are small. The next difficulty above this is another bulge which was surmounted by a strong pull on the arms, as

Alison Higham,
Pinnacle Ridge,
Sgùrr nan Gillean,
Skye, August 1976

Photo: John Higham

the hold, a rounded knob, is nearly six feet up. The last pitch is unpleasant. It consists of worming one's way left, round under an overhang on to footholds, whose consistency for climbing purposes is as dependable as Gorgonzola. The same applies to the handhold. The rest of the climb, though completely rotten, is easy.

Just looking at that picture of Lucy Smith in her long skirt and imagining what it must have been like trailing a weight of damp mud-sodden wool around the hills makes one reflect on the changes that have taken place in climbing gear. At the first AGM of the Club a 'Club Climbing Outfit' of rope, lantern, compass and a selection of maps was to be made available on loan. Ropes of course were made of twisted hemp, usually 100 or 120 feet long. When it is wet, hemp becomes heavier and heavier, and if iced becomes almost impossible to coil, having a mind of its own entirely independent of any attempt to control it. Climbers simply tied this rope around their waists using a bowline knot, with no harness or other concession to comfort or support should one have the misfortune to fall off. Members of the Club were encouraged to acquire a rope of their own and also a pair of nailed boots.

Anyone born of the generation old enough to have possessed a proper pair of climbing boots nailed with 'tricounis' will know what purgatory they were. Guaranteed to give large juicy blisters before they were broken in, they scarted and clattered around on the rocks, sometimes striking sparks and requiring very delicate placing to grip on the holds. Indeed one way of finding one's way among the rock routes was to follow the white scratch marks left by earlier boots. The exact pattern of nails on the soles of one's boots was quite an exclusive business, and the LSCC had its own particular design made especially by a cobbler in Argyll Street in Glasgow. Often when attempting a particularly delicate piece of rock climbing, the boots were removed, and progress was made in stocking soles – even better when wet!

What a relief it was in the 1950s when rubberised Vibram 'Commando' soles came in with their ridged moulded soles and padded soft leather ankles. Boots have become increasingly lightweight and comfortable and one almost takes it for granted that at least one's feet will be dry and comfortable. Even more joy for rock climbers when lightweight tight-fitting 'rock boots' came into style, allowing for delicate footwork and giving maximum friction on the rocks. Grades suddenly seemed easier, even although the tight-fitting boots often rubbed all the skin off one's toes. Even a rock climbing rabbit fitted with such boots could feel a rush of (misplaced?) confidence. One can only admire the skill of these early climbers who put up hard classic routes using such awkward gear.

For many, Skye is the Mecca of rock climbing, and with good reason. The Black Cuillin shows a magnificent skyline, with a superb long ridge of almost continuous rock climbing, containing 12 Munro summits. The rock is gabbro, a dark-coloured coarse-grained igneous rock with a remarkably rough adhesive quality, giving very pleasurable rock climbing. (Perhaps 'abrasive' is a rather more accurate description, as a week's rock climbing in Skye leaves one with very little skin on the finger-tips and urgent need of patching the breeks!). The magnificent corries abound in fine climbs, many of which were pioneered in the 1890s by such SMC worthies as Naismith, Ling, and Collie.

The Ladies were not slow to follow – indeed were very likely companions on many of these climbs – and the early Records read like a catalogue of classic rock routes in Skye. Take for example Ella Mann's entry in the 1926 'Member's Doings'; Pinnacle Ridge of Sgùrr nan Gillean; the Bhasteir Tooth; Naismith's and Shadbolt's Route; Cioch Direct; Collie's Amphiteatre Climb. This is her description of one such route.

> There is one ascent that everyone who climbs in Skye should be made to do. It is a climb with a sense of humour, a climb unique – Shadbolt's Chimney on the Bhasteir Tooth. The most sensational route is the descent. One starts off by getting flat on one's back, then, feet first, one slides down a sort of rabbit-hole, which ends in a manhole with a drop into – nothing, almost! All this in darkness. At this point the leader with a *flair* lights a match. But I shall give away no more secrets of this climb, except to say that one emerges into the light of day with the worst still to come.

An ambition of many climbers, then and now, is to do a complete traverse of the whole Cuillin Ridge from end-to-end. Usually this will begin at the easiest end with an ascent of Sgùrr nan Gillean and proceeds along pleasant ridge scrambling over Am Basteir and Bruach na Frithe – pausing to admire the Bhasteir Tooth – over Sgùrr a' Mhadaidh, Sgùrr a' Ghreadaidh and Sgùrr na Banachdaich, and so to perhaps the climax, Sgùrr Dearg and the Inaccessible Pinnacle – not really inaccessible, but hard enough to have daunted the worthy Sir Hugh Munro himself, and cheated him of one of his Munros. It is usually ascended along its steep coxcomb of the longer east ridge and involves abseiling down the west face. Another challenge on the route is the famous Theàrlaich-Dubh Gap which involves a tricky climb down one side of the gap and then a climb up the other side to finish on Sgùrr na Eag.

If one is not thoroughly worn out by such endeavours, then the Greater Traverse is an option, including the additional delightful summits of Blàbheinn and Clach Glas. A challenge often undertaken is to complete the whole traverse within 24 hours, an expedition often planned with military precision requiring helpful allies leaving discreet caches of water and other comforts at strategic points on the route.

Joan Tebbutt has an amusing description of doing the Ridge in 1938 with Nancy Ridyard and Nancy Forsyth, two of the Club's keenest rock climbers of the day.

> I now lie (quite contentedly) in a pool of water, as the rain beats unremittingly on the sagging tent. But do I care? Not a bit. It's so heavenly to do nothing but be completely still in a horizontal position with nothing whatever demanded of one's arms or legs or feet; it seems to me the very height of bliss at the moment – having for twenty hours or so been clambering up gabbro faces and teetering down, up and down, after the flying feet of the Nancies.
>
> I forget exactly who was to blame for this Ridge idea, but it came to the boil at eleven one night as we crawled into bed after a day in Slanting Gully, and we decided to get up at three next morning...Darkness and a cold wind met us as we peered out of the tents at the dim dawn. Even Ridyard, always at the top of her social and physical form the moment she wakes, merely grunted as she crawled out and looked up at Sgumain....

Anne Littlejohn, Theàrlaich-Dubh Gap, Cuillin Ridge. In 1964 she set up a record for an unroped solo traverse of the Ridge in 17h 22m

LSCC Archives

'Not much of a day.'

'Foul,' said Forsyth.

'Blowing up for rain.' But there was no getting away from the fact that the Ridge was clear, something phenomenal for the spell of weather we'd been having.

I've dim recollections of a super breakfast made by the indomitable Ridyard, and of nauseating sandwiches that we cut as in a dream and stuffed mechanically into our rucksacks (and hardly had time to eat anyway!) and of dividing the weight equally as Forsyth drove us with a glazed look in her eyes along to Sligachan – and of plodding conscientiously up the rocks of Sgùrr na-h-Uamha, and back onto Gillean, where we sat down for what must have been at least five minutes and simultaneously offered one another whatever one happened to be finding heaviest. I thought a tin of grapefruit would be the very thing, and why not have a good long drink out of my aluminium water bottle? We changed into rubbers there, and no matter how you packed them, your boots felt like a couple of wringers on your back – all knobs and what a weight!

From where we stood grimly resigning ourselves to these frightful burdens we could see the countless peaks of the great Cuillin Ridge swinging away southwest to Ghreadaidh, round to the Inaccessible, Sgumain, and beyond the Dubhs to Sgùrr nan Eag and Gars-bheinn, blue in the distance, dim and far and incredible as heaven, and always as we moved, crawling up and clambering down and padding silently along, we were conscious of those shapely peaks strung like beads on a necklace in a wide curve against the cloudless sky, the silver sea running in among them at either end.

'Naismith's Route,' said Ridyard, as I came puffing up to find the two of them calmly contemplating the descent of what seemed to be at least a super-severe dropping some millions of feet down to a scree slope that appeared to leap up and meet you, sway dizzily and dissolve and resolve itself again as you looked.

Me: Whew! (removing pack to think about this).

N.R.: Down you pop. (making a belay).

Me: Oh, yes – er – I see – you mean – just straight down here? (knotting my rope a little tighter.

N.R.: That's it – just straight over the edge – *lovely* holds – just like walking downstairs.

And so it was – only to a mere pansy it seemed the stairs had been left out....

After this came a series of what seemed like dozens of absurd little knobs that must be traversed, and then all the Mhadaidhs, Ghreadaidh and Thormaid. My mental picture of every peak includes a clear but distant view of the rear patches of the swift Nancies and the soles of their four rubbers, vanishing upwards, lightly skimming each cairn and positively flying on to the next....

Now and then we allowed ourselves judicious sips from the water bottle. Never have I been so thirsty – the glugging of the half-empty bottle in one's pack was very trying to the self-control! By the time we reached Banachdich I had ceased to look on this as a 'nice day out' and was beginning to tire of the way this confounded Ridge would rear extra pinnacles up here and there for sheer cussedness it seemed...It was demoralising, and when I looked up again there were those two just streaking up the Inaccessible!

But what a supreme moment it was on the top of that pinnacle. We felt very grateful to the powers that be for having set us at that particular moment on that particular spot. The sun by this time was very low (ominously low!) shining from below a bank of dark clouds, throwing its golden light against the soaring Cuillin peaks with a background of shimmering sea. Macleod's Maidens seemed to stand in a pool of gold, and as we turned we had a wonderful glimpse of the Brocken Spectre of our great pinnacle surrounding and almost obliterating in its ethereal colour the summit of Sgumain.

That was the peak of the day, in more respects than one. The weather deteriorated very quickly, and by the time we reached the Thearlaich-Dubh Gap darkness had fallen with wet mists and a cold wind. We took the line of least resistance and decided to wait for daylight. The boulder we chose to shelter us from the wind was not at all accommodating, and I must admit it was quite a rest to get up and move again when the light came. With dawn came rain and thickest mist: and somehow or other we found ourselves gravitating towards the top of such an inviting stone shoot that, before we knew where we were, we were at the bottom, among the great iceworn whalebacks of Coire Lagan, lying on our tummies mopping the burns dry.

Cocks were beginning to crow as we waded across the moor below the Lochàn Fhir-bhallaich, and a hearty person in immaculate slacks said 'Getting up an appetite for breakfast?'

This valiant attempt so nearly succeeded and gives some indication of the amount of energy and stamina required to complete the Ridge. After all in the 1930s it was well-known as the 'biggest mountaineering expedition in the British Isles'.

All climbing clubs go through phases of activity when there are many keen climbers putting up new routes or pushing up the grades on known routes, and equally times when there is less interest in rock climbing and a greater emphasis on hill-walking. Molly Johnstone mentions the Club being 'lifted out of the doldrums' by the new young blood coming into the Club from a group of keen rock climbers emerging from both Glasgow and Edinburgh universities. GUM Club and EUMC both provided recruiting grounds for able new members of the LSCC. In the 1950s a new rock climber appeared on the LSCC scene in the shape of Anne Littlejohn, who, in spite of working as veterinary specialist in Surrey, somehow managed to drive (rapidly) north almost every weekend to put up a huge list of rock climbs in Scotland, Wales and the Lake District. There is an almost methodical nature to her list of climbs as she 'polished off' routes systematically, leaving very few of even the hardest routes of the '50s and '60s without a tick.

In 1956 a harrowing 29 hour failed attempt on the Cuillin Ridge had rankled with Anne Littlejohn. Determined not to be defeated, she teamed up with Betty Stark and Anne Clark (later Murray) to have a go at the Skye Ridge together. Laden with gear they met up at Kyle of Lochalsh and carted it all laboriously over the hill on an evening so beautiful that 'we forgot the weight of the packs in the joy of being once again on the threshold of a struggle so worthy of an opponent.' Setting off at different times the evening before, the three met up at the Theàrlaich-Dubh Gap at 6.15am poised to tackle the main difficulties of the day. On a perfect day, all went well, until Anne realised that in order

Anne Littlejohn pioneered many of the early rock climbs on Rum

Photo: Eilidh Nisbet

NE Face of Ben Nevis from Càrn Mòr Dearg

LSCC Archives

to complete the Greater Traverse in 24 hours, she would have to speed up and continue on her own. Valiantly the other two shouldered her pack, and, stuffing apples, dates and biscuits into her pockets, Anne pressed on alone, fortified with the last of Anne Clark's glucose tablets.

> Whether it was Anne's glucose tablets or sheer desperation, I don't know, but I climbed Gars-bheinn in twenty minutes, less than I had ever done before, reaching the summit at 8.30pm. The last two hours were among the pleasantest of the day. It was a perfect evening and the scramble over Clach Glas and up the steep little wall and sixty-foot chimney on to Bla Bheinn were easy enough to present no danger but sufficiently interesting to make one forget one's tiredness...I hirpled into camp at exactly midnight.

As she took off her boots, Anne described her feet as not so much blistered as flayed. However, a glutton for punishment, eight years later in 1964 Anne was to set up a record of 17 hours 22 minutes for an unroped, solo traverse.

Lounging in the sun at the end of a long day in the Cuillin and gazing southwards, the curvaceous outline of the Rum 'Cuillin' offers an irrestistible invitation. Although not as long, as high, or as technical as the Skye Cuillin, the rocks are ultrabasic types with a coarse texture similar to that of gabbro and there are numerous climbs of all grades affording excellent climbing.

Anne Littlejohn was captivated by the Rum hills, and soon they became almost her personal friends as she worked over several successive visits compiling a card index of climbs to be used in the Rum guide book. A glance at Hamish Brown's guide book shows a wide range of new climbs put up by Anne Littlejohn, Mora McCallum and Eilidh Nisbet, mostly in the fine amphitheatre of crags on the south-east face of Allival.

With the acquisition of Blackrock and the building of the new road, Glencoe became the focus of much of the Club's rock climbing activity from the 1940s onwards. Not surprisingly considering the magnificent view from the west end of the cottage, Buachaille Etive Mòr was always a favourite with the Club. Many excursions were made both up and down Curved Ridge and Crowberry Ridge. Some of the most challenging routes, however, are on Rannoch Wall, a steep face of red rock with many fine cracks and lines giving long hard mountaineering routes. It is still great entertainment for those no longer young or agile enough to swing around in a harness to perch comfortably on Curved Ridge and watch the acrobatics of the gymnasts on Rannoch Wall.

One of the classic lines on Rannoch Wall is Agag's Groove – so called from a passage in the Bible when Agag 'trod delicately before the Lord'. Nearby is another long route that zig-zags interestingly across the face and is aptly named January Jigsaw, which is one of the few climbs to have the accolade of being a four-star route. This enjoyable classic was first climbed by LSCC member Esme Speakman in 1940.

Further down the road in Glencoe itself Club members frequently climbed on some of the easier routes on the East Face of Aonach Dubh, where many novices were enticed up such classics as Lower and Upper Bow, Quiver, or Archer Rib. Eilidh Nisbet graphically describes the struggles of herself and Mora McCallum up the crux pitch of a more challenging climb on the Church Door Buttress of Bidean nam Bian .

Next we came to the dreaded crux chimney with its awful aura of warnings from J.H.B.Bell and a man with a fractured skull to prove it. Certainly the stance and belay below are perfect, the second could undoubtedly hold a falling leader, but what one would do if the leader bounced off the ledge is a problem, for it's a sheer drop of nearly 200 ft. underneath. However, Mora romped up it, declaring it to be quite easy, and even finding a runner-point in it. However, I was surprised to see her suddenly turn to face outward and disappear under a chockstone. I was even more surprised when I myself reached the chockstone. To go under the chockstone I too found I had to turn on my back, but even so I couldn't get through past the waist. Mighty struggles, wriggles, kicks (nothing for hands to grip). Panic. Another effort – no success – but an idea! My right arm was pinioned above my head, but with my left I painstakingly removed all the contents of my anorak pockets – hanky, cigarettes, matches, chocolate, line slings, knife, gloves, etc. – and laid them one by one on top of the chockstone. Then at the next attempt I got my bottom through the hole quite easily. Mora, who couldn't see this performance, must have wondered what on earth was going on. So carried away were we with elation that we quite forgot the bit above was supposed to be a 'steep face pitch', and sailed up it unbelayed carrying coils of rope over our arms.

*Esme Speakman on
the Chancellor,
Aonach Eagach Ridge,
Glencoe, May 1973*

*Esme Speakman Collection,
LSCC Archives*

No Scottish rock climbing record would be complete without mention of the towering northern corries of Ben Nevis, and indeed the Club records are full of accounts of ascents (and descents) of all the classic routes. Tragically it was on these very cliffs that Nancy Forsyth, one of the ablest Club rock climbers, fell to her death in 1944. Especially poignant in that the Ben was her favourite mountain for rock climbing, as her extensive list for that same year shows.

Ben Nevis: Long climb, Orion Face, descent by N.E. Buttress; Rubicon Wall; Indicator Wall; 1944 route on Central Trident Buttress; Route 1, the Castle, descent by Castle Ridge; Italian Climb; Gardyloo Gully; Bayonet Route, descent by Ruddy Rocks; Slab Climb on middle tier of Central Trident Buttress.

In total contrast to such serious climbing, only six years previously Winifred Roberston led a meet at the CIC Hut which reads more like a housewifely picnic than a serious climbing expedition.

Mrs Robertson was the first to arrive, and was coping with the stove when N.F. and N.R. reached the hut about one o'clock, immediately followed by the pony with provisions. The latter had had a very hazardous journey over the moor, but only the cream for the strawberries had disappeared in the bog...Mrs Robertson was a perfect hostess and spent the days, ably assisted by Mrs Standring, cooking delicious meals, sweeping the Hut, and shaking the blankets.

Mind you, in between such domestic chores, they managed to do Tower Ridge, Observatory Ridge, NE Buttress, the Càrn Mòr Dearg Arete, and even had a swim in Lochan na Ciste!

Most of the Club's climbing activities seem to have gravitated towards the West, possibly because there has never been a great preponderance of members around the Aberdeen area; however, there were some members enjoying some of the fine long climbs in the Cairngorms. In particular Eagle Ridge on Lochnagar has offered sport on a number of occasions. Pat Bell's husband, Jim, and the redoubtable Nancy Forsyth had made the first ascent of this fine climb, and Pat has a thrilling description of crux of the climb when she climbed it later with her husband.

The Crux itself is most impressive. The rocks on the left of the ridge fall precipitously down to a gully, and the ridge itself abuts on a nearly perpendicular face, perfectly smooth on the right, while a few cracks slope up towards a shallow scoop into which one must climb, and below which the rock falls perpendicularly for some thirty feet to steeply sloping slabs. Of course the cracks slope the wrong way. There is no easy way round. I stood by the wall, some thirty feet below the knife edge, on its right, and for once had a good belay! The first time that Jim had climbed this pitch he had put a piton into one of the cracks and used it first as a handhold then as a foothold, for he was unaware that there was a good handhold in the scoop. Since then the cracks have opened, and we found them too wide to wedge in a piton firmly. The cracks sloped tantalisingly in the wrong direction and gave little comfort as hand or footholds. When I used the crucial handhold at the top of the wall I fancied it moved slightly. Since then, I am told, it has come away, but its socket gives a satisfactory substitute. I arrived at the top with a feeling of considerable satisfaction that I had not fallen off and dangled!

In 1964 while enjoying a happy day in Arran on the A' Chir Ridge, some of the younger members of the Club, keen to climb together and improve their rock climbing standards, while at the same time recognising their modest limitations, formed an unofficial group called the 'Mod Rockers', playing on the current theme of Mods, Rockers and Teddy Boys then in vogue. Eilidh Nisbet, Alison Dinwoodie, Mora McCallum, Alison Higham and the author were the originators of this ploy, and some grand days were had together on the rocks, their initial training ground being the sporting crags on the Cobbler, Beinn Narnain and A' Chrois. Indeed, to quote the words of someone who watched them disporting from the top of Narnain.

> You looked like little children running up and down, in and out; with the sound of your voices and your laughter, it would have made a good colour cine, especially with sound attached.

Beinn Narnain in particular has some interesting little scrambles, with a system of cracks and fissures splitting the rocks at the summit and giving great sport on short climbs. Jamblock Chimney, as its name suggests, is a narrow fissure blocked half-way up by a large rock which requires some interesting gymnastic activity to surmount. Engine Room Crack is another such fault line. The start involves lowering oneself down into the bowels of the earth (although in fact it is only a matter of a few feet), then, looking up, daylight can be seen at the top of a long crack, which is ascended mostly by extensive use of back, knees, elbows or any other convenient part of the anatomy. The author recalls an incident when her climbing companion had struggled, somewhat inelegantly, half-way up, and had suddenly felt in urgent need of a psychological rope. Her companion had to slither down the crack, rush round to the summit, pass by the bemused picnickers at the top, and 'halloo' down several cracks until the right one was identified!

On another occasion, in the first flight of enthusiasm for 'Mod Rocking' Eilidh, Jane and Helen left their companions on the top of A' Chrois at 3.30pm on an October evening and headed off for a recommended easy route on Creag Tharsuinn. Or rather it should have been easy, only rated Difficult, but what the intrepid group failed to take account of was the fact that the clocks had changed that weekend; darkness descended with relentless inevitability, and they started up the wrong route. Only having one torch between the three, and that only held together by dint of stuffing its innards with old bus tickets, didn't help their progress. In spite of all adversity it was a fine route, especially in starlight.

Soon the Mod Rockers had progressed from Difficult to Very Difficult, and eventually to Hard Severe. Many enjoyable days were spent down Glen Etive on the Etive Slabs on Ben Trilleachean, where the rock climbing is of quite a different nature, requiring infinite belief in one's properties of adhesion rather than any craven longing for that 'jug-handle' hold. As Alison Higham describes Spartan Slab in the Journal.

> For the first pitch you feel most insecure, balancing up with few positive holds, but on granite there is tremendous friction. By the top of the pitch you are getting the hang of it and from then on it is superb. You never stop wondering why you are sticking to the rock.

Sue Blair and Helen Moore at Ibrox climbing wall, Glasgow, 2009

LSCC Archives

Sadly the Mod Rockers dispersed to various corners of the globe, and Alison Higham, Cynthia Grindley, Sheila Cormack and June Ross, each in somewhat isolated situations kept rock climbing alive in the Club. In the 1980s Mary Lothian, Helen Geddes and Julia Banks joined the Club, followed some years later by a whole new generation of enthusiasts; Lizzie Potts, Marieke Dwarshuis, Jean Hunter, Ann-Marie Henderson, Fiona Hutchinson and Diana Preston, to name but a few.

The sport of rock climbing itself was changing. Whereas previously rock routes were viewed as part of a long mountaineering day out in the hills, younger climbers were viewing the gymnastic activity of rock climbing as a sport in itself. Climbing on shorter and harder routes on crags became more popular, and in many ways more accessible, as many crags are at a lower level, don't require a long hike in, and can easily be enjoyed on a mild June evening out of Edinburgh, Glasgow or Perth. Traprain Law, Craig Y Barns, Polldubh, Ben A'an, Loudon Hill, and that old Glasgow favourite, the Whangie, once again became popular venues.

Even quarries and railway embankments became suitable targets for frustrated rock climbers, although sometimes such spots were somewhat lacking in aesthetic appeal.

> Once one becomes immune to the aesthetic limitations of the place – rusting abandoned cars and other rubbish at the foot of the crag and slogans painted on it – the climbing is good and the graffiti serve as useful reference points for locating routes – 'start six feet left of "Shoot Thatcher" or ten feet right of "Ban Religion".'

It was a logical step to move from climbing as a gymnastic sport in quarries and on outcrops to the creation of indoor climbing walls. Nowadays almost all good leisure centres have a good climbing wall and regular week-night meetings at the wall have become a regular feature of club activities.

In contrast to such urban wasteland and indoor exercise, the pleasures of climbing the sea cliffs has a huge attraction. Travel west from Ullapool, past prickly Stac Pollaidh to Achiltibuie, and keep going to the westerly tip of Rhu Coigeach and one comes on the magnificent, layered sea cliffs of Reiff. These provide an ideal playground of short climbs of all grades, and what can be more pleasant than climbing with the blue waters of the Minch at one's back, sun-warmed rock beneath the fingers, and a belay point that has the full panorama of the Sutherland peaks from Quinag to Ben More Coigeach?

An altogether more serious proposition is the climbing of some of the famous sea stacks, the most famous being the Old Man of Hoy in Orkney. Club member Cynthia Grindley recounts her ascent of the Old Man of Hoy with Angela Soper of the Pinnacle Club – an ascent made doubly difficult by the antics of a cagoule in a high wind.

> After climbing up the first pitch, I belayed Angela as she romped across the traverse and began to climb the crack. After a few feet she began to have problems as the crack was too wide to allow for a handjam but too narrow to get into. The technique was a sort of arm lock. Her Gore-tex cagoule was causing trouble and she shouted down that she would have to take it off in order to lead the pitch. She tied it by the sleeves to the rope below her and finished

Helen Geddes on the classic Ardverikie Wall, Severe, Binnein Shuas in 1996

Above: Helen Steven at an idyllic campsite on the 2008 stravaig

Below: Nicola van Rijsbergen and Rachel Kennedy ascending The Cobbler, Ben Lomond behind

the pitch in good style. All went well as I climbed across the traverse, but as I began to climb the crack, I realised that three layers of sleeve were restricting my ability to get my arm into the crack. Then after I took out a runner, the Gore-tex cagoule slid down the rope and hung over my head like a circular blue curtain. My vision restricted to about a foot above me, I became ever more angry with the offending cagoule. If I could have taken both hands off the rock, I would have untied it and sent it to join the seals in the sea below who were watching my antics with interest if not amusement.

However, overcoming all obstacles, they made it to the top, and their pleasure was all the more when they learned that they had made the first women's ascent.

Although based in Scotland, the LSCC has always looked further afield, and every year meets are arranged in the Lakes, Wales, or crags in Northumberland. The availability of cheap air travel too has brought the world into our back yard. One club member recently praised the cliff-climbing in Spain – 'guaranteed good weather, warm rock, and NO MIDGES'. How could one resist?

This chapter began by describing Edinburgh Castle Rock as a dramatic backdrop defining the Edinburgh city skyline. Too big a temptation for members of an adventurous climbing club. A challenge indeed, but by no means a first ascent.

The first recorded ascent was in 1305 when a small band of intrepid Scots, armed to the teeth, inched their way slowly up the rock to surprise the English garrison, and reclaim a vital strategic gain for Robert the Bruce's struggle for Scottish independence. In 1973 the stakes were not so high, but secrecy was still vital as Edinburgh bye-laws prohibit any climbing on the Rock

Dodging marauding police cars, a team of three Club members (who had better remain known by their pseudonyms) foregathered on Castle Terrace ready to face the first obstacle – an awesome iron fence topped with fearsome spikes. They found the rock slippery, the grass even more slippery, the light afforded by street lamps inadequate, and the belay points even more inadequate. At the top, brought up short by the man-made bastions of the Castle itself, they had to resort to twisted ivy roots for their security. The last word on the climb remains with the criminals themselves.

Ere long they were back at base in that quiet Midlothian village, sipping tea around a vase of willowherb which 'Ella Nibble' had thoughfully plucked from the rock during the ascent…All agreed, wearily, that it was nice to have done it but that they would not like to do it again. They also agreed that it had been not only foolish but (whisper) perhaps a little dangerous. Not only is the rock slimy with the reek of ages and covered with loose gravel in places, but its vegetation is the abode of numberless starlings which naturally object to disturbance of their slumbers. As responsible members of a senior Club they would earnestly recommend that no attempt be made to repeat this illegal and foolhardy exploit.

Somehow this kind of crazy adventure epitomises the light-hearted attitude of the Club and one cannot help thinking that an admonition such as this can only be taken as a challenge to future generations.

Ice axes at the ready,
Pauline Ranken,
Anna Ranken and
Joan Smith descend
Clach Leathad, Meall
a' Bhuiridh, Black
Mount, 1909

LSCC Archives

5: Winter Playground

ALTHOUGH THE SCOTTISH MOUNTAINS are not particularly high by European standards, in winter they can offer unique climbing opportunities recognised and respected by noted Alpine and Himalayan climbers. Scottish hills do not have glaciers or crevasses or year-round snow-fields, but the climate above 2000 feet is sub-arctic – indeed it often *feels* totally arctic – and the wet state of the mountains becomes a positive advantage when waterfalls and runnels in gullies freeze over to hard blue ice, and rough rocky plateaux become crisp shining highways of scrunchy snow. Such, of course is the ideal. More often than not great plans can be laid for epic climbs and a warm, wet Atlantic hurricane sweeps in from the west washing away both snow and high hopes. Add to this the short days of a northern latitude, where the sun – when it is seen at all – starts setting in mid-afternoon, and winter climbing is a serious sport requiring a commitment to early rising, a degree of stamina, and imperviousness to weather.

Small wonder then that many photographs of the 'Ladies' show a pretty rugged bunch, rosy-cheeked and (dare we say it) somewhat leathery after a good battering in January blizzards. To protect themselves against the elements in the days before Gore-tex and breathable synthetics, climbers would be well kitted out in many layers of Shetland knitting, tweed jackets and Burberry rainwear. Knitted balaclavas, snow goggles, long ice-axes, woollen mitts and perhaps silk gloves would complete the outfit. And of course nailed boots, often with puttees (long bandages of woven cloth wrapped around the legs as used in the trenches in the First World War). Nor was it as primitive or inadequate as might be supposed. Now, almost a century later, it is well recognised that warm natural fabric with a 'wicking' property which allows the moisture of sweat to escape from the body is one of the best for keeping warm. The advent of synthetic waterproof has undoubtedly helped enormously in battling the elements and has the advantage of being so much lighter than a sodden tweed jacket, but one cannot be too disparaging of the garments worn by our founder members. After all Mallory and Irvine may have reached the summit of Everest wearing such gear.

Early climbing equipment. Long axes and hawser-laid ropes, May 2008

Photo: Rik Higham

As far as nailed boots were concerned, they may have seemed heavy and ungainly on summer rock, but in winter they came into their own for the remarkable grip they gave on ice and snow. When 'Vibram' rubber-soled boots began to be used, there was a school of climbers who maintained vociferously, and with some justification, that such boots were absolutely lethal on snow. By the 1950s and '60s many people were moving over to using crampons in winter, but many of the old school maintained that, on the mixed terrain in Scotland, crampons were often not used until too late, when one was half way across a steep snow slope, suddenly gripped, and hopping about on one leg trying to put on crampons with fumbling frozen fingers. However, once introduced, and with ever-improving technology, crampons became a winter-climbing essential and as a result the standard of grades in snow-climbing increased enormously.

The early members of the LSCC spent almost every summer in the Alps and were experienced in alpine techniques, so it was little wonder that right from the start they were intent on exploring the Scottish mountains in winter as well as summer. The first New Year Meet of the Club was held at Crianlarich and there is a fine photograph of a row of determined women, ice-axes up to their chins, booted and muffled up (complete with motoring veils) preparing to set off for the tops. Not for them the easy way up either.

> Peaks ascended – Cruach Ardrain, North Face by snow gullies; Stobinian, from Luib to Crianlarich, via Snow Gully; and Ben More, including the 'Water-Cave Chimney' from Ben More Farm.

They were tough, these Ladies. One account describes cold so severe that their eyelids were frozen; another tells of a member who went on her own for a New Year 'tramp'. She covered a distance of 36 miles, from Lochan na Lairig near Ben Lawers to Loch Rannoch and back again to Killin, accomplished when daylight only lasted until 4pm, and then casually brushed off as if it were a Sunday afternoon stroll. One intrepid pair set off to climb Curved Ridge on the Buachaille, but when they discovered themselves floundering waist deep in soft powder snow before they had even started the climb, sanity prevailed and they turned back.

Just as sledging gives pleasure to youngsters, the art of glissading down mountains affords endless fun. It could be said that glissading is simply a fancy name for sliding down the mountain, but well done, there is rather more elegance and style to this method of descent. One either sits or stands at the top of a steep snow slope, with a good clear run-out at the bottom, and, using one's ice-axe both as brake and steering mechanism, one can accelerate rapidly to the bottom. Done safely it can be enormous fun. One account in the 1929 Journal came to be known as the 'Tam O' Shanter Glissade' after an episode at the 1911 Meet in Glencoe.

> The following day the writer (Jane Inglis Clark) and her party had a narrow escape on Gearr Aonach, the central sister of Glencoe. We were late in our start owing to the wagonette being late in driving us down the glen. It was a day of fine seasonal weather after the storm. We had climbed to the summit without special difficulty, and were enjoying the view, when suddenly it occurred to me that, as the sun was nearly set, unless we made a very rapid descent it would inevitably mean a night out for all of us. As we ascended I had noticed a snow couloir. Keen frost had now set in. There was no choice but to glissade down the icy slope of the couloir. All my party were novices, and having given them instructions how to follow, I screwed up my courage, took a firm hold of my ice-axe, and led the way. Down I shot; never shall I forget the terrific speed of that glissade, or the fervency of my hope that all would go well at the foot. Very pluckily did the party follow my instructions, and fortunately the angle eased off sufficiently to allow us to pull up. I shall always remember the look of that last scarlet Tam O' Shanter as its wearer came safely to my side.

Snow can be just as severe at Easter Meets as the first Club Meet at Kinlochleven held in 1914 shows. Describing the weather as 'bad, as usual, if not a little worse', the Club activities were in no way diminished.

> The usual method of reaching one's destination by train and steamer was on this occasion entirely abandoned in favour of motor cycle and foot, and this contributed greatly to the feeling of novelty and adventure which permeated the whole Meet...on the 9th April, Miss M.I.Newbigin and Miss R.Raeburn with one of the members of the Scottish Mountaineering Club, starting from Steall in Glen Nevis, crossed the col between Ben Nevis and Carn Dearg to the head of the Allt a' Mhuillinn, and returned to Steall in a soaked condition, the weather being particularly unfavourable. The next day, the same trio set out for the high pass of Coire Gabhalach, which is the most direct route from Steall to Kinlochleven. At the top of the pass, the two members parted from their companion, who acted as a most convenient anchor at certain exposed parts of the route. Immediately on turning the corner into a region of calm, the battered and breathless travellers encountered several members of the Club proceeding in a leisurely manner up the other side of the pass. Greetings were exchanged, experiences related, destinations enquired about, and in the minds of the two who were returning was the thought, 'when you get round the corner you won't look quite so tidy!'

However 'bad as usual' is hardly a fair description of the Scottish hills in winter. Sometimes the most memorable climbs can happen on a crisp blue day of hard frost and sparkling snow when even the little spicules of moisture dance as frozen specks in the sunlight. Then it is good indeed to be alive.

In the early days the LSCC had a considerable amount of help and encouragement from their husbands and brothers in the SMC as is acknowledged by Ruth Raeburn, writing Mollie Bell's obituary. (Not the same as Pat Bell, mentioned elsewhere). Here Ruth describes an early climb on Stob Ghabhar;

> In the distant past, even before the LSCC came into existence, I met Mrs Bell – Mollie – for the first time at Inveroran. We were a party of five – my brother Harold, Mr and Mrs Bell and Mr Ling. I had already done a good deal of scrambling but had never before seen a snow climb; Mrs Bell had only recently been introduced to the hills and might truthfully be described as a complete novice.
>
> Led by my brother and supported by Mr Bell and Mr Ling, we started our initiation by struggling up the snow-covered sides of Stob Ghabhar as far as the famous Couloir, which happened to be in a shocking condition. Here steps had to be cut, and we shivered on the edge, sticking like flies to the slippery surface. We returned from this, our first serious expedition, inexpressibly weary, but aglow with a feeling of exhilaration, which on my part has never entirely left me

LSCC party approaching Stob Coire nan Lochan, Glencoe, January 2001

Photo: Julia Banks

Mabel Jeffrey, writing in the 1929 Journal, gives a thrilling account of a climb at the Easter Meet at Inveroran in 1909.

> The weather was still perfect and we joined a large party of LSCC and SMC. at Bridge of Orchy station. Our objective was the northern corrie of Beinn an Dothaidh, where the cliffs rise imposingly in a semicircle, and these were nicely plastered with snow and ice…It was bitterly cold in the shadow of the corrie, but hard kicking up the steep snow kept the leaders warm. All went well with my party until we were faced with a very steep rock face entirely plastered with ice and slightly overhanging at the top. Here my leadership broke down entirely, and Mr Collins (*an SMC member*) had to take the lead. He cut handholds and footholds on the icy face, and as if by magic he was soon over what had appeared to me as an insurmountable difficulty…
>
> Meanwhile the other members of the party had become so numb with cold that they had the greatest difficulty in climbing up the icy face. Standing on one foot in a small ice-hold while using a jammed-in ice-axe as a hitch was an unusual experience for me, and one which I did not much enjoy as time wore on. Gradually fingers and toes lost all feeling, and when at last I had to move all power had gone out of my limbs…I moved cautiously along, with a sheer cliff of several hundreds of feet on my right; I had gained about half the distance when both foothold and handhold, on which I had put all my weight, suddenly gave way, and I slid with them to the very edge of the precipice. My companion, who was occupied bringing up the fourth member of the party to the tiny ice-step, saw what was happening, and quickly pulled in such slack rope as she could. At the same moment I came to a standstill, and was able to step forward quickly on to firm snow.

Perhaps this incident explains why Mabel Jeffrey was always so keen to pass on step-cutting and ice-axe techniques to new members of the Club.

Often with gully climbs one of the hardest parts can be at the top climbing out through the cornice – the great build-up of wind-driven snow which often overhangs the top of a gully. Mabel Jeffrey tells of further adventures at that Meet in 1909.

> As the snow conditions remained ideal, two parties decided to tackle the northern corrie of Ben Achaladair, each selecting a steep snow gully. After the prolonged spell of fine weather the sun had partly softened the snow, and so it was with difficulty that we made footholds sufficiently firm to be safe. As we ascended we heard sounds of avalanches falling off the rocks, making us realise that snow conditions were changing.
>
> A large cornice projected at the top of the gully, and as there was no way of escaping it we had perforce to cut it down with the ice-axe. A perpendicular wall of snow towered high above our heads, and while I was negotiating this it was necessary to hitch me securely by passing the rope round an ice-axe driven into a crack which ran along the base of the wall directly under the cornice. A second ice-axe was driven horizontally into the snow wall, and, with the aid of a shoulder and using the driven-in ice-axe as a foothold, I was able to cut handholds and footholds, and then to hack away at the cornice. Soon it was possible to ascend, and quickly I was on top, only to find that the cornice was entirely detached from the mountain, and a wide gap stretched between me and safety. I said nothing, but hastily jumped across and drove my axe into the solid snow beyond and brought up my companions secured by the rope. Luckily the mass of snow was not dislodged by our ascent, and we all safely reached the cairn.

There are several classic snow climbs in Scotland which appear again and again in the annals of the Club as great favourites, and because snow conditions are never the same from one year to the next, these routes stand repetition. For example, some classics are: Y Gully on Cruach Ardrain, a gully on the north face, branching into a Y and offering a steep little exit at the top; Central Gully on Ben Laoigh, taking a direct line up the face and emerging in classic style right at the summit cairn; the Upper Couloir of Stob Ghabhar with quite a long walk in, but a good climb at the end of it.

As with rock climbs, snow climbs are also graded as to severity, starting from Grade I upwards. For most of its history, until more recent times, Club members didn't profess to be hard snow and ice climbers. As one Journal article put it.

> It seemed to be sufficient for us to pick out a gully with a cornice at the top, a buttress of ice-covered rocks, or a snowy ridge of peaks; and to enjoy the day conquering these.

In the days before crampons enabled one to walk on steep snow or front-point up ice pitches, ice-axes were used to cut laborious steps up the slopes. This required practice and a strong arm, as one perfected the art of cutting an adequate groove for placing the foot with a couple of vigorous, well-placed swipes with the axe. Soon a long line of well-spaced steps would lace their way up the slope to the accompaniment of a steady chop-chop-step; chop-chop-step. This is easier to do on the way up than leaning out of balance on the descent, and is hot work indeed for the leader. It was said that Barbara Macfarlane was so expert that she could cut steps up a slope, swinging her axe in seemingly effortless rhythm, talking non-stop to her breathless companions.

At the New Year Meet at the Ben Lawers Hotel near Loch Tay, Barbara Macfarlane, along with Ilse Bell and two guests was involved in an epic be-nighting on Ben Lawers, which attracted a great deal of media attention, much to the embarrassment of the Club. After all the Constitution itself stated:-

> Remember, above all, that each Member has the reputation of the Club to make and uphold, and that even the slightest mishap would immediately bring the Club into disrepute.

A grave code of honour indeed, and this adventure seemed to some to be bringing the 'good name of the Club' into disrepute. Questions were asked and Barbara asked to give a full explanation of events to the Committee – both in vindication of her own actions and as a corrective to media hype.

The episode begins with a concise, matter-of-fact account in the log of the Meet.

> Dec. 28th – 29th. I. Bell; B.P.Macfarlane; W. Barlow (guest); B.Burt (guest)
>
> Traverse of Ben Lawers, 3984, Creag-an-Fhithich 3430, and An Stuc 3643. The route followed was from Lawers north of Meall Odhar by the S.E. Ridge to Ben Lawers and north by main ridge to An Stuc. In dense mist a descent was attempted to the S.E. by a slope increasingly steep and craggy, but it had to be abandoned above a sheer drop of about 200 ft. to the corrie. After moonrise the ascent was commenced over iced rocks and turf with a covering of new snow and the summit of An Stuc regained. A successful descent was then accomplished S.W., then S.E. through a break in the crags to Lochan-nan-Cat, whence Lawers was reached across the moor.

A perfectly matter-of-fact account, with a sensible decision taken not to attempt the crags in the dark and the mist, and then an orderly retreat the next morning.

However, a rescue team had been organised, and inevitably the adventure made it into the newspapers. Headlines such as 'Party of Lady Hill Climbers lose their way in the mist', 'Ladies' Pluck on Scots Ben', 'Exciting Experiences of Mountaineers' all added to the sense of drama and exaggeration. *The Scotsman* account told of a large search party of men being called out and escorting the ladies to safety after their thirty hours on the hill in freezing conditions. *The People's Journal* of January 5th offers a fuller account.

> Caught in a thick mist away up on the snow-clad heights of Austue (sic for An Stuc), the neighbouring peak to Ben Lawers, the mountain monarch of Loch Tayside, four ladies had a holiday ordeal which they are not likely to forget.

Interviewed by the press, Barbara Macfarlane gave this account;

> It was perilous, it is true, but we were not rescued. By the time that the men arrived we had extricated ourselves from our precarious position.
>
> The peak afforded absolutely no foothold whatsoever. There were no ledges and the slope was sheer, covered with frozen snow. All the rocks hung with icicles, and even such things as tufts of grass, where they appeared through the snow, were frozen hard as cast-iron...I had my compass bearings, but these

were valueless on the ridge…The only thing was to get back to a position of safety. I had to make certain of every step before I could venture up and invite my friends to follow.

At times there was nothing between us and a fall to the bottom of a 200 feet slope but the two inches of our ice-picks in the ground. I had to hang on with one hand while I scraped the frozen snow with the fingers of the other in order to determine a safe place for our next step. That is why my fingers are all worn through, although I did not discover that until day-light.

It was for this reason that we took so long to get up the slope. One false step and I would have plunged my friends to their doom.

We did get up to the top all right, and extricated ourselves from our difficulties. I did not haul the others up. I got up and held the line. It is incorrect to say that we were rescued. We were all fully equipped with Alpine gear and spare clothes. All that was wrong was the lack of food. We had some bread-and-jam sandwiches and five sweets.

It's certainly a dramatic account, but from its slightly defensive tone, one can almost hear the eager probing of the journalists for good 'copy', perhaps trying to expose some incompetence on the part of the ladies where in fact they acquitted themselves well.

Blizzards are frequent on the Scottish hills in winter and there is always that little surge of relief when emerging in a raging snow-storm to find the cairn where it ought to be. It is often a source of wonder that this should happen so often, although of course it shouldn't be if one is trusting the compass and navigating accurately. However there are many tales of wandering around a desolate mountain top searching for a cairn that may be deep buried in snow.

Monday, April 2nd, was our last chance for Ben Alder and five of us, Grizel, May, Elisabeth, Catharine and Janet were able to seize it. Having left the hotel car at Ben Alder Lodge, we followed the most direct path to Culra Lodge, took the advice of the Guide Book and climbed from just before the Bealach Dearg. This proved an excellent and very easy way up. The snow line was not far above the Bealach and there were extensive snow fields on the top. The mist rose and fell as we reached the cairn, and we had some short but lovely glimpses of lochs and distant hills. A somewhat heated argument arose on the comparative magnificence of Ben Alder and Braeriach for we were all struck by the likeness between those two massive giants. Perhaps a spirit heard and whistled up the blizzard. At any rate, just as we turned to leave the cairn, the blizzard struck us with a blinding and almost numbing violence of wind and snow. As one member of the party described it, 'If you opened one eye and saw a pair of legs in front of you, you were thankful!' Unfortunately the blizzard blew that pair of legs some way round the mountain and when we saw the path below us we also saw some delightful views of lochs which we should not have seen. We were only on the other side of the pass and greatly enjoyed the walk back over the Bealach Cumhann and the Bealach Dubh, with their beautiful views of Loch Ericht and Loch Ossian. In spite of the length of the expedition, twenty miles at least, we were not late for the car at Ben Alder Lodge.

The summit of Creag Meagaidh is notoriously hard to find in bad weather. One cold winter's day, Alison Higham and two friends were climbing Raeburn's Gully in Coire Ardair. Conditions were so icy that they had to pitch the whole climb, belaying each other up the gully, making progress painfully slow, so that it was dark by the time they reached the top. Knowing the difficulties of finding the summit cairn for bearings, they remained roped together and headed for the distinctive notch of 'The Window' thinking it the easier landmark to find. However, in the darkness they came to the edge of a sheer cliff and decided to find a place to bivouac. Being so near the edge, they spent the night tied to a fence post and shivered, and shivered and shivered. Alison felt that it was only really dangerous when the shivering stopped. By morning they were so frozen with the cold that it took them an hour just to rouse themselves. Suddenly a big mountain rescue dog came bounding up to them, and they were escorted safely down the mountain to the inevitable press interview. As an indication as to how time had moved on, there were no requirements to report to the Committee.

Perhaps the significance of both stories lies in the fact that, although temporarily in difficulties, both parties coped with the situation in a competent way.

Although not a ski-ing club, some LSCC members have always been proficient pioneers of the sport. For most of them ski-ing was not an end in itself, but simply another exhilarating way of enjoying the mountains. The Inglis Clark family pioneered many adventurous ski routes in the Alps, and Mabel Jeffrey was still enjoying ski-ing in her 80s.

When the Scottish Ski Club installed a generator-driven rope tow at the back of Ben Lawers, Janie Cameron, Christina Macnair, Irene Addie and others were among its early users. Then a chair-lift was built on Meall a' Bhuiridh right on the doorstep of Blackrock and many more Club members took to the slopes. However downhill ski-ing was never the most favoured pursuit of members of the LSCC. Competent skiers were soon deliberately adventuring off piste to go cross-country exploring over the tops. Trips in the Alps included the challenging Haute Route, and many enthusiasts such as Alison Dinwoodie, Karin Froebel, June Ross, Sarah Mackay and Kate Ross made regular visits to Norway for high level ski-touring. Club members are also members of the Eagle Ski Club, well-known for adventurous high-level routes. LSCC member Joy Turner is currently President.

One rather more original way of travelling involved an epic journey through the Làirig Ghrù in the Cairngorms, using snow-shoes. Suilven Strachan, then aged 19, describes the adventure in a letter home to her mother, written in 1953.

Here is my tale – the Doing of the Lairig Ghru.

It was with great relief that Betty (Stark), Rhona (Weir) and I climbed onto the train for Aviemore on Thursday night. The elderly members of the Club, holding a meet at the Tilt Hotel, were decidedly against our doing the Lairig – highest mountain pass, and forty miles if you end up coming down Glen Tilt; and it means 40lb. rucksacks for three days, through very deep snow...But once at Aviemore there was no turning back. Betty, our leader, had the two groundsheets and the primus, I had the tent, and Rhona had the extra tins, in addition to our snowshoes, sleeping bags, dry clothes, and heaps and heaps of food.

In 1953, Suilven Strachan, Rhona Weir and Betty Stark snowshoed through the Làirig Ghrù

Photo: Rhona Weir Collection

Rothiemurchus forest was deathly still as we scrunched through the snow, taking turning after turning, with each successive path getting smaller and smaller, until we had to guess our path by the lie of the land under the snow. Thus to the edge of the forest to camp above a quiet river, with the moonlight throwing long shadows from the pines, and bringing distant hills so near, you wanted to touch their slopes.

Betty wakened us at seven – to go and be sick. She had burnt herself on the primus. We resignedly thawed out our iron hard nailed boots over the primus before getting out of our warm sleeping bags. We wore snowshoes all that day, taking frog-like steps, to go ever higher right up onto the top of the Lairig, through soft, deep snow. It was very heavy going, but the differing tracks of deer, fox, ptarmigan, winter hare, and the textures of the wind-blown snow, were lovely to watch – and the dark woods below us against the gleaming snow.

Betty was decidedly miserable however. We had two miniatures of Martell Cognac for emergencies. So we fed Betty on whipped egg and cognac and sugar. This, she liked!

By evening my left nailed boot had ground through the string of the snowshoe, and in the morning we discovered that Rhona's feet were so badly blistered from her snowshoes that we had to pack her off to Inverey (nearest civilisation), and Betty and I went on walking right down the bed of the frozen Dee, eight miles to Bynack Lodge, and then another seven right down into Glen Tilt, which here is very steep and narrow. We had to go very carefully once it got dark.

We found the bothy we were looking for...and I remember that night best by the wonderful punch we brewed with our emergency cognac, two oranges and some honey.

(Next morning) our boots were very hard indeed and I couldn't get either hand into my frozen and unbendable mitts. We discarded our snowshoes and walked the last dozen miles down Glen Tilt.

It was rather fun getting to the Tilt Hotel just as the elderly members were starting afternoon tea, and being congratulated by the President!

The Cairngorms are not always so benign, and the plateau in winter can become a white hell of screaming blizzard. In 1971 in what came to be a much-debated tragedy, a party of schoolchildren and their teacher died in a ferocious blizzard on the Cairngorm plateau. Among the many opinions offered at the time some wondered why they had not attempted to dig a snow-hole for shelter. December snow is rarely sufficiently consolidated to make this possible, but the following February a group from the Club decided to see for themselves just how much effort and skill were required to dig an adequate snow-hole. Being the LSCC this inevitably turned into something of a party.

Snow conditions were ideal and, suitably equipped with ice-axes, snow shovels, four-season sleeping bags, candles and stoves, a party of six set off for the deep gash of the Chalamain Gap where there was a suitably deep build-up of snow banked up the side. Working in pairs and digging hard, it took the group a good two hours to make three well-designed and very adequate caverns in the snow. They reflected that this was a strong group, well-equipped, fresh at the start of the day, working in ideal conditions; not a group of exhausted, frightened teenagers, struggling in the teeth of a blizzard.

Each snug little cave had a trench down the middle of its floor to allow the cold air to escape; a couple of ice shelves as bunks, and the roof just high enough to melt a little in the heat of the candles and then freeze over giving a glistening crystal ceiling that reflected back the light and heat. So entranced were they with their shining palace, the architects decided to link the caves together with a connecting room. This may have improved the social amenities, but it did nothing for the air-flow system as a whistling draught necessitated closing up the ends. Placing someone on guard with an ice-axe to ensure an opening for breathing, the group settled down to a surprisingly snug night of music and refreshment.

One hazard of a blizzard is the 'white-out' when the combination of unbroken snow slope and flat white light create the effect of a complete blanket of white cotton wool. In such conditions the eye is unable to focus and it becomes impossible to tell at each footfall whether one is going uphill or down. Sometimes simply tossing a snowball ahead or having someone walk out a few paces in front on a compass bearing is sufficient to bring the white world back into focus again. But one of the dangers of having someone in front is that they themselves are walking completely blind and could easily step over the edge of a cornice.

This was exactly what happened when the author as a very young and inexperienced climber encountered her first white-out on Ben Challum – surely one of the safest hills in Scotland. She and her friend, Jane

Mora McCallum, Ann Winning and Rosemary Duncan settle down for a snug night in a snow-hole. Cairngorms, 1972

Photo: Eilidh Nisbet

Kate Ross on
Broken Gully, Coire
an t-Sneachda,
Cairngorms, March
2002

Photo: John Higham

Rennie, were keen to do everything exactly right so, although quite disconcerted by the feeling of disorientation, Jane was prodding her way cautiously a few yards in front, while her companion was reading the compass and keeping on the bearing. Thinking that it might be time to turn back (a wise decision in hindsight), the two came together to consult. At that point with a sickening 'whump' and a roar the cornice gave way beneath them and both fell through. The author (well schooled by Mabel Jeffrey) stopped herself almost immediately with her axe, but the avalanche swept Jane out of sight down the slope. Calling anxiously, the author followed the snow tracks down the steep side of the mountain and, thankfully, found Jane sitting near the edge of a large drop nursing nothing worse than a sprained ankle. Huge relief and many lessons learned.

It is remarkable when one considers the seriousness with which avalanche risk is, rightly, regarded in Scotland to read of the reckless, devil-may-care attitude of our founder members. Hamish MacInnes, writing in the preface to *Scottish Winter Climbs*, has this.

> Avalanche accidents have become such a major source of Scottish winter accidents that some guidance is necessary to avoid further possible trouble. The simple rule of not climbing in gullies or on dangerous slopes, i.e. steep, open slopes, especially convex ones, during or immediately after a heavy snow fall, should be strictly adhered to.

He then goes on to enumerate the various conditions and types of avalanches which can occur regularly every Scottish winter. Indeed nowadays one cannot visit a hostel or climbing hut without being made aware of avalanche danger, and often avalanche risk will be posted at all major climbing centres.

Contrast, then, the happy-go-lucky behaviour of the Ladies in their early days. This is Mabel Jeffrey writing in 1909 about a Meet in Inveroran.

Five of us, roped together, climbed a snow gully on Beinn Achaladair. The weather, which had been brilliant, turned cloudy and mild, and we noticed that the snow was continually sliding off the ledges, only we had not sufficient experience to know that an ascent under these conditions might be dangerous. We had almost reached the top when suddenly, with a hissing sound, the snow in the gully slid down, sweeping the whole party off their feet. Down we went, helter-skelter, some five or six hundred feet. I tried to gain control with my ice-axe, but the rope tugged me right and left and every way. When at length we came to a stop down in the corrie, I was afraid to look round at the others. Imagine my joy and relief to find that no-one had received even a scratch! Three ice-axes were amissing – that was all!

A telling example of beginners' luck, and partly due to a mistaken belief common amongst climbers at the beginning of the century that avalanches were an Alpine phenomenon. Even as late as 1936 an article on *Snow Conditions in Scotland* written in the Record states categorically that 'Experiences of avalanches in Scotland are rare' and that 'the condition of the snow known as "wind-slab" which is common in the Alps is somewhat rare in this country'. Not so, as this account illustrates;

On February 23rd, 1936, Ilse Bell and Iris Blaikie were descending Stuc a' Chroin during a blinding snowstorm, when they were carried down about 200 feet by an avalanche, definitely started by themselves. The snow conditions were treacherous and difficult – dry powdery snow lying on old icy neve, the former being blown into drifts by a raging gale – and as the light was failing and the weather severe, it was essential that they should reach the valley with the least possible delay. Ilse, having had experience of snow climbing abroad, was aware of the danger of avalanches, and accordingly decided to cut steps down into Coire Chroisg until they could see the nature of the ground between them and the glen. It was iced, with channels running down it filled with soft powdery snow, but having ascertained that there was a good run-out, and having decided that even if an avalanche did occur, they were not likely to get hurt, they took to one of the snow channels, Iris leading. They had not taken more than a few steps when there was a grunting noise and the snow started to slide, carrying them with it. It moved slowly at first but quickly gained speed, and when they stopped Ilse's legs were buried and it took some time to dig herself free. Iris, who had stopped some 60 feet lower, was more enveloped in the snow, which had probably packed itself round her, with the result that she had a slightly bruised rib. They were otherwise unhurt and *were greatly thrilled by the experience.* (Author's italics)

However this article then goes on to give good solid advice to members on the kind of care to exercise when climbing in winter. Never at any time does it suggest that attempts at snow climbing should not be made, and members are encouraged to keep trying new routes.

To choose a sporting route, not necessarily difficult, adds greatly to the fun and pleasure of an expedition and certainly extends one's experience. A ridge, which in summer would be a simple walk, may present an interesting or even a difficult problem when hard frozen, covered with snow and corniced, while a good snow gully has a fascination all its own. Knowledge of the varying conditions of snow must be learnt by practice, and cannot be gained only by reading books.

Avalanche debris. below The Comb, Coire na Ciste, Ben Nevis

Photo: Greg Strange

*Lizzie Potts,
Ann-Marie Henderson
and Brenda Roddy
skiing into the
Monadh Liath*

Photo: John Higham

Over the years climbers have learned the lethal potential of a Scottish avalanche, and all members now take seriously the necessity of being well-equipped and well-acquainted with snow conditions in order to take suitable precautions. Conditions for full membership of the Club were made more stringent to take account of the need to be thoroughly competent on the Scottish hills in winter. Thus it was a doubly cruel blow to the Club when Margaret Taylor was avalanched off a gully in Glencoe in 1960 and confined to a wheelchair for the rest of her life. Her immense courage and determined spirit, however, refused to allow this tragedy to ruin her life. Rejecting the option of walking with callipers and crutches in favour of a wheelchair, saying, 'A chair you can fly around in', Margaret continued her career in bacteriology, worked tirelessly on behalf of other paraplegics, and stood for election to her local council. To cap it all she triumphantly brought home a gold medal for table tennis and a bronze medal for fencing at the Paraplegic Commonwealth Games in 1962.

The development of more advanced equipment has made winter climbing more and more ambitious. Shorter ice-axes with dropped heads, ice hammers which enable the climber to use both hands to hack a line up steep ice; ice screws which mean that the leader no longer has to rely on traditional rock belays, but can continue straight on up an ice pitch; and of course crampons with front points eliminating the need to cut laborious steps, have all advanced snow climbing standards immeasurably.

One such piece of technology is a shield-shaped plate known as a dead man, which can be hammered into deep snow to give a belay point from the wire attached to it. One party of members, keen to try out new gadgets, took one with them on an ascent of Tower Gully on Ben Nevis. The climb completed, the party decided to split up, four by abseiling down Number Four Gully, and two continuing down the path. An ideal time to try out their new toy.

What our innocent friends didn't realise was that there is a certain amount of skill required to place a dead man at the exact correct angle. Gaily they whammed it in, clipped on a sling and offered a safety line to the descending friends who were using the old-fashioned method of abseiling with the rope around their bodies. Going over the cornice, one member caught her crampon on the edge and came with her full weight on the safety line.

Slowly her companion was dragged to the edge, her feet making deep grooves in the snow, until the not insignificant weight of both came on the casually hammered in dead man. 'I hope we put that thing in right' said Esme, jumping up and down with anxiety. They must have – it held, and all lived to tell the tale of marvellous technology, which they then went and learned how to use properly.

All of which cautionary tales point to the need for training and the passing on of skills. In the early days skills were passed on by Club members Often training weekends were organised with snow and ice skills, ice-axe practice, rope management and navigation being passed on to younger members. More often this was done informally on days out with the Club and indeed such sharing of experience is often one of the main reasons for joining a club.

Sadly, however, with the onset of a culture of blame and litigation, it becomes more difficult even to hint at accepting responsibility for the safety of others. 'Duty of care' has become the watchword of the day, and now clubs expect professionals who are suitably covered by insurance to undertake training. The Mountaineering Council of Scotland has met this need by providing excellent training weekends with subsidised places for affiliated club members. Of recent years the LSCC has invited professional instructors to organise weekend courses specifically tailored to Club members' needs, and these have often ended with a day of great enjoyment doing one of the Cairngorm winter routes together.

However, while skill and expertise must never be belittled, it is to be fervently hoped that the spirit of independence and challenge are never stifled by over-protective legislation, and that the next generation of climbers can enjoy the freedom of the snows as much as their predecessors.

Alison Higham on Jacobs Ladder, Coire an t-Sneachda, Cairngorms 2007

Photo: John Higham

6: Stravaiging the Tops

THE DICTIONARY DEFINITION of the Scots word 'stravaig' – to wander about idly – is not exactly appropriate for the energetic activities of the LSCC on the Scottish hills, but there is an element of enjoyment implied in the word, which most certainly does reflect the ethos of the Club.

Scotland's mountains may not be particularly high, rising to no more than 4406 feet but there are still wide areas of wilderness with lonely hidden corries laced with burns with swirling brown pools and winding tracks through dusty pollen-rich heather, known only to the deer and the buzzard. In 1908 most of the Scottish hills were still relatively untrampled, frequented mainly by gamekeepers and shepherds. There was an aura of remote romance about the annual 'Highland Meet' that is lost forever nowadays in our era of fast cars and easy access.

The founding members of the Club were mostly ladies of leisure and they certainly knew how to enjoy that leisure to the full in a context of unspoiled beauty – if not one of reliable weather! Almost every summer a group of friends would set out, booted and ready, to spend two or three weeks simply walking and exploring little-known areas of the Scottish hills. Always there seemed to be an abundance of friendly shepherds' wives offering cool drinks of milk, home-baking and a bed for the night, and often the opportune farmer's wagon or dog-cart seemed to materialise just at the point of giving up, all adding to the spice of adventure.

When one follows their journeys on a map, it becomes apparent just how fit they were and what long journeys they undertook all in the days before 'West Highland Ways' and other upland trails were established. It is well worth getting out a map of Scotland to trace the long-distance walk undertaken by Mrs Sang in 1919.

> In June, with the President and Secretary of the SMC I had a cross-country tramp from Dalwhinnie to Glenbrittle. From Dalwhinnie we walked up Ben Cuich (sic) – a disappointing Munro. The next day (the 2nd) we drove to near Loch Pattack, past Loch Ericht Lodge, followed the Stalker's Path, and climbed Ben Alder by the ridge that contains Loch Bealach nam Bheidhe. Wide view and pleasant weather. Descended by the ridge which flanks the path to the Bealach Dubh, and walked through Glen Pattack to Laggan. On the 4th we visited Coire Ardair, and thence up to the 'Window' in a downpour of rain. To the summit cairn of Creag Meagaidh by compass, and thence along the east ridge in dense mist to Sron a' Ghoire. Saw a newly born deer, and were glad of a blink of sun to dry us up when we had tea by the burn side. The next day we started, in passable weather, for Garva Bridge. It commenced to rain as we ascended the Corrieyairack road, and got gradually worse until we were within three miles of Fort Augustus. We saw nothing and arrived completely soaked. The next day we took the steamer to Temple Pier, and drove from Drumnadrochit to Cannich. Later, after waiting in vain for the weather to clear, the President left us, and we walked through Glen Affric and down Glen Licht. Luckily a splendid day for it. The grandest glens I have seen, and the finest walk in Scotland. On the 11th we left Loch Duich in a torrent of rain, and got the steamer from Kyle to Broadford. We were again soaked to the skin, and very cold. We walked to Glen Brittle, where the weather did not improve very much. We had a chilly day of climbing on the Cioch by the slabs. We used rubbers, and found the climbing very entertaining, and at times almost sensational. Turned out of Glen Brittle, we went to Sligachan, and from there we climbed the Pinnacle Ridge of Scur nan Gillian (sic) twice. The traverse of Mhadaidh once, Bruach na Frithe, Blaven, Clach Ghlas, and several other moderate excursions usually in very cold weather.

One cannot help thinking that lesser mortals might have given up in face of such foul weather. However, it takes more than bad weather to deter the LSCC. As one member remarked in the record 'The forecast for the weekend should have sent right-minded people deep into their alternative 'inside' hobbies!' Right-minded or not women have set out in all weathers, perhaps having their founder, Mabel Jeffrey's admonition ringing in their ears; You have to climb in bad weather as well as good if you want to keep fit enough for all you want to do.

Easter Meet 1939.
Ben More Assynt

LSCC Archives

Just a quick glance at Mabel Jeffrey's own exploits in the Cairngorms leaves one in no doubt that she must have followed her own advice.

August and September – Cairngorm from Aviemore; Cairngorm and Ben Macdhui, and back by the Lairig Ghru to Coylum Bridge; Sgoran Dubh four times from Kincraig; Carn Ban Mhor, also Meall Dubhag from Kincraig; two days excursion from Kincraig to Inverey, the route followed being Kincraig to Loch an Eilein, Lairig Ghru, ascent of Creag an Leth-choin, over Ben Macdhui plateau (fully six inches of snow), descent to Shelter Stone at Loch Avon, ascent of Ben Mheadhoin, descent to head of Glen Derry, thence by Derry Lodge to Inverey. Returned the following day to Kincraig via Glens Geldie and Feshie.

Many Club members remember the days of catching the 4am mail train from Glasgow to Fort William, and others recall catching a bus organised every weekend by the JMCS which also left at an unearthly hour of the morning. Frequently Club members found interesting and original ways of arriving at Meets. Cynthia Marr was well-known for turning up on her motor-bike, often long after dark, burning up the miles of the twisty Loch Lomond road between Glasgow and Glencoe. Mora McCallum's little VW 'beetle' was often to be found parked in remote unlikely places with helpful little notices on the windscreen reading, 'The owner does NOT wish to be looked for by the Mountain

Rescue'. On one occasion, after the Beetle had remained in a field unvisited for a week, a herd of ponies, obviously deciding the owner was never coming back, and unable to resist temptation any longer, chewed off all the paintwork. The car was never the same; history makes no mention of the health of the ponies.

Mora enjoyed long expeditions on her own in the remote parts of the Scottish hills. This is her account of ten days camping in Ross-shire.

The advance of the motor age has brought most of the Scottish hills within easy reach of the moderately active walker, but there still remain a few remote mountain districts where one can travel for days without contact with tarred roads or tourists, areas whose exploration offers more challenge and interest than a car-based holiday can give. This is why I found myself trudging up Glen Elchaig from Killilan, Ross-shire, one inauspiciously wet Saturday in the summer of 1966, carrying a light tent, a strictly rationed ten days' supply of food for myself and six tins of dog meat for Bess, my canine companion.

Fortunately the rain went off after I had reached Iron Lodge and crossed by a hill path to the head of Loch Mullardoch, where I camped in a sticky heat which made the midges active for the next few days. My first day's climbing was the round of the hills to the south of my camp: Creag a' Choire Aird, Sgurr nan Ceathreamhnan, An Socach, MamSoul, Carn Eige and Beinn

Misses E.S.Mann and F.M.Macleod. Nailed boots on a hot day could produce sore feet

LSCC Archives

Annette and Janet Smith enjoying the view from Stac Pollaidh. Early LSCC members often covered huge distances on their summer walking holidays

LSCC Archives

Fhionnlaidh. It was clear and very warm and I looked enviously at the tea being brewed by a party of boys on the top of Carn Eige – I had still another Munro and 2000 ft. of steep grassy descent, the hardest work of the day, before my meagre supper.

After climbing all the hills in the Mullardoch area, Mora packed up her tent and moved on to Loch Monar, where she described an exhausting journey over unrelenting peat hags to the head of the Loch. To her dismay, her boots showed signs of giving up the struggle, and she had no other footwear (fortunately they lasted the trip), but she was rewarded by a beautiful camp-site with soft, flower-studded grass to lie on in the warm sunshine. Surely these are the moments that make the effort worthwhile.

Some days of hard slog in varying weather, sometimes in thick mist, sometimes in thundery downpours, and Mora nears the end of her epic journey;

Saturday brought my return to inhabited regions with an eighteen mile tramp to Achnashellach. After a damp start, the sun emerged warmly when I reached the River Meig, and my wet clothes soon dried on the pleasant path over the watershed behind Moruisg and down a forestry road with magnificent views of the Coulin Forest hills to the north – very different country to what I had just left. But the road was hard and stony after days of bog-trotting and by the time I reached Achnashellach my feet were rather the worse for wear. I collapsed thankfully outside the telephone box and, having assured my family that I was still alive, crawled painfully to the River Lair to camp on a very boggy shelf for the next two nights. Sunday was spent on a very wet round of Ben Liath Mhor and Sgurr Ruadh, and Monday's breakfast was a few sardines and dried potato – my last scrap of food, before I caught the train to Strome Ferry.

Some of Mora's ideas, however, were worthy of more careful scrutiny. Picture a scene on a wet, windy weekend in Knoydart, when Ann Winning, Alison Dinwoodie, the author and Mora were lying in a tent, bored and frustrated, waiting for the wind to abate so that they could continue canoeing up the west coast. Mora, thinking to lift their flagging spirits, said, 'How about walking across country sometime from Blackrock to Milehouse (the two Club cottages)?' Knowing Mora's energetic flights of fancy that should have been the moment to get out the map and check the route. Poor innocents that they were, they didn't realise that from Black Rock in Glencoe, over the Devil's Staircase to Blackwater Reservoir, up Loch Treig to Loch Ossian, over the Bealach Dubh to Culra Bothy, then down Loch Ericht, across the A9 at Dalwhinnie, down Glen Tromie, finishing with 11 miles down the road to Milehouse was a total distance of 72 miles – all to be completed in two days! Add to that one of the hottest of August weekends and legions of bloodthirsty midges, and a pleasant cross-country walk becomes a misery. It became known as the Saga of the Bloody Blisters.

It was on the stretch of railway line between Loch Treig and Corrour Station that realisation began to dawn on us. The sun reflected off the water and the white oven-clay rocks and beat down on us trapped in our own personally heated kilns. Alison had tied a handkerchief round her head and draped her own cagoule and mine over her back and legs so that she looked like some strange scarecrow. Even from the depths of her garish camouflage she emitted a kind of rosy glow that made me keep my distance. We plodded along the railway track hardly exchanging a word except to comment that railway sleepers are never the right distance apart. I became lost in my own private hell of endurance, miserably speculating whether it was worse to be a navvy staggering blindly through the blizzard to the railway, or a Touareg coming home from a weekend at the next oasis.

However women are notoriously good at surviving and by the time we had reached the far end of Loch Ossian we were once more able to appreciate the beauties of the scenery. The sun was sinking by now and flushing the tops of the old Scots pines with a deep russet glow. The heather flamed vivid purple, birch trees held their breath, and it was a pleasure to sit and look at the polished copper of the loch before rolling over for another gulp of pure burn water. We commented on how pleasant the track over the Bealach Dubh was going to be.

At least it would have been pleasant had the there been one. Mora had assured us that there was an excellent path over the Bealach Dubh, and I'm sure she's right, but we didn't find it. As the light faded from the glen I have a lasting picture of Alison floundering from peat hag to bog hole singing 'Lead Kindly Light'.

The journey continued the next day – thirty long weary miles of it, mostly on roads, to the detriment of feet already afire.

Dalwhinnie was reached conveniently by morning coffee time, when our feet just seemed to stray inadvertently into the Tartan Tuck-In Tearoom. People stared at us strangely as we gulped down pot after pot of tea, but it wasn't until I hobbled painfully into the Ladies Room and saw myself in the mirror that I realised why. An exhausted face stared back, eyes rather glazed, trails of sweat through the dust of the track, hair full of bits of bracken and heather. I suppose they thought we had just popped down for tea from Cluny's Cage.

At the end of it, all were agreed that it would make a wonderful cross-country expedition over at least three days if not perhaps a week!

Going back to earlier days, Kate O'Dwyer Shepherd remembers an epic journey in 1920 with the redoubtable founder-member, Lucy Smith. Starting in Glen Affric, their journey took them up Glen Cannich, over to Loch Mullardoch, into Glen Affric, through to Loch Duich, past Ben Attow and the Falls of Glomach, over the top of The Saddle, along Loch Hourn, into the Rough Bounds of Knoydart via Inverie and Loch Nevis, to Mallaig. A brief interlude on a train, and they finished up crossing from Rannoch Station to Loch Tay, over Ben Chonzie, finishing up at Crieff. The whole journey, which takes one all the way from Ross-shire to Perthshire through some of the most arduous mountain country only took them a week. Kate enthused about the magnificent scenery and, indeed, visiting the Highlands seems to have been a new experience for her, but one significant remark reveals the down side of the trip; 'I had ascended many Scottish hills in my youth, but it was Lucy who first showed me what feet were made for.' One can almost feel her agony as she follows the stalwart Lucy on their cross-country tramp, and ever more drastic measures have to be taken with her boots, first slitting them down the toe-caps, then marking on the boots where the blisters were and cutting holes around them, finally jettisoning them altogether, because as Kate said, 'It is not quite 'done' to take a good pair of boots and slice them in all directions!'

In the 17th and 18th Centuries soldiers' boots didn't have a right or left foot made to measure. Apparently feet were stuffed in regardless and padded out with paper or straw. It must have been torture tramping the military roads in search of rebellious Highlanders with feet like raw ham. One can still recall early climbing boots, pre-ergonomic design, that felt remarkably like that. Blisters were a common complaint, pulling the socks off at the end of the day reminiscent of Torquemada's torture, and helpful suggestions for dealing with them by pulling thread through or soaking the feet in methylated spirit, were not much better.

Perhaps it is a tribute to the vast improvement in comfortable footwear that the Great Outdoors Challenge has become such a popular event. In May 1996 Lorraine Nicholson rose to the challenge and walked from coast to coast across Scotland, describing it in the Club Journal.

It's not the 'mass' event that many think it is. It can be as individual as a finger-print and there were plenty of these left on the many OS maps I pored over prior to the event, plotting my route West to East. I chose Shiel Bridge as my starting point in May 1996 and set forth on the longest back-packing trip I had ever tackled, my sights set on St Cyrus...I was to meet up with friends old and new *en route* and pass through some wonderful scenery: Glen Affric, Glen Moriston, the Corrieyairack Pass, Glens Banchor, Feshie, Lee and Esk and so to the East coast at St Cyrus...Many of the cross-country routes were

Nailed boots on Curved Ridge, Buachaille Etive Mòr. While heavy, they allowed a good purchase on small holds

Photo: Rik Higham

completely new to me, and in the course of a fortnight, I was to be reminded just what a fantastic jigsaw Scotland is. Accommodation varied: camping, bothying and hostelling...I was caught in a snow blizzard on Morrone above Braemar, had to wade through the Water of Mark and then face a dramatic hail storm on Muckle Cairn but it was all part of the 'challenge'.

Not content with doing it once, Lorraine repeated the exercise the following year with a partially sighted friend. Nearing the triumphant end of their marathon walk, Lorraine relates the quote of the trip:

> 'Can you see the sea yet, Lorraine?' Ivan asked somewhat anxiously.
> 'No, not yet,' I replied.
> 'Oh, Lorraine, you could have lied and said, "yes"'

> It had been quite a profound experience for both of us and we were well satisfied with ourselves as we arrived at the finish. By walking across the land, Ivan had gained a far greater insight than most who visit Scotland, as expressed in one very sad commentary overheard in a Scottish hostel. An Australian girl asked two Americans where they had visited in the north of Scotland. 'Well, we hired a car in Glasgow and drove up to Fort William but there wasn't much there so we drove on up to Inverness and there wasn't much there either and there's only hills in between!'

Another epic journey was the 'Great Trek' carried out in 2001 by Pam Johnson, Moyra Hawthorn and Ruth Hannah. Over a period of three weeks they tramped from Glenfinnan via Glen Dessary, Knoydart's 'rough bounds', Kintail, Kinlochewe, Ullapool to Oykel Bridge and all the way up to Kinlochbervie and Sandwood Bay. The trio would have gone on to Cape Wrath, but were prevented by a military exercise. As Ruth pointed out, they took satisfaction in the fact that it took 14,000 soldiers to deflect them from their ultimate goal. They used bothies, tents and occasional luxury stops at B&Bs; they arranged food drops at strategic points, but they also caught trout and cooked them. Ruth's diary entry captures some of the trials and contrasts of the expedition as they traversed the wild country at the back of Ben More Assynt;

> One stumble after another all day, into and out of a wild rout of streams, peat hags, rivers, peat bogs. With heavy sacks, we leapt, waded, stumbled, tripped, and trotted as fast as we could. The path quickly disappeared, as we knew it would, but there were great problems in finding it again after the bealach. A terrific example of getting absolutely soaked through but not cold – all day, and it was the first day without any footache whatsoever. We looked for paths, at the map, at the scenery, reading in the rain, we gazed at the foaming waterfalls, and dodged round rocks in an effort to find the best way to cross the streams in spate. And again. And again. It was exhilarating and challenging and fearful. My lunch-time oatcakes became crumbs; we walked eight hours on two mugs of coffee. At last we found the path above the Eas Coul Aluinn waterfall (the highest in Britain) and marched down to the road. Hurrah! We marched down to Kylesku – a day ahead of our timetable. Fortunately there was space, the hostel was not crowded, the sitting room was cosy and the showers were hot.

Altogether the trip was about 300 kilometers and they climbed over 6000 metres in height. An epic indeed.

Pam Johnson river crossing en route to the remote Munro Seana Bhraigh

Photo: Ruth Hannah

Early winter snow on
Stob Bàn, Nov 2002.
Sarah Richards and
Mary Lothian

LSCC Archives

Readers may be wondering by now when mention will be made of the most popular 'stravaigs' of all, namely the addictive sport of Munro-bagging, not to mention Corbetts, Grahams, Docherty's, Donalds, Marilyns and any other list of tops with a name attached.

In 1891 Sir Hugh Munro's now famous list of Scottish mountains over 3000 feet (914.4m) in height was published. When the list was completed there were 276 Munros, 277 with the addition of Creag Tarsuinn, which Sir Hugh omitted, and indeed he himself fell short of completing his own list by a mere two tops. Over the years mountains have been re-surveyed and promoted or demoted accordingly, so that the list currently stands at 283. Following Sir Hugh's ideas, John Rooke Corbett, who in 1930 was only the second person to complete all the Munros and tops, brought out a list of all the tops in Scotland over 2500 feet (762m) high. The floodgates were opened and ticking off the tops soon gained addiction status. All peak-baggers give as their rationale that ticking the tops takes them to areas of the country they might never have visited, and certainly this used to be true of the Munros, although sheer pressure of feet nowadays is making even the more remote Munros well-trampled, with resulting impact of erosion and parking problems. However, the sheer variety and scope of the mountain ranges allow Munro-bagging to remain a truly delightful challenge.

For a challenge it undoubtedly is. The 14 Munros of the Cuillin Ridge include a significant amount of reasonably difficult rock climbing; the rocky ridges of Torridon are not to be taken lightly; one can encounter snow on the Cairngorm plateau any month of the year; some tops are so ill-defined that they require serious navigation skills, and some like Lurg Mòr or Seanna Bhraigh are remote enough to require a bivouac. But what delights they offer, from the sparkling glimpse of Hebridean islands from Ben Sgriol or the wild hills of Knoydart, to the wind scoured high plateau of the Cairngorms, sheltering tiny alpine plants in its pink granite outcrops; from the sociable accessibility of Ben Lomond or Ben Lawers, to the aloof loneliness of Ben Hope or Ben Klibreck.

The first to complete all the Munros was Rev A.E.Robertson. His second wife, Winifred, was a member of the LSCC so it is a fair guess that she must have accompanied him to many a top. Certainly Winifred had an intimate knowledge of the Scottish hills, not only as peaks to bag, but as treasured flower gardens and monuments to history. Her description of the hills around Ben Alder brings their Jacobite history vividly to life:

> A wisp of wind came over Ben Alder and soughed around the cairn stones; and with it came voices. Voices of men hunted by their fellow-men, crossing and re-crossing by these bealachs through the hills between Badenoch and Lochaber. Lochgarry and Locheil – who was 'bad of his wounds' Cluny and the tragic Dr Cameron, how well they knew it all!
>
> How gallantly, with prices on their heads, and Loudon's Militia in barracks but a half-day march away at Garvamore, did they travel to and fro to meet the Prince, to fetch the Prince, to carry the Prince's message.
>
> And here the Prince himself arrives almost without escort upon the 20th of August, 1746, having missed Cluny and Lochgarry somewhere between Achnacarry and Badenoch...We are told that first he lodges in a 'smokie bothie' and thence was guided to Cluny's carefully prepared 'very romantic comichal habitation' woven among the roots of an ancient holly high above Loch Ericht.

Cluny, knowing the difficulty of obtaining food in that countryside, combed and ravaged by the Saighdearan-Dearga, cached a store of meal in a sheiling by the Uisge nam Fichead...but first they must leave the fastnesses of high Badenoch, go warily down the glens and ford the Spean.

Many a fierce thrill would there be! Stones rattling on the hillside in the dusk – an English patrol? No! only a hind and her calf crossing a patch of screes. A 'thing' looming out of the steamy mists in the throat of a pass – a spy? No! naught but an ice-split rock up-ended in the path.

Is it a wonder that the hill winds carry still the voices of these men? And sometimes, on grey evenings, they carry too the weeping of a wife, a sweet-heart. But on blue days, when gallant cloud-galleys sail the skies, there is young brave laughter in the wind, the laughter of a Prince.

Moyra Hawthorn, Pam Johnson, Alison McLure and canine friend enjoy a brew at a bothy during their 'Great Trek' from Glenfinnan to Sandwood Bay in 2001

LSCC Archives

Decades later, perhaps inspired by Winifred's royalist romancing, an intrepid band decided to test out the comforts of Prince Charlie's cave in Glenmoriston. The royal doss was supposed to be situated somewhere on the slopes of Sgurr nan Conbhairean, and believing that the Bonny Prince's residence could not fail to be luxurious, the gang carelessly left their tents behind – a move soon to be regretted as they spread out over a rock-strewn hillside hunting for anything that might remotely be described as a cave. Eilidh Nisbet recounts their adventures:

L.Forrest, Sue Vaughan, Pam Johnson and Ann-Marie Henderson in heavy snow conditions on the Easains, February 2005

Photo: Alison Higham

It is not really a cave but a huge boulder shelter, commodious but decidedly damp in parts due to the water-supply trickling through it. The upper corrie, which we christened 'Trogladal' (on account of us being troglodytes) is full of little hideouts formed by tumbled boulders.

Howffs were graced with names such as 'Troglets', 'Trogwash', and 'Troghaven', and were soon adapted and made habitable by carefully building up the floor with stones and deep moss. In no time they had converted the unlikely ground into a most desirable residence – fit for a Prince even? Eilidh's diary continues:

> There was rather a lot of giggling in Troghaven as we settled into our sacks enjoying a final brew of whisky-laced tea and admiring the decorative effect of the banded gneiss and the mica-filled flakes on our roof and walls glittering in the candle-light. I can't speak of the others, but we four slept like trog-logs and didn't wake up till nine o'clock.

The first LSCC member to complete her Munros was Annie Hirst, only tenth on the list of 'compleatists' and the first woman to do so. There was then a long gap in the story of woman Munroists, and then in 1960 Anne Littlejohn completed all the Munros, all the tops and all the Munros furth of Scotland, followed in the same year by Nan Miller. In 1967 Mora McCallum not only completed all her Munros and tops, but was the youngest to do so. From then on there was a spate of LSCC members doing all their Munros, with some doing them more than once round.

Perhaps one of the greatest Munro-bagging achievements for the Club was Kathie Murgatroyd's completion in 1982 of all the (then 276) Munros in one continuous trip using only a folding bike, kayak, car support and her own feet (apart from ferries to Skye and Mull), most of it on her own.

The idea came to Kathie in Shenavall bothy inspired by a chance entry in the bothy book: 'Passed through on Long Walk, 1976, Hamish Brown.' Kathie discovered that no woman had yet tried to emulate this and began to wonder if she could manage. By the spring of 1982 she made up her mind to give it a go.

It was a huge gamble. Not only did it mean giving up her job as organiser of outdoor education for Grampian Region, but it also meant giving up her house. Kathie knew that she was fit and competent, but there was no precedent, no-one to whom she could turn for advice, and she wasn't at all sure if it was possible. In fact so unsure was she of the outcome, that even LSCC members weren't told until she had completed the challenge. However, her friend Ivan offered vital car back-up, and that was enough. It was on!

At the start the weather did all it could to be discouraging. The expedition began on Ben More on Mull on 1st May, when one might have expected balmy spring days. Alas, not so! Kathie was blown off her feet several times on her way up Ben More, and then storm-bound for four days at the foot of Ben Cruachan while Force 8 gales and full blizzards raged outside. So much for Scottish spring weather! Desperate at the loss of valuable time, Kathie made an attempt on Ben Eunaich where she developed a technique of running with the wind, listening for the gusts coming, ready to fall on her ice-axe when it became overpowering. At last, on May 5th, all alone, she managed Ben Cruachan which was still deep in snow with alarming cornices on both sides of the ridge.

Then, just as suddenly, summer began and less than a week later it was possible to canoe across Loch Lomond in shirt sleeves. This was the auspicious start to one of the best summers on record, and from then on there was no holding her.

Being on one's own in the mountains gives rare glimpses of wildlife in its natural environment. On one occasion a mallard took a run at the tent, tucked in its legs, and used the fly-sheet as a slide. Less welcome was the cat that tried the same trick in the Fannichs. Once, cycling without lights down Glen Lochay, Kathie was startled by thundering hooves and nearly collided with a whole herd of deer in full flight. Often high camps were shared with herds of deer, and in Glen Geuseachan a female reindeer with a newly born calf passed quite close. Whether the helicopter-load of Cairngorm Mountain Rescue dossing in Culra Bothy should be described as 'wildlife' is debatable.

An expedition lasting nearly five months calls for a huge amount of organisation. Ivan with his support car made the whole thing possible, but food had to be carefully divided into five-day packs and then left at various arranged points. After three weeks Kathie found her energy level dropped alarmingly and realised that a diet of dehydrated food

Ben Nevis and the Càrn Mòr Dearg arete from the Mamores

Photo: A.Dinwoodie

simply was not adequate, so she arranged for fresh food at weekends. Although spending long periods on her own in the wild, Kathie made full use of the benefits of civilisation when appropriate. Accommodation ranged from bivouacks, tents in the wild, the back of the car, bothies, club huts, youth hostels, friends' houses, B&B and, on one luxurious occasion, a hotel. On reaching Loch Ossian Youth Hostel she was told that it was full, but when the warden realised that she was a lone female, he told her there was one female bed. He just hadn't believed that a woman would have undertaken such a trip on her own!

The walk was planned to end with a party of four on top of the Inaccessible Pinnacle on 11th September, but things don't always turn out as planned. The wind was so strong at the Theàrlaich-Dubh Gap that they had to turn back, so the last long day turned out to be Mhadaith, Ghreadaidh, Banachdich, Sgùrr Dearg, the Inaccessible Pinnacle, with a triumphant finish on Sgùrr MhicCoinnich.

So Kathie's Mountain Walk was over. The bicycle tyres were worn down to the fabric; Kathie herself was lean, tanned and incredibly fit, but filled with a mixture of elation and sadness. 'No need to set the alarm'; 'Look at this mountain of washing'; 'How do I sleep in a bed?'; 'What does the future hold?'; 'I've done it!'.

So what magic is it that attracts such an obsessional ticking of little piles of stones at the tops of bare summits? This extract from the 1998 Journal perhaps sums it up;

> Scotland's Munros are unrivalled anywhere in the world for delightful variety of weather, colour, birdsong and situation. The joy of crampons creaking on firm snow and the blue-green hole left by the ice-axe; the weary boots, dusty with heather-pollen on bee-droning evenings in the Rothiemurchus pine; the quiet satisfaction of navigating to the cairn in the right place after long-staring through moisture-rimmed eyelashes in the muffled closeness of the mist; the hooded isolation of a head-down battle against a West-coast blatter; or the delicate wrinkle of sun-warmed rock with Rannoch Moor at your back.

For the dedicated top-ticker, the lure of 11 Munros linked by a pleasant connecting ridge that drops very little between summits is irresistible. Such is the South Cluanie Ridge, starting from its eastern end at the highest point of the old road over to Loch Quoich. The first top is Creag a' Mhaim, thence over nine other magnificent tops to finish at the western end on Sgùrr na Sgine, or even, if there is any spring left in the knees, continuing on to The Saddle. This high-level jaunt along the tops features in many Club accounts, both summer and winter, snow, hail or sunshine.

One hot June day in 1967, 11 Club members and a dog set off in fine spirits, but one by one heat overmastered them, until only three members remained, kept going only by the leader's promises of a fine deep pool for swimming in the burn at the end. Even this promise came to be doubted, as the heat-wave raised spectres of drought and dried-up puddles. Fortunately for the leader's safety, hopes were well and truly fulfilled as three hot, dusty bodies plunged into the delicious cool depths of the pool at the foot of Faochaig, even emulating salmon as they attempted to swim up the waterfall.

The North side of Glen Sheil also possesses a fine array of Munros culminating in the much-photographed range of the Five Sisters of Kintail. The wearisome toil up to the bealach on Sgùrr nan Spainteach is more than rewarded by the fine rocky scramble over five fine tops finishing with a western sunset over the distant outline of the Cuillin of Skye.

Another happy hunting ground for Munro-bagging stravaigers is Torridon. The long ridge of Beinn Eighe with its ten tops offers a fine day's walking; the great bulk of Liathach is said to be one of the hardest of the mainland Munros offering few easy ways up or down; and the Horns of Alligin provide a dramatic accompaniment to a good day out. They are heroic mountains, made for epics.

An Easter Meet in 1971 provided perfect conditions for such epic outings. The Record describes a grand traverse of Beinn Eighe.

Saturday gave Mora and Sue perfect conditions for the original route on the Eastern Buttress of Coire Mhic Fhearchair and the main peaks of Beinn Eighe. Janet, Erna, Catherine, Dick, Vera and Margaret climbed the Beinn by Coir' an Laoigh, while Christina, Isabel, Helen, Eilidh and Mona attacked it from the east. Combining a Steven (an exceptionally energetic day!), an Easter epic and an initiation ceremony for one of the Club's newer members, their day started with deceptively long rests, while Eilidh committed her latest lyrics

LSCC group snatch a sparkling day on Beinn a' Bheithir and the Ballachulish Horseshoe, February 2005

Photo: Alison Higham

to paper. This was followed by a direct ascent of near vertical scree – an ordeal mitigated for some by memories of worse slopes encountered in East Greenland. After traversing the Pinnacles and Sgurr Ban and before the Steven spirit took over, Christina and Isabel wisely left the party. Hours later, with all the peaks of Beinn Eighe in the bag, the survivors staggered into the Ling Hut. Mona collapsed in the corner with food and a bottle of cider.

Liathach must be one of the finest mountains on the Scottish mainland. One particularly memorable Easter, Mora and Helen had a most enjoyable epic on Liathach. After ploughing their way up the steeply tiered rock bands festooned with deep soft snow, they slumped down thankfully on the summit ridge, and had a delightful scramble in warm sunshine to the top. By this time the sun was setting magnificently in the West, when Mora suddenly announced that she still had a top that she hadn't done. It so happened that it was at the far end of the Northern Pinnacles, a sharp bristly ridge of unstable and dramatic rock towers. Nothing daunted the pair set off, but found that the pinnacles were glazed over with a thin film of ice on the north-facing side. This slowed them down somewhat, so that by the time they thankfully reached the end of the ridge, darkness was falling. Mora confidently asserted that there was a full moon. There was, but it shone on the other side of the ridge! However, after a dramatic glissade into the unknown down the north side of Liathach, they finally emerged onto the road at about midnight, to creep stealthily into a sleeping camp.

The Cairngorms show a totally different character to the rugged mountains of the West. More subtle perhaps, keeping their secrets tucked into lonely corries gouged out of the rolling expanses of high plateau, and contrasting the bald wind-swept high tops with sweet scented ancient Caledonian pine forests and gleaming lochans around their skirts. This is a stravaiger's paradise, with the great heaving plateau above 4000 feet, split in two by the great gash of the Làirig Ghrù, and bordered by four of the highest mountains in Scotland. Although Cairngorm itself has become a ski resort, with all the paraphernalia of mechanical uplift, cafes, car parks, and even a railway, it is still easy to lose oneself in the remote hinterland of the high massif. Tucked in behind Braemar and Tomintoul, Ben Avon and Beinn a' Bhùird are splendid in their aloofness and there is something most fitting about the name of one of the tops of Ben Avon, Leabaidh an Daimh Bhuidhe, the Couch of the Tawny Stag. Stand quietly at the top of the March Burn where it plunges down into the Lairig and hear the sound of silence, broken only by the low whistle of wind over dry grasses and the occasional rumbling of a ptarmigan. Or mark where the boots tread to discover tiny shy *Silene acaulis* creeping over grey granite boulders or the startling white of *Dryas octopetala*. Or wallow in luxury on a hot June day in the clear mossy spring of the source of the Dee near the summit of Braeriach and know perfection.

On the Braemar side of the Cairngorms, Derry Lodge, now alas no longer in use, and Muir of Inverey, belonging to the Cairngorm Club, have provided welcome venues for many a Club Meet. A Club record of 1952 well illustrates the pleasure and variety offered by a spell of fine weather.

Sunday, 29th June. The fine warm summer morning allowed us to appreciate fully the fine situation of Derry Lodge. At the front door the road ends; at the back the tracks to the Cairngorms begin – the famous tracks through the Lairig Ghru and through the Lairig an Laoigh, winding first through the old Caledonian pines and eventually reaching Coire Etchachan, the Shelter Stone, the Wells of Dee and the Macdhui ridge.

Helen Steven enjoying a high camp near the summit of Ben Macdui in the Cairngorms

Photo: Julia Banks

The Club made the most of a wonderful weekend, traversing most of the high tops, doing some good rock climbs in Coire Sputain Dearg, but also finding time for sketching, swimming, cooking omelettes over a wood fire, and brewing up endless cups of tea. All the ingredients for a memorable weekend.

On another meet two Club members cycled their way up to Derry Lodge, left their bicycles secreted amidst the heather and toiled heavy-laden with camping gear up the long slope of Ben Macdui to within a hundred feet of the summit. A welcoming patch of soft moss presented an inviting camp-site, but a sharp May blizzard drove them into the warm shelter of their sleeping bags. Emerging into the sunset at about 10pm it was a rare experience to sit with feet dangling over the edge of Coire Sputain Dearg clutching steaming mugs of chocolate. Surely, at over four thousand feet, the highest hot chocolate in Scotland that evening! The next day dawning cold and crisp, the two were ideally placed to wander all day over the high tops of the Cairngorm plateau.

*Julia Banks' last
Munro –
Buachaille Etive
Beag, June 2001*

Photo: Alison Higham

East of Braemar lies Lochnagar. One memorable trip comes to mind. It was Easter of 1969, blue and cold, with plenty of good snow. The author and Mora MacCallum, having left the car near Braemar, plunged through deep snow to the fine northern corrie of Lochnagar and climbed the Black Spout, a pleasantly easy snow gully, plastered with magnificent whorls and patterns of ice on the black rocks on either side. Emerging through the cornice at the top, they were met with an array of shining white tops, and a long plod through soft snow over Toll Mount and Tom Bhuidhe down to Glen Clova where the Club was meeting. A fine long day out.

This Meet was Ann Winning's introduction to the Club as a guest. On the arrival of the exhausted two, Ann engaged in conversation in a friendly sort of way. She was soon invited to join them going to fetch the car. Little did Ann know, as she casually agreed, that the journey to retrieve the abandoned car involved traversing Mount Keen and a walk out to Braemar past Loch Muick of about 25 miles! Ann's producing rum-flavoured Kendal mint cake at a strategic point on the journey no doubt ensured her membership of the Club.

For many, once they have completed the Munros, drunk the champagne at the summit and added their names to the ever-growing list of 'compleaters', they then go on to do the Corbetts, or to complete the Munros in a different way, or to complete all the tops, and so the top-ticking continues.

In 1987 Sheila Cormack reported that she had finished her second round of Munros on Christmas Day with Slioch, on a wet and windy day. On Christmas Eve she had completed her Corbetts with Beinn Airigh Charr near Poolewe. Not content with this, on 4th May she finished the Donalds on Saddle Yoke near Moffat, and announced that she was ready to start all over again!

Others however, consider it a kind of liberation to be freed from the self-imposed restraints of lists. As someone aptly described a Meet in Glen Clova.

> Sunday dawned delightfully sunny and everyone was looking forward to one of these delicious days on the hills when it seems vastly more important to bask in the sun on one's first Munro than to add several to the bag.

Sometimes a sense of proportion does prevail. These are some reflections of the author on completing her Munros.

> And so at last the libations were suitably poured on the summit of Beinn Teallach, my last Munro. What next? Corbetts? Tops? Do them again? Hang up my boots? So many of my contemporaries were also completing their Munros, I briefly contemplated only counting it if it were someone's last Munro party. In fact, I was agreeably surprised at my reaction. I suppose I must have been a slave to The List, no matter how vehement my denials, because suddenly the whole wide vista of Scotland and its mountains lay at my feet. Hills I hadn't visited since I was a teenager became available again; rounded enigmas shrouded in mist could be revisited in fine weather; I could accompany my friends anywhere without a furtive checking of the List first. I had been awarded the Freedom of Scotland.

Some of the most enjoyable 'stravaigs' arise on a whim, on the spur of the moment. Like the time when someone suggested a moonlight

Above: Monica Jackson and Sherpas Mingma and Ang Temba on the summit of Gyalgan Peak, Nepal on the first ascent in 1955. The expedition included Betty Stark and Evelyn Camrass (McNicol) and was the first expedition by British women to the Himalaya

Below: Greenland 1970 – Eilidh Nisbet (front) and Helen Steven making the second ascent of Ardvreck, a shapely peak of rock and ice above Alpefjord and the Sandgletscher

Above: Helen Geddes, Sarah Mackay and Mary Lothian on The Monch, Lauterbrunnen meet 1995

Below: Kate Ross on the summit of Ama Dablam, Nepal in 1999

trip up Càrn Bàn Mòr, and then, after settling in comfortably by the fireside at Milehouse, had their bluff called. A great idea, only there happened to be no moon, just starlight, though the glint of the starlight on the white stones of the path sufficed. Fine, until one of the party tripped over the summit cairn.

Indeed moonlight, and even pitch darkness, seem to present an irresistible challenge to some members. Many a time, stepping out of Blackrock for a breath of fresh air before turning in has led to an urge to wander the tops. This is an account by Betty Stark of the classic route from Stob Ghabhar to Meall a' Bhuiridh.

> Why waste a lovely spring day sleeping off a climb? they said. Better start by moonlight, see the sunrise, then enjoy it all day up on top... and we nearly took this counsel, but just then the moon came up, magnificently huge and golden and, with our eyes fastened on it, we picked up our wee sacks, reached for our axes, and set off as summoned.
>
> We had never done anything quite like this before, and we talked excitedly at first about all sorts of things, till the moon, contracting into brilliance, softened the dark landscape below and silenced us.
>
> I remember we crossed a flashing stream and stopped a long time to look at a waterfall; and there was a narrow snow arête, I remember, leading to a great corniced dome below the summit, which we reached just on the dot of midnight...It was too cold to linger and anyway we had a marvellous world to walk in.
>
> We could see and recognise peaks miles away, and near us the snow gleamed like taffeta in the moonlight. Later it became hard and icy, and sometimes a crust would flake off as we kicked, and go down with the sound of running water. We found that the darkest hour was not before dawn at all. Walking along the top of Clach Leathad to Sron na Creise and back we watched the sky lighten in the east long before sunrise.

As the years catch up and the knees lose their spring and the breath comes in shorter gasps, it is good to know that the mountains always offer an alternative. For some it is to be found lingering over the plants and mosses at their feet, for others it is bird-watching.

Members can still recall Eleanor Lloyd moving slowly and painfully with two sticks, but always returning with a keen-eyed list of birds and plants observed. Some in the Club are accomplished artists in the sure knowledge that sitting at an easel painting, the memories of the tops are still there behind the canvas.

In 1980 a group of Glasgow members started the Tuesday walks, and every second Tuesday a group finds new territory to explore at a gentler pace and gradient than the high tops.

Then there have been the regular Island Meets in the summer, usually organised by Rhona Weir. Colonsay, Rum, Jura, Gigha and Orkney have all been thoroughly explored from shoreline to rough rocky summits.

It may be a love of the mountains that brings the Club together, but lasting companionships are formed in their company. It was said of Elspet Mackay, one of the early members of the Club – 'Elspet would never tick off mountains; they were her friends.' and it is perhaps this attitude which has led the Club to explore the mountains in all aspects and weathers.

LSCC group in
Zermatt before
climbing the
Breithorn, c. 1920

LSCC Archives

7: Alpine Adventures

DURING THE LATE 19TH CENTURY walking and climbing in the Alps became almost as much a mark of distinction as making the Grand Tour in an earlier era. Wordsworth and the Romantic poets played their literary part, and after Whymper's acrimoniously competitive ascent of the Matterhorn in 1865 becoming an 'alpinist' was almost part of a rich young man's coming of age.

Needless to say, women were in there as well doing their alpine ascents as is amply illustrated in some of these famous old prints. How awkward it must have been with long skirts trailing through the deep soft snow of the glaciers, becoming ever more heavy and cumbersome as they tangled clammily around one's legs. Pictures show women with wide skirts, nipped-in waists, and even bustles clambering over crevasses bridged by precarious ladders, the women still clutching their hats and veils, ice-axes reaching up to the chin.

One could almost argue that the LSCC had its source firmly in the glaciers of alpine climbing. The friendship that grew up between the Inglis Clarks, the Smiths and the Raeburns was fostered and nurtured during the long summer weeks spent together in the Alps almost every

year. Often they would book together into a hotel at their chosen venue
– Chamonix, Zermatt, Arolla – and then engage the services of a guide,
often the same one year after year, for the duration of their stay. The
list of achievements during these energetic summer weeks was prodi-
gious. They may have been rich, but they most certainly were not 'idle
rich'.

It is obvious from the accounts in the Club Record that these early
climbs were often done in the company of their men-folk, however, the
whole *raison d'etre* of the Club was to encourage women to take the lead
and take off on their own adventures. By 1912 the list of individual
members' doings in the Alps had grown, including several trips made
by women on their own, some guideless climbs and even a few first
ascents. This is Miss S.Last's entry for 1912;

> Switzerland, August – Saas – Ascent of Sudlenzspitze and over Arete to Nadel-
> horn. Miss Last with her sister carried out a successful guideless walking tour
> in a part of the country little known to English (sic) climbers. From Saas Fee,
> they crossed the Monte Moro to Macugnaga, a good deal of snow on the Pass.
> Over the Col del Turlo to Alagna, easy Pass, snow at the top. Walked up to
> the Colle d'Olen in mist, and stayed the night but had no view. Went down,
> still in mist, to Gressonay la Trinite. Went over Colle di Betta Furka in mist
> to Fiery. Went over the Col des Cimes Blanches to Breuil, great quantity of
> snow. Over the Col de Valcournera to Praraye, pass in bad condition, rocks
> iced, and some step cutting necessary. Over the Col Fenetre de Balme to
> Mauvoisin, a long day, easy pass with some snow.

1912 must have been a good year for energetic long walks, as a total
of nine members – one third of the membership of the Club – spent
time in the Alps. In July of that year Lucy Smith and Helene Greiner
had a three week walking holiday in the Tyrol, on their own without
menfolk or guides. It is apparent that these trips to the Alps did not
necessarily include many summits but were often high-level walks
involving the crossing of mountain passes, the negotiation of glaciers
and crevasses, and staying in mountain refuges or huts. These trips could
be done guideless, but often in those days at the expense of raised
eyebrows and such comments as 'But Mesdames, where are your *men*?'
However, a certain Miss Lowson (one of the original Club members)
climbed a total of 18 alpine peaks, including a casual mention of the
Matterhorn by the Zmutt Ridge. The LSCC's growing reputation for alpine
climbing was suitably recognised when Mabel Jeffrey (Inglis Clark) was
invited to attend as a guest of honour at the Ladies Alpine Club annual
dinner in London in 1912.

There is a specific timetable for alpine climbing that is partly necessitated by snow conditions, and hence has not changed with the passing
of the years, but could be said to be almost part of the alpine allure (at
least to those with an affinity with larks and other early birds). It is usual
to leave the cafes and fleshpots of the valley behind and climb up to
one of the high mountain huts arriving late afternoon or early evening.
These huts are usually staffed by a 'guardien' and often cooked meals
can be obtained. Not much time for loitering over the evening drinks,
however, as preparing and packing one's gear and early bed is usually
the order of the day (always hoping that the other occupants of the hut

are of the same mind!). Sleep at this stage is a somewhat rare commodity, as anticipation, worries about the weather, stereophonic snoring, and concerns about waking betimes are not good nightcaps. An 'alpine' start involves getting up any time between 1am and 4am, grabbing a hasty breakfast – usually not much more than coffee or tisane and setting off up the glacier before dawn.

One reason for this precipitate departure is of course to be one of the first ropes on the hill, and this can be particularly important for a climbing party without a guide, as other faster parties can overtake and leave one with a long wait at the harder sections. Of greater importance, however, is the condition of the snow. Early in the morning, before the sun reaches it, the snow will be hard frozen. Vital, delicate snow bridges spanning crevasses will be firm and trustworthy early in the day, but in an ever-increasing state of collapse as the sun melts the snow. The later in the day, the greater the risk of avalanche or of being hit with a fusillade of stones from the melting slopes above – or, let it be said, from careless parties higher on the route. The aim therefore is to depart in relative safety, reach one's summit by lunch-time and be back in the hut in the afternoon in good time for those welcome buckets of tea.

There is something of the essence of the Alps to be filing quietly, absorbed in one's own thoughts, up a glacier trail, following the flickering light of a torch – candle-lit storm lanterns then; tiny, intense LED lights now – and watching the candles grow dim as the light increases, flushing the tops to golden rose, and then flooding the glaciers with dazzling white light, throwing rocks and crevasses into dark relief. No wonder people return summer after summer.

It is interesting to note that the anniversary Journal of the Club, published in 1929 makes no mention of any Alpine exploits, confining itself entirely to descriptions of hill days in Scotland. This may possibly reflect an attitude expressed at the AGM in 1923 when a proposal to hold Meets furth of Scotland was actually turned down on the grounds that this was a Scottish climbing club. Such may have been the policy of the Club at that moment, but it most certainly did not reflect the activities of Club members.

Barbara Macfarlane who became a member in 1922 was one of the most intrepid and far-travelled members of the Club. Her list of climbs in the Alps was impressive. Indeed in the year she joined the Club during the months of July and August she climbed 20 peaks over 10,000 feet in height in addition to a whole range of lesser expeditions. Perhaps even more impressive was her original and adventurous list of countries visited. She climbed in the Bernese Oberland, the Tyrol, the Tatra, the Caucasus, Norway, Germany and Corsica, and was climbing on the Continent every year between 1922 and 1939. Most of these climbs were done without guides but in the company of local climbing enthusiasts, which resulted in a host of friendships all over Europe. Even in her late 80s Barbara Macfarlane's array of Christmas cards testified to her enormously wide circle of climbing friends. Small wonder then that she was the only foreign guest at a dinner in Berne for the Swiss Everest Team, and was asked to speak on behalf of the LSCC, and that she was awarded a Fellowship of the Royal Scottish Geographical Society.

Dressed for dinner at the Hotel Central in Kandersteg c. 1920

LSCC Archives

In 1926 Kate O'Dwyer Shepherd was also carrying the skill of the Club well beyond the borders of Scotland. Her entry that year is impressive;

From Chamonix – Aig. de Floriaz; Aig. de Belvedere; traverse of la Nonne and l'Eveque; Dent du Requin; Aig. de l'M (by the face), Pic Albert; traverse of Grands Charmoz; Aig. de Grepon; Aig. du Geant; Grandes Jorasses; l'Innominata; Mont Blanc (turned 20 mins. below the summit by blizzard). From Zermatt – Zinal Rothorn (by the Trifthorn Ridge); Wellenkuppe (guideless); Trifthorn (leading); Riffelhorn (Corner, Glacier and Skyline routes, leading). In the Dolomites – Cinque Torri; Punta Croce, Punta Erbin; Testa di Bartolo (on Pomagagnon – new climb); ...Kleine Fermeda (easy way); Grosse Fermeda (twice – S. and E. routes); Marmolata (S. Wall); Grosse Zinne (leading up)

She leaves one quite breathless with her energy, but at least she admits to one easy way up to encourage lesser mortals.

Obviously many Club members were already having regular climbing holidays in the Alps as individuals, and it only remained for the Club to promote an Alpine Meet to bring these members together. The first organised Alpine Meet was held in Arolla in 1928. It seems to have been something of an anti-climax as only three members attended, although they seem to have had a grand time, with an ascent made almost every day of their week together. However, a precedent had been set, and in 1930 three members again headed for the Alps, this time to Chamonix. According to the record the weather that year was the worst experienced in the Alps for many years, with fresh snow and ice making the more difficult rocks very treacherous. The Record states that 'the more ambitious climbs were impossible'. As they achieved a remarkable amount in their time together, one is left wondering what a 'more ambitious programme' would have looked like. Their programme included the Aiguille de l'M, the Petits Charmoz, the Aiguille des Grands Montets, the Aiguille du Tacul, and the Aiguille du Plan. Quite enough Aiguilles to keep even the less ambitious happy.

It takes more than a season of bad weather to keep the LSCC off the mountains, and the following year saw them returning to the Alps, this time to Zermatt. This was well-attended with eight members and two guides, four out of the eight returning to their second Meet, obviously undaunted by previous experiences. Although described as a 'Novices' Meet, they all seem to have acquitted themselves well, climbing the Rimpfischhorn, the Breithorn, the Petit Mont Cervin, and the Unter Gabelhorn. The guides Joseph and Anatole Georges provided welcome leadership, and on a subsequent occasion Iris Blaikie and May Green availed themselves of their expertise.

> Next day was our last with Joseph and Anatole, and we were to end up with a big climb – the Grands Charmoz. We started at 4.0 a.m. and dawn found us steadily ascending the Glacier des Nantillons. Roping up when we came to some large crevasses, we soon left the lower glacier, and after a halt on the summit of the rognon, we climbed up the steeper part of the glacier for an hour or more, until we reached the rocks below the famous Charmoz-Grepon col...we pushed on to the summit, first on steep but easy rocks, then up a crack in a shallow trough to the foot of the final chimney, which we all found difficult. The lower section was very holdless and exposed, while the chimney proper seemed to be made to fit no mortal dimensions. Once over the chockstone however, some judicious back and knee work, and pushing and pulling and puffing and blowing brought us on to a narrow steep ridge of granite, up which we scrambled, and perched on the delightfully airy summit of the Grands Charmoz.

One of the reasons that people join climbing clubs is to learn new skills and techniques from the more experienced members, and although people expected to benefit from the professional skills of a guide in the Alps, to dyed-in-the-wool amateur climbers the idea of actually going to an alpine school to learn techniques was somewhat frowned upon and was decidedly controversial in those early days of alpinism. This may seem somewhat surprising in our current age of Mountain Leadership Certificates, professional climbing tours and well-run training courses, but back in 1938 the debate between amateur and professional was a keen one.

Club member Ann Sheriff challenged these conventions by writing of her visit to a School of Alpine Technique in the 1938 Journal:

LSCC party with guides on the Gornergrat, 1921

LSCC Archives

> Among cherished events, a week of Ice and Snow Technique with the Zurich Section, SWAC (Swiss Women's Alpine Club) stands out, ringed around with glowing colours. To me anything is worth trying once – the unknown is always an adventure. There was no worry that I should later on walk into controversy, bitter and mordant, as to whether a climber is born or made. Does it matter, so long as one is happy on a mountain? They are to be envied who are born knowing tricks – or are they? There is much fun in learning, and moving on from (easy) conquest to (easy) conquest. So I had no compunction about attending a course, and, were it possible, I should add a week of the course to my efforts each season.

Ann learned the skills of step-cutting on steep snow, escaping from crevasses, (in which she said she felt like a piece of cheese being cut in two), moving together with a coiled rope, and, (another controversial piece of equipment in the 1930s) the use of crampons.

> At first amazingly clumsy, we could trip ourselves up and set ourselves flying so easily. As we learned to raise our feet and keep them clear of one another,

a new confidence was born. We threaded our way across the glacier, on the edge of crevasses balancing on the most narrow of ridges. We were led across the most broken-up parts of the glacier, and gradually acquired, if not contempt for it, assuredly a familiarity with it at its worst, which is perhaps the best mental equipment. The glacier was given to us.

Not surprisingly, the onset of war in 1939 set the Club's activities back considerably and membership remained static with climbing rather in the doldrums. Post-war, there was a deliberate attempt to recruit new members, and both Glasgow and Edinburgh Universities proved fertile recruiting ground. A whole list of new names appeared in the late '40s and '50s. Janie Cameron, Christina Macnair, Elma Wrench, Molly Johnstone, Cynthia Stewart, 'Ikes' Dickson, Betty Stark, and Anne Murray all joined at roughly the same time, bringing new life and energy into the Club. They had all recently been students and were mostly in their first jobs, so not for them Alpine climbing from hotels. They were just as determined to make regular visits to the Alps, but it had to be done on a shoe-string, and they had to rely on their own initiative and develop their own skills.

Betty Stark, newly qualified as a speech therapist, on a student budget and with a thirst for adventure, was not to be deterred by the restraints of finance and describes a camping holiday with Flora Geddes in the Alps. Lamenting the restraints of their budget, Betty remarks;

> I see that I wasn't allowed a cigarette in the month of July, and that we sneaked a glass or two of wine when we came down from the Aiguille du Plan. But more important we proved that, both on this year's holiday and last, we managed by camping out to live on roughly 9/6d per day. That includes everything except fares and the cost of a guide...
>
> Outside Dieppe we camped one night on a farm near the aerodrome...the farmer's wife gave us milk and eggs, though this was just an excuse to come and inspect our proceedings, saying' "Et vous dormez comme ca! Sans messieurs! Quel courage!"
>
> Camping abroad means travelling with a heavy load, though no extra equipment is necessary, but for some of us it can make possible or greatly extend an alpine holiday. Moreover it is fun; the shopping is fun whether you manage by pointing, or on resuscitated French by getting a tin of fruit in mistake for jam...
>
> On reaching the mountains we made the tent our base, and left our spare gear in it when we went up to the huts. Nothing was ever taken or disturbed...Sleeping out in the Alps is a wonderful experience and often a wakeful one...in 1949 we made quite a habit of it against the advice of Luc, our guide. Luc had a personality as vivid as his blue eyes and shock of black hair and gay moustache. He went very quickly and was often impatient with us, but we soon discovered his prodigious appetite and that the best way to stop him was to produce a tempting morsel. "Cinq minutes", he would say severely, and half an hour later he was still scraping happily with his ice-axe at a tin of jam!
>
> On one occasion we slept out below the Glacier de St Sorlin in Savoy when the Pic de l'Etendard was our objective. We had a wonderful camp fire as the full moon rose over the Aiguilles d'Arves. But it was less romantic at 3.0 a.m. trying, in a heavy dew, to re-light the fire with toilet paper and to coax the lumps out of the porridge.

Possibly in the light of this influx of keen new members, all anxious to acquire alpine skills, Iris Blaikie organised a Club Meet at a Mountaineering School in Pontresina. Although the unfortunate Iris broke her arm right at the start of the Meet, it was obviously a great success. Herr Vetter of the Mountaineering school had laid on special instruction tailored specifically to the needs of the LSCC members, and they had a glorious fortnight walking, climbing, admiring the flowers, and trying to avoid the temptation of cafes. (This was still the post-war period of restricted currency abroad). The climax of the trip came in the ascent of Piz Palu on 22nd July.

Janie Cameron, abseil on the Riffelalp 1948

Photo: Janie Cameron Collection

> At 3.20 a.m. eight of us set off with Vetter and a second guide for Piz Palu (3912m). For half an hour by lantern light, we skirted the dark rocks of Arlas, then picked our way down to the glacier. As dawn came in we strapped on crampons and roped up. Vetter led Riona, Annette, May and Grizel; his colleague, Morf, led Billie, Janet, Christina and Janie. The weather was very fine, and the views, especially in the early morning light were superb. To some of us, at least, the snow slopes were of the steepest, the ridges of the narrowest, and the tops far removed above the lowlands of everyday existence. We traversed the three tops and the rock ridge to Fuorcla Bellavista in good time for so large a party. From there we came down over the upper Morteratsch Glacier with its fantastic scenery of seracs and crevasses. Here the guides had to search for safe snow bridges though conditions seemed good and easy. Down at the Boval Hut we gazed in wonderment at the tops we had traversed and at the many summits still beyond us. We were very happy and all agreed that the Meet had reached a fitting climax.

Soon the Club was branching out into joint meets, and in 1953 Esme Speakman, Elma Wrench and Janie Cameron attended a joint meet in the Chamonix area with members of the Swiss Women's Alpine Club. They only had a week, and the weather was not promising, but virtue, or at least perseverance, was eventually rewarded and they had three sun-baked days of climbing, reaching peaks so small that they had to take it in turns to stand on the top, and returning home with tender, throbbing fingers.

Whereas one goes to the Swiss or French Alps for snow and glacier climbing, it is for fine hard rock climbing that the Italian Dolomites are famous. Anne Littlejohn, one of the Club's finest rock climbers, spent the summer of 1957 in the company of members of the Pinnacle Club, doing an astounding number of hard routes. Anne describes the sheer exhilaration of reaching her first Dolomite summit;

> Delight was heaped upon delight as wall, chimneys and arêtes followed in quick succession. A final steep pitch and we were on our very first Dolomite summit. The guide, a wonderful character called Johann Demetz must have seen the pleasure that was registered all over our faces, for he solemnly stood on his head on the topmost rock. He was a trifle disconcerted, I think, when Eileen and I, with equal solemnity, also proceeded to invert ourselves upon the summit. So ended my first climb in the Dolomites and literally, I didn't know whether I was on my head or my heels.

Regular Alpine Meets were now firmly on the agenda – 1958 Fafleralp; 1959 Zermatt; 1962 Saas Fee; and in 1965 back to Chamonix again. The 1958 Meet at Fafleralp marked the Club's Jubilee and was attended by a record 18 members, with their guide Herr Roth. They had an amazingly energetic time, with many of the members leading a second rope, and indeed, when Esme completed a particularly fine lead of the second rope on a difficult traverse of the Aletschhorn, she was greeted with an ovation by the climbers already foregathered at the top.

Some of the most adventurous exploits in the Alps, however, were carried out not at official Club Meets, but by individual groups of Club members planning their own trips. Monica Jackson describes an exciting moment while climbing in the Dauphine with her friend Eileen, and it should be noted that this was done without guides, indeed on several occasions, as Monica put it 'We were the only *cordee feminine* on the mountain, and we did not want to get involved with gallant offers of advice and help'. They enjoyed a series of successful hard ascents, but perhaps this made them over-confident;

> We were soon to be humbled. The mountain we were now after was the Aiguille de Sialouze, which was a serious undertaking for a guideless party of our standard….Everything went wrong from the very beginning of our attempt on Sialouze. We started at 6.0 a.m. – much too late – and I was still very tired. We had insufficient rappel rope and, of all shameful admissions for a mountaineer to have to make, we forgot to take a torch! It was a long way to the peak and we had to cross two glaciers, the second of which was in a dangerous condition by the time we got there. When at last we embarked on the climb we found route-finding harder than we had expected. At last we came to a traverse described optimistically, I think, as Grade IV in the guide book. It looked very unpleasant, and we spent a lot of time trying to find a place in which to hammer a piton. Once this was done and Eileen tied to it I started out along the beastly traverse, which, naturally, wouldn't have been complete without a sinister overhang below. It was not easy...and I had already run out quite a lot of rope. The route now appeared to go straight up a groove which I followed, finding an increasing dearth of hand and foothold, till I was climbing by friction of hand and foot alone. At last I reached a resting place, but by now it was clear that there was no way up above me. Neither was there anywhere to hang a runner or knock in a piton. I had to manage without safeguards and climb down the way I had climbed up. Meanwhile Eileen could do nothing for me. I had run out at least eighty feet of rope, and below us was the overhang. On these occasions one is too busy to be aware of fear, and one climbs neatly because one has to.
>
> At last I reached the traverse, which seemed easy now compared with what I had been doing, and was soon able to creep round the corner to Eileen's side. Reaction set in immediately, and I realised that I was too exhausted to be capable of thinking constructively. It was up to Eileen to organise the retreat, which she did with great coolness and resource.

The pair struggled on down the glacier long after darkness had fallen, by the light of the stars, and eventually huddled together until morning wearing all the warm clothes they could find, and thumping each other to keep the circulation going. By dawn they were on their way thankfully, and somewhat chastened, back to the hut

Perhaps one of the most noteworthy events during this burgeoning enthusiasm and skill was Esme Speakman's ascent of the South Face of the Grand Cornier in 1957. She did this with a guide, but it was a totally

During a quiet period for Alpine meets, Lyndsay Urquhart kept up the tradition of annual visits to the Alps. On the Feejoch, with Alphubel behind

Lindsay Urquhart Collection
(LSCC Archives)

new route, a very creditable first ascent – male or female – and Esme was climbing more as a companion than as a client, as is obvious from this account;

Half way up the last slope we halted, turning to look up at the great golden granite sweep of the south face of the Grand Cornier. Henri pointed to a slight ridge running from the highest point of the glacier below the summit to a big, reddish gendarme on the S.W. ridge, just to the left of the summit. "I should like to try and climb that one day" he said, "it would make a fine first ascent for the south face has never been climbed". I remained silent, filled with envy of the lucky client who should tackle it with him. After a minute: "Would you care to attempt it with me today?" asked Henri. It was unbelievable, and I nearly fell down the glacier with surprise and excitement. Henri went on to explain the problem: he had hesitated to suggest it because, though he did not think the route would present any very great difficulties, we only had our 100 feet of climbing rope with us, and no pitons, and if it became too difficult we should have to retreat. In this case, there would be nothing for it but an ignominious return to Mountet, and we should have lost all chance of doing a summit.

It was well worth risking that – even an attempt on an unclimbed face would be fun – so, the decision taken, we hurried down the slopes of the Col and across to the foot of a large couloir, on the east side of which our route began. I have not, unfortunately, the sort of memory which after a climb can recall it pitch by pitch, so my description of this one is extremely vague. It was delightful, though never really hard. The rock was good, the holds were small but adequate. Time seemed suspended, and one lived and climbed in golden light. This, indeed, was Tir-nan-Og!

Strangely enough after this spate of activity, there followed a gap of some years when the Club was not so active in the Alps, although Lindsay Urquhart kept the Club flag flying by continuing to climb in

Margaret Graham on Dent de Ruth crux pitch. Lauterbrunnen Meet 1995

Photo: Marion Boyle

the Alps summer after summer for as many years as she was able. In 1973 an Alpine Meet was proposed, but there were not enough takers, and in 1974 only three members foregathered in Arolla.

A combination of factors came together in the early 1980s to revive interest in alpine climbing One was Molly Johnstone's enthusiasm as President which led to the organisation of a Club Meet in Austria in 1985. The choice of Austria as a venue was well-considered. The Austrian Alps, although high and presenting glacier crossings, rocky ridges and alpine style climbing, are not quite as demanding as the Swiss or French Alps. The intention was to enable Club members to explore the alpine peaks without having to rely too heavily on alpine guides.

The idea was popular, and the Meet well-attended. Molly herself was accompanied by her family, and Ruth Baird, Maureen Brocklehurst, Pam Cain, Jean Galbraith, Livia Gollancz, Christina Macnair and Lindsay Urquhart made up the party. In the LSCC there is mercifully no age or fitness barrier. Some of the group had been to the Alps many times before; for some, such as Ruth and Jean, it was their first visit. None of them was in the first flush of youth, but they covered huge distances, crossed high passes, wandered through seracs and crevasses, and actually reached a 3,600 metre peak – the Grosse Venediger. All this as well as enjoying alpine meadows and flowers, cafes and villages, even finding enjoyment in Austrian-style food shopping in Spar!

A second factor in the Alpine revival was influx of new blood into the Club. Karin Froebel, Helen Geddes, Mary Lothian, Kate Ross, and Margaret Graham all joined around the same few years. They were joined in their enthusiasm by Alison Higham, freed from family responsibilities, and Eve Gilmore. Together with the growth of cheap air fares, there was no holding them. Indeed Club members were climbing all around the world in the Yosemite, the Atlas Mountains in Morocco, in Kenya, Corsica, Sardinia, Norway and the Karakoram – all had become accessible, and over the next ten years Club members tended to go in their own groups rather than as an official Club Meet.

It was Sarah Mackay who saw the value of meeting together as a Club, and brought the idea of a Club Meet in the Alps to the Committee in 1995. Her idea was that they would engage the help of professional guides Mick Tighe, his partner, Kathy Murphy, and an 'aspirant' Robbie. Mick and Kathy had already been very helpful in providing good instruction to the Club back in Scotland, and they agreed to come. They proved staunch friends and allies in their enthusiastic encouragement of group, enabling them to take leadership themselves.

The Meet was organised in Lauterbrunnen and proved an immediate success. The teaching was thorough and exacting. For some members it was their first time in the Alps and there was much to learn. Speed is of the essence in alpine climbing and Club members' memories are of Mick and Robbie constantly cajoling, threatening and otherwise urging them to make more speed. Where the terrain is not too steep or hazardous climbers will 'move together'; that is stay roped together but not spend valuable time belaying or putting in protection. Coils of rope are held in the hand ready if necessary to check a small stumble by looping the rope around a rock or an ice-axe. It is a tricky business requiring some skilful rope handling. It was Marion Boyle's first time in the Alps, and she had to work hard at her rope-work;

> Sarah led the way along the ridge in a very confidence-inspiring manner, although being brought up short occasionally by the tendency of the Alpine rookie in the middle of the rope to entangle various permutations of axe, rope, slings, legs, arms, rucksack, rocks, etc. – thus bringing proceedings to frequent temporary halts. I am working on this 'moving together roped' business – honest!

After their first week Mary Lothian, Karin Froebel, Sarah Mackay, and Helen Geddes set off on their own and climbed the Gross Fischerhorn, their first 4000 metre peak, accomplished in guidebook time. They returned four very happy women. They were then joined by Kate Ross. Kate and Mary had never climbed together before, but along with Helen Geddes they excitedly planned a serious route up the Lauterbrunnen Breithorn. Kate assured a somewhat diffident Mary that the route was *peu difficile*. It was only some time later that Kate confessed that her guidebook was about 100 years old and rated everything easy. They were eyed somewhat askance by the grumpy hut *guardien*. Three women on their own – not only without men, but without guides – would they make it? This was a recognised serious climb, Mick had so impressed upon them the need for speed that Mary practically ran up the glacier, calling anxiously over her shoulder, "Am I going fast enough?" The others were too breathless to reply. The whole expedition only took six hours of hard slog, and although the climbing was never more than Very Difficult they were all delighted to have done it. On their return there was a distinct indication of respect from the *guardien*. "And it was good?" he asked. "Very, very good" replied three beaming women.

Sometimes the learning experience at the Lauterbrunnen Meet was a little bit more exciting than they anticipated. This was certainly the case for Marion Boyle, when Mick Tighe took a group of the Ladies off for a day's rock climbing practice.

> We would go rock climbing (said Mick), but not, he assured us, Scottish style. We would head for the Dent de Ruth. Mick showed us the route in the guide-book, but I wasn't any the wiser. Just as well as it turned out. Most of the pitches were Grade V. OK, I thought, we've done some Vs this week already. I didn't know that the guy who graded this had a system all his own. And I was too daft to notice the number of Vs – each denoting a separate pitch – over 400 metres in all...Sometimes we bridged up chimneys, hands and feet on the cool of shaded rock. Then out to sun-warmed rock with little fingery holds and a few jugs. Occasionally water-worn flutings added interest. Most of the rock was gabbro-rough...Then we came to the traverse. The other team seemed to be moving rather slowly. When our turn came, I saw why. Blank vertical rock, occasional bolts, from two of which hung slings – footholds, I was told. To make matters worse, I was last across, so had to collect the gear. Try hanging from an extender with one foot flailing wildly in a long sling while the other paws frantically at the rock for some vestige of a foothold, and with the other hand remove a karabiner from a small bolt, at finger-tip stretch distance. Yes, you will want a tight rope. A very tight rope...

> A lovely delicate step round on small holds led to the last pitches. We finished the climb tired but happy. I think I felt the same about the Dent de Ruth as the others felt about the Eiger. I came here to learn about glaciers, crevasses, speed, how to look after myself in the Alps. I have learned a lot, but I love rock climbing, and the Dent de Ruth was the hardest and best route I've ever done.

And so a new Club tradition of going regularly to the Alps was born. The Dauphine in 1996; Randa in 1997; Aosta in 1999; Saas Grund in 2001; Arolla in 2002, Switzerland again in 2004; North Italy 2005; Saas Grund in 2006 and Grindelwald in 2007. More and more people joined the group, with Meets of 15 – 17 members, following a similar pattern of 'mix and match'. Snow, rock, hard climbing, pleasant walking, guided and independent, there was enjoyment for everyone, beginners and experienced alike.

1999 at a Club Meet in Aosta – Mary Lothian describes another epic;

> Two o'clock in the morning and we were wearily following the beam of Kate's head torch, slowly picking our way up debris and snow and up the heavily crevassed Glacier de Planpincieux. Kate and I started up the rock, following in a slow procession up the mountain. At daylight we reached the traverse and I was delighted to let Kate lead out under the ominous seracs and ice cliffs,

*Mary Lothian on
The Monch. LSCC
Lauterbrunnen
meet, 1995*

Photo: Karin Froebel

creaking in the strengthening sun. We cast a few nervous sideways glances as we hurried over the long snow slopes.

Kate, Margaret, Mary, Helen Copeland, and David were climbing the Grandes Jorasses which tower splendidly above the Rifugio Baccalette. Even the ordinary route is famous as a '*grande course*' – a serious climb, long and demanding. They left the hut at 1am and almost immediately were plunged into knee-deep snow, the consistency of porridge. Crossing this they were dismayed to find that they had taken more than twice the guidebook time. However, after scrambling up a steep rock buttress, they were onto perfect hard snow and they soon made up the lost time. Soon they came to a band of south-facing seracs which they could hear creaking and groaning ominously. Pausing apprehensively before launching onto the dangerous traverse, they were urged on; 'Run' shouted Kate, and they ran for their lives across the gap. The whole day they moved fast, with Kate leading the crevassed snowy sections and Mary leading rapid pitches on rock – a combination that they found worked well. They finally reached the summit by 9am. 'The best thing I've ever done', said Margaret. That same Margaret on reaching the valley, felt that their efforts merited a 'wee thimbleful' of malt whisky

As far as Kate and Mary were concerned the high point of their

Kate Ross near summit of Castor, Pennine Alps 2003

Photo: Sarah Mackay

climbing so far was an ascent of the Mitteleggi Ridge on the Eiger. The Eiger, of course, has become famous in climbing history and legend. It conjures up the names of Heinrich Harrer, Dougal Haston, Catherine Destivelle, Alison Hargreaves, and recalls the tragic deaths of so many, making the Eiger into something fearful and full of dread. However most of these stories centre around the darkly forbidding 'Nordwand'. There are other ways up than the north wall, some of them quite straightforward. The Mitteleggi Ridge is a classic, quite hard route, providing a complete and exacting mountain experience.

Even reaching the hut is an experience in itself. Perhaps the most hazardous part of the climb is the simple action of escaping from the station. Taking the Jungfrau Railway, one leaves the train at Eigergletscher Station. Sounds easy so far. One then walks down a tunnel often almost completely blocked with snow, sticks one's head out of a window that looks out over the sheer rock face, wriggles out head first, swings the feet round, and kicks in immediately to begin the traverse across the east face of the mountain. Because the glacier has shrunk the first pitch to the hut is now a rock scramble, followed by a traverse across a buttress on appallingly loose scree. All this is before one even starts on the ridge itself. Not for the faint-hearted. Even going to the toilet at the hut is an adventure as one has to traverse along a rope above a steep drop.

The day of the actual climb dawned with perfect blue sky, and an enjoyable route of fixed ropes led to the summit. However, sitting in the sun enjoying being on the summit of the Eiger was only half the story. The real difficulty of the route lies in the fact that the descent is at least as long and difficult. Kate and Mary decided not to use the tourist route down as it is notoriously loose and dangerous. Instead they decided to cross over to the Eigerjoch. The descent was technical all the way, demanding the utmost concentration on their climbing, and there was no turning back if the weather broke. At one point they had a massive abseil from the South Ridge to the col, involving two ropes tied together. Relief all round when the ropes reached the bottom and didn't jam in the rock. After ten hours constant climbing they saw figures running to greet them from the hut. Exhausted, beaming and triumphant they could relax.

Another popular classic is the superb arete between the Aiguille du Midi and the Aiguille du Plan. Margaret, Kate, Mary and Jim Lothian traversed it on one of those days of absolute perfection when row upon row of peaks rise in glittering array. It is perhaps indicative of the over-riding need for speed, that Margaret's hopeful comment on emerging from the *teleferique* was 'If we get somewhere with a good view, can we stop to take a photo of our route?' The route is mixed corniced snow and knife-edged rock with very exposed climbing out on the face. Instructions to Margaret were 'Face in, kick down, and you can see Chamonix beneath your feet'. One wonders if she stopped to take a photo at that point.

After a thoroughly enjoyable day, the group realised that they were probably going to miss the last cable-car down to the valley. In the distance announcements were being made and a few tourists were

Irene Kelly, Dauphine Alps, 1996

Photo: Marion Boyle

already on the bridge to the station. Panic! None of them fancied a bivouac at the cable-car station, so they began to run the last few hundred yards. Still wearing their crampons, and roped together, they vaulted the gate into the station, to hear the announcement "This lift is running 20 minutes late"!

So why does the Club keep returning to the Alps? The last word remains with Kate Ross:

Wherever I climb in the world, the Alps always has a special draw. Even easy routes are dramatic and as I acclimatise I can tackle something more technical. From the valley the peaks tower upwards looking scary and impossible, but every summit won has one looking to the next – "I can do that!" Winter nights spent poring over maps and guidebooks. The excitement of arriving in the Alps with training walks on good paths, warm sunshine and cheap wine. The hard pull up to the hut in the heat of the day with sacs too heavy. A busy international throng in the hut; too hot in the dorm and too many snorers. In the dark the stomach churns visualising the route and trying to dispel the demons of crevasses, steep ice and loose rock. It's a relief to get up in the early hours, force down food and coffee, crampons on and rope up...

Suddenly two dimensions become three. The sky becomes red and gold. We're high amongst the peaks and as we gain warmth from the sun, we scramble over rock, balance along knife edges of snow to arrive at summits which are small and sharp.

The descents require total concentration, abseiling, moving together, checking ropes and belays – total trust in your climbing partner. Back on the glacier it's hot and the snow is soft. Watching for crevasses and testing every step; it's amazing how far we climbed in the pre-dawn hours. Why is it always uphill to the hut? Litres of *teewasser* before the knee-grinding descent to camp. Only now can we relax, reminisce and revel in the satisfaction of a perfect day – 'What route do you fancy next?'

8: Opposite Extremes – the Arctic and Antarctic

PERHAPS IT'S JUST THE VIKING BLOOD singing in our veins, but there has always been a strong pull from the arctic northlands. Or maybe it's just that magic quality of light as the white bog cotton dances in the cold, clear air and the June sun at midnight casts its long shadows over the heath; or the sharp tang of cloudberries and blueberries, heralding the onset of the lean winter months, and bringing the knowledge that all the joys of spring, summer and autumn have to be packed into a few short weeks.

Whatever the reason, over the years many Club members have travelled in Arctic Norway, Lapland, the Canadian Arctic, Greenland, and at the other extreme, southwards to the Antarctic.

The earliest record of Arctic adventures was a mention in the 1927 Club record under *Members' Doings* of a two-month journey by Margaret Murray, in which she describes a now much-visited area of Norway as 'the trackless Jotunheim'. As ever with the Ladies, she modestly describes as a 'walking tour' a journey which included most of the highest peaks in the area, including Store Skagastolstind, Galdhopiggen and Glittertind, not to mention several high passes and glacier crossings.

Brief mention is made of Barbara Macfarlane's journeys in Norway in 1939, just on the eve of war and occupation, but it was in 1954 that Club members began to explore what was to become a favourite haunt of lovers of Arctic Norway – the Lyngen Alps. This is how it is described by Betty Stark in *Mountaincraft, the Journal of the Mountaineering Association* in 1955.

> The Lyngen peninsula in Arctic Norway is the very place for a party of some experience – yet not enough to climb in the Alps without guides. So it proved for myself and four other girls this summer.
>
> The mountains there are 5000 to 6000 feet in height, glaciated and rising sometimes to their full stature from sea-level. The rock is mostly gabbro, and it can be delightfully sound, though it has a trick of being just as difficult close to as it appears from a distance.

The 1954 expedition members were Cynthia Marr, Evelyn Camrass, Betty Stark and Elma Wrench of the LSCC, and Angela Hood of Glasgow University Mountaineering Club. In those days an all-female expedition created quite a stir in the press. The *Sunday Dispatch* had the following.

> Five Scots girls dressed in mountaineering outfits left Glasgow yesterday for the Arctic Circle. Their trip will make history – it is the first time an all-girl expedition has ventured so far north...They are heading for the northern mountains of Norway and weeks of climbing among the glaciers, ice-falls, and 6000 foot peaks...While exploring the wilder regions they will live in tents and fish for food in icy fjords. Among the provisions they took yesterday was a large supply of porridge oats.

Predictably they set their sights on Jaekevarre by a route which Evelyn

Ann Cordiner and Pam Cain on the Alpefjord, Staunings Alps, during the 1970 Ladies Scottish East Greenland Expedition

LSEGE Archives

described as; 'Jaekevarre via moraine, deeply crevassed glacier, rock ridge and ice cap' – a little bit of everything in fact. One of the joys of climbing in the arctic in summer is that there is no such thing as darkness, time ceases to matter, days on the hill can last as long as one wants, only being bound by food and sleep. In fact it is quite easy to get completely out of step with other expedition members, and arrive back at camp after a long day all ready for a good meal and sleep, to find the others just tucking into breakfast! Cynthia describes the timelessness of their lingering on the summit of Jaekevarre.

> The ascent of Jaekevarre was undoubtedly the climax of our Norwegian holiday, and this was not only because it was the highest peak in the Lyngen peninsula where we were climbing, standing some 1840m. above sea level. My diary records that we left the summit at 9 p.m., but gives no time of arrival. Probably all three of us were too tired to notice the time, and anyway it mattered little in that land of midnight sun. I do know that we spent a long while on the summit, at least two, probably three hours.
>
> The summit itself was a huge dome of ice and snow, the remains of the great ice-cap which had long ago covered the whole area. The top was cairnless, and it was rather hard to determine exactly what was the highest point. From the centre of the dome one could see little of the surrounding peaks, which added to the enchantment of this unique summit. Here was a plateau

*Alison Dinwoodie
summits Trollvastind,
Lyngen Alps, Arctic
Norway, 1969*

Photo: Mora McCallum

of virgin snow, seldom climbed by anyone and probably untrodden on that year by any save ourselves, for we had neither seen nor heard of any other climbing party in the peninsula. The only living creatures on the summit were a few moths, blown there no doubt by the wind, and still bravely alive despite the lack of vegetation.

When one traversed two or three hundred yards in any direction, however, what a wealth met the eye! All around were jagged peaks, sharp ridges of rock and snow flanked by steep buttresses rising darkly from the rapidly shrinking glaciers. Some twenty miles to the north we could distinguish the peaks of the area where we had been climbing the previous week. There was the shapely point of the Lenangentind, which we had approached by a delightful rocky ridge giving us good climbing but whose final five hundred feet had been treacherously loose and too risky to justify our completing the ascent.

There also we could see Store Jaegervasstind, on which we had been more successful, and a horde of other peaks. Between them and us were other mountains and valleys bearing fascinating names like Store Goalsevagegeissa, and offering hundreds of possibilities for climbing and exploration.

To the south-west lay the wonderful area of the Laxelvtinde, which had caused many a backward glance on our ascent of the summit ridge, and on which we feasted our eyes on the way down. What superb buttresses and summits! How we wished we had time to explore there also! West and east were fjords, and beyond them still more mountains. Standing there, I had a glimpse into the past of our own Scotland. This was what it must have been like at the end of the Ice Age.

Ten years later Club members were once again exploring Arctic Norway. Heather King, her husband Graham, and a friend Douglas Barclay, went climbing in the Romsdal, although hampered by a distinct scarcity of reliable maps and weather rather too reminiscent of wet, misty days in Scotland.

Next year, in 1965, it was back to Lyngen with a distinctly casual approach to Jaekevarre. Alison Dinwoodie wrote.

Well, as Jaekevarre is the highest mountain in Arctic Norway, we had better do that tomorrow or the next day, and then we can spend the rest of the time peak-bagging or pottering as we feel inclined.

With that kind of tendency towards decadence it was hardly surprising that, as daylight merged into daylight, and one day slipped into another, they were left with only thirty-six hours in which to achieve their objective. Not that attempts had not been made. Maps being somewhat unreliable, some time was spent in reconnoitring a route up. Twice they were turned back by misty weather and rock, which they described as not only brittle, but like asbestos fibre. The final calamity was when wild goats trampled all over the tents and ate any available food that was not sealed in a can, including quantities of whale meat, onions, polythene bags and a tin of Nivea cream. It certainly confirms the indestructibility of a goat's digestive system. At last, however, a concerted effort was made.

Ascending Jaekevarre, highest peak in the Lyngen Alps, Arctic Norway, 1965

Photo: Heather King

Time was running out, but Graham and Douglas were not to be defeated. Heather and Edna decided that, pleasant though the glen was, three times was enough. I said that if the weather looked reasonable at 3.0 a.m., I'd be the ladies' representative. One thing about Arctic climbing; it doesn't much matter when you set out. It does get cooler at night, but there isn't the same strength in the sun during the day, so that there is a fresh cool all the time, which leaves one with the energy to go on far longer and harder than usual. However, it was as well we started early on this particular day, because as we climbed the mist gradually appeared in the valley below, and we were laying bets as to whether we'd beat it or not. By the time we were on the south ridge it was thickening up, but as the ridge was not too difficult we managed to keep ahead of it, until finally we reached the plateau and found ourselves in brilliant sunshine, surrounded by island peaks in a sea of mist. Jaekevarre is really an ice-cap, so that there is hardly a top as such – the excitement is in reaching the plateau. So must the Cairngorms have appeared a few thousand years ago.

The rest of the way, apart from negotiating a couple of bergschrunds, was a plod through knee-deep soft snow, until at last after four hours or so, each member of the party stuck his or her ice-axe in the snow at different points and announced that this was the top!

Such dogged determination merely whetted Alison's appetite, because four years later, in 1969, she was busily enthusing other Club members to return to the Lyngen Alps. As the record for that year somewhat ironically puts it: 'Miss Dinwoodie had been responsible for seven members arriving at the same spot in Arctic Norway by various routes, as planned, and when expected – no mean feat!' The seven members enjoyed the arctic to the full, some travelling up the magnificent Norwegian coast in the local boat, on arrival, pitching their tents close to a lake where frequent dips could be enjoyed (as long as there was enough wind to deter the blood-thirsty mosquitoes). Perhaps the highlight of the trip was enjoying the view of the fantastic rock pinnacles of Jaegervastind silhouetted against the glowing disc of the midnight sun. Yet another attempt was made on Jaekevarre, but bad weather thwarted their efforts.

In July 1972 Mora, Pamela, Ann Winning and Eilidh finally made it up Jaekevarre at the first attempt, despite Eilidh's getting soaked (including maps, cigarettes and other essentials) fording a glacial stream on the approach. On their descent they encountered a mass of avalanche debris which had not been there when they went up. Which gives pause for thought

An even more intrepid undertaking was Mora McCallum's solo visit to Norway in 1973. She wrote.

> I can still see that silent, undulating expanse of moonlit snow dropping to dark valleys with shadowy peaks silhouetted beyond; sunrise on haze-filled fjords; morning light on the Jotunheim peaks from Hamrane, the nunatak where I camped for the night at 6,000ft.; and the black tip of Lodalskapa appearing over the last interminable snow-dome.
>
> The S to N traverse of Jostedalsbreen, Europe's largest icefield, was a slightly rash undertaking, but it was worth all the effort of carrying a 60 lb. rucksack up from Fjoerland in a burning heatwave, slogging 30 miles through ankle-deep snow for two days, and losing all the skin off my face. Even the ferocious night of storm which blasted my frail camp high on the moraine just off the north end after a hasty ascent of Lodalskapa and the following four days of rain and snow, sodden clothes and sleeping bag and subsistence rations, could not quite erase the memory.

Mora walked a total of 170 miles in three weeks, and was still tempted to return.

The 1970 Ladies Scottish East Greenland Expedition really began with the author's longing to go to the Antarctic! No she wasn't particularly challenged by map-reading; it just took some time for her to realise that it's cheaper and easier to do one's adventuring in one's own hemisphere.

Eventually, being pragmatic, she turned her sights towards Greenland. No sooner mentioned than excitement grew and other Club members became enthused. The LSEGE was born and formally adopted at the Club AGM in 1969.

Plans began to be made. First an area had to be chosen. The Staunings Alps area of East Greenland seemed particularly attractive. Two Club members had already visited the area in 1968 as members of the Womens' East Greenland Mountaineering Expedition – the first-ever women only expedition to Greenland. Although no mountains of great note were climbed, some valuable exploratory work was undertaken. Eilidh Nisbet had the frustrating, if somewhat sybaritic experience of being dropped by helicopter high up on a glacier with all the expedition equipment, complete with most of the food, sun-cream, and even, if you can believe it, sun-loungers, while the other three struggled and failed to cross the river separating them. Both Eilidh and Esme Speakman had been captivated by Greenland and were keen to give it another go. The mountains are steep and alpine, reaching a height of over 7000 feet, huge glaciers gouge their way from the interior ice-cap to calve dramatically into the sea, and there are still many unexplored areas. Maps could be obtained, but they were based mostly on aerial photographs and were largely inaccurate, showing many interesting blanks.

The Scottish Mountaineering Club had organised several previous expeditions to the Staunings Alps area, as is obvious from many of the

names given to the peaks – Dunottar, Merchiston, Stirling, – and SMC members were generous in their sharing of information. There is a Danish meteorological station and airstrip at Mestersvig, and it was possible for groups to get together and charter a flight from Iceland.

Excitement grew. Evenings were spent poring over maps and photographs, climbing gear was checked, chucked and sorted and applications made for free offers and sponsorships. Applications for funding were made to the Royal Geographical Society and to the Everest Foundation. One august body asked in their application form; 'State the number of men and the time to be spent on each'! The expedition was quite unable to frame an appropriate answer. Esme's mews flat in Edinburgh was used as a storage depot and Pam Cain soon had everyone organised sorting food into boxes divided into one-day, two-day, three-day packs – and the most popular 'treats box'. Everything had to be weighed down to the last gram, as the weigh-in for flight involved swinging from a hook wearing one's rucksack. A situation where being a petite woman is a distinct advantage.

The Ladies Scottish East Greenland Expedition 1970. From left back row: Alison Dinwoodie, Helen Steven, Edna Stewart, Esme Speakman, Greta Sumner, Ann Cordiner. Middle row: Eilidh Nisbet, Pam Cain, Chris Pattie, Ann Winning, Mora McCallum. Front: Christina Macnair with a musk-ox skull

LSEGE Archives

There was some talk during the planning stages as to the wisdom of being a women-only expedition, particularly with regard to carrying a rifle as a precaution against polar bears. The expedition members had no doubts at all as to their mountain competence, but decided that a gun would present more danger to themselves than to any unsuspecting polar bear.

To return to preparations in Edinburgh, at last all was ready. There were 12 expedition members, Pam Cain, Ann Cordiner, Alison Dinwoodie, Mora McCallum, Christina Macnair, Eilidh Nisbet, Chris Pattie, Esme Speakman, Helen Steven, Edna Stewart, Greta Sumner and Anne Winning. The plan was for six to fly out at the beginning of July and the other six to join them at an agreed rendezvous four weeks later, all leaving at the end of August. Ann Cordiner, who worked for the Outward Bound in Wales had organised an inflatable dinghy with outboard, and the initial plan was to launch this as soon as possible and motor round to a hitherto unexplored area known as Nathorstsland where a base camp would be established. However, as the pack-ice was very late in breaking up that year this plan had to be amended.

It was decided to go inland from Mestersvig, cross the Skel River and explore the climbing possibilities at the head of the glacier. It is interesting to note that this was the point at which being a woman suddenly became a disadvantage. Owing to a seeming reluctance from the men at the base to give a group of women any kind of encouragement to wander too far from home, the expedition was virtually grounded at Base Camp. Somehow no boats were available, fuel couldn't be obtained, and several other obstacles suddenly appeared. Fortunately a party of geologists came to the rescue and offered to drop a load of food from their helicopter near the head of the glacier. All the expedition had to do was cross the Skel River to reach it.

All! The Skel was a huge, brown, rumbling glacial torrent, often braiding into many swift streams, and this was the obstacle that had prevented the previous expedition from linking up. In some ways this was to be the testing point of the whole expedition – hesitate and it would be relegated to the annals of a failed female expedition. Hours of searching discovered a small cairn marking a crossing point, and Mora, Eilidh and Helen managed to pick a way through thick mud and strong currents to a steep glacial moraine on the other side. Foureen miles of hard slog up the heavily crevassed Berserkerbrae, and the camp was finally established on a rocky platform with a spectacular outlook to the head of the valley and the soaring cliffs of Merchiston, reminiscent of the fluted ridges of the Grands Jorasses.

One of the most attractive peaks beckoning from the head of the valley was the Berserker Spire, a graceful needle of rock and snow which had only been climbed once before. Three LSEGE members set off from camp at almost the same time as a separate party of Italians. The race was on!

> The rock was lovely, very solid and very easy so that we moved together most of the time. It was most exposed and sensational, but very good fun. About two thirds of the way up we met the Italians on their way down, and were slightly amazed that they were hammering in a lot of pitons. They said that

there was terrible ice at the top which was very dangerous without an axe, which rather worried us, as we had deposited ours at the bottom of the ridge. However we bashed on up and evidently appalled the Italians by moving together. At last we reached the first rock pinnacle on the ridge. It was in a magnificent situation with a 5000 foot drop down to the Dunnottar Glacier. The snow was sensational but not far and not difficult, and at last we emerged at the top of a lovely pointed granite slab, with only just enough room for the three of us. First women to the top – what an exhilarating feeling! Elated, we staggered down, floundering through deep soft snow to the camp, where the others greeted us with a huge meal and a celebration ceilidh.

Helen Steven and Eilidh Nisbet reconnoiter a route up the Berserkerbrae glacier, en route to the ice cap, 1970

LSEGE Archives

The morning after a ceilidh can always be a problem, and 17th July was no exception. The group groaned stiffly awake to find the sides of the tent collapsing under the weight of new snow which had fallen in the night. The returning three had been so exhausted that they had dropped most of their gear where they stood, and after a decision to evacuate camp, a couple of hours were spent rummaging around in the snow for ropes, crampons, spoons and mugs. An exhausting trek back down the glacier and over the Skel River, greatly helped by a trail broken by the SMC expedition, brought the company back to Mestersvig, where it was discovered that the pack-ice had now receded, making the next phase of the expedition possible. Honour had been vindicated, women had not only survived but acquitted themselves competently, and suddenly doors opened, boats became available, and part two could begin.

Ann Winning looks over ice-floes in King Oscar's Fjord, East Greenland, 1970

LSEGE Archives

The expedition's next objective was Alpefjord, a long narrow fjord, almost dammed at one point by the snout of the Sporregletscher. A fine campsite was found on the shores of the fjord, a rendezvous was made with the six new arrivals, and exploration of new territory began. One particularly exciting trip was taking the rubber dinghy through the narrow channel of Dammen past the glacier snout. A strong wind made the waters dark and choppy and every now and then huge chunks of ice would break off from the glacier creating tidal waves that surged back and forth across the narrows. Once through, crossing a remote glacier to glimpse the inland lake of the Fureso, the whole isolation of the situation made itself felt – uncharted territory, no-one else for miles around, no mountain rescue.

In fact the expedition was involved in a rescue of a Frenchman, a client with two guides, who had seriously injured his arm. By the time members of the Ladies' expedition, one of them being Chris Pattie, the doctor, had canoed through the narrows, crossed the glacier, treated the casualty, carried him back over the glacier, ferried him out by sea to a point where a helicopter could pick him up, the whole exploit had taken a total of 72 woman hours, and altogether counting everyone involved, over 400 hours. A stern reminder of the need for self-sufficiency.

Perhaps the climbing highlight of the expedition was the ascent of Ardvreck, a shapely rock and snow ridge rising straight up from just behind the high camp site. The mountain had been climbed once by a Scottish party, but again this was the first women's ascent. This account is from the author's personal diary.

The ridge was very long and went on unfolding one rocky bluff after another with some quite sensational bits of narrow balancing. The first difficulty came at a big pinnacle which proved hard to climb down. We roped up and Eilidh went down a chimney on the right and started cutting steps up the snow, but she found hard ice underneath. Mora and I abseiled down onto the ridge to join her, but by this time Eilidh had found a way round to the left. After a very little more rock scrambling, we came to the snow and stopped to put on crampons. The ridge looked absolutely magnificent; a beautiful curve with the sun lighting up one side and then a long sweep of a snow slope to the summit. The ridge was quite simple, but dramatic with the snow sweeping down for about 3,000ft. to the Sandgletscher below. The slope was steep and we had to belay each other up, but it was quite straightforward, and by 3.30 p.m. we had reached the summit.

From the top of Ardvreck it could be seen that there was a whole valley and several peaks that simply were not on the map, so a group was ferried round by boat across the river mouth and two successive groups made their way up a valley surprisingly like a Scottish glen, to the expedition's first unclimbed summit, which was a shining dome of snow, quite easy and only lightly crevassed. The sense of elation at reaching the top was mingled as always with a slight feeling of anticlimax as the group stands around wondering what to do to mark the occasion appropriately. The new summit was named Glenhead in memory of the home of Janie Cameron, who would have been a member of the expedition, but was tragically drowned on a Club walk through Glen Feshie just a few weeks before they left.

Mora McCallum was undoubtedly the most intrepid member of the party and, possibly despairing of her weaker companions, she made her way solo to the top of two other unclimbed summits, which she named Sgurr Ban and Sgurr Breac.

By now there were unmistakable signs of the end of summer. Everywhere the ground was carpeted with autumn russets and gold of blueberry bushes and creeping willow; thistledown was drifting in the colder air, and on 12th August for the first time there was a brief spell of darkness at night. It was time to go home, and no time to waste as the pack-ice was closing in fast and the frail rubber boat had to thread its way alarmingly between gleaming icebergs with the sea freezing over in between. It was said that the week after the expedition left the fjords would be frozen over again and dog teams would be sledging over the ice. Seven unforgettable weeks, from the glories of spring alpine flowers, through blazing heat on the glaciers, to the long golden shadows of autumn, were over and Greenland could return to ice and snow.

Greenland held its spell, and soon other Club members were turning their feet northwards. In 1979 Esme Speakman returned to Mestersvig for the third time, mostly spent exploring many of the coastal huts. One of the interesting attractions of the East Greenland coast was the scattering of tiny hunters' huts all the way up the coast. Sadly many of these have fallen into disuse and been dismantled and in the 1970s the Danish government commissioned an artist to do a series of paintings of these huts as a lasting record.

These tiny huts, some only large enough for one person to squeeze into, must have literally saved lives, and there is an unwritten rule that each occupant leaves the hut in slightly better order for the next, with kindling chopped by the stove, and even the box of matches left with one sticking out so that it can be struck with a cold gloved hand. It is not hard to imagine creeping in out of a savage blizzard, grovelling around for the life-saving box of matches, then sinking back onto a warm bunk of musk-ox wool, listening to the steady thrum of the chimney as the stove glows red.

Imagine then the agonising hours spent by the author, who having spent a night in one of these huts and cleared the ashes carefully, looked back across the fjord to see a thick pall of smoke hanging over the hut! Painfully framing her grovelling apology for having burnt down a survival hut, she had to wait until the wind dropped to take the boat back across the fjord, to discover a low-lying bank of mist. O happy day!

Soon others were finding their way to Greenland. In 1986 Margaret Graham joined a small expedition to Milne Land, a previously unexplored region in East Greenland. In the course of two six-day back-packing trips the group managed to scale a total of four unclimbed peaks. From the 1980s onwards Sarah Mackay and her husband Peter began a long and happy relationship with the Arctic, returning to Greenland some eight or nine times.

The joys of real exploration in untrampled territory, where maps were sketchy, to say the least, and there were no convenient paths or bridges, but where time was always on their side, became addictive. Their first few trips were to East Greenland, where Sarah commented that the air was so crystal clear that glaciers and mountains which seemed close could take hours to reach. As ever the rushing glacial meltwater torrents caused real problems, with crossings thigh-deep in bone-numbing icy water. The down side of constant sunshine was that snow became soft and mushy – add to that carrying all one's food and equipment for ten days or more, and one almost levitated when rucksacks were finally removed from aching backs. Often too, even low down on the glaciers, they would be faced with huge chasms, necessitating long detours, or even sometimes retreat. Nothing was ever easy.

Partly because of the difficult river crossings, Sarah and Peter chose West Greenland for their next six visits. Here the feeling of remoteness was lacking, but there was the added fascination of human habitation and village life. Sarah's notes give an account.

> Silent little boys watching every move as we erected kayaks. Dogs everywhere. In summer they take a lot of male huskies to an offshore island and feed them twice a week just to get them out of the way. Sledges all over the village, abandoned until next year at the sea edge when the ice became unsafe the previous spring. Skins and fish hanging up to dry, and kayaks.

Sometimes there were unexpected encounters with wildlife, as on the occasion when four friends were paddling their kayaks on a reconnaissance, when they suddenly realised they were on a collision course with a whale. A tense moment indeed, but to their relief the whale changed course and left the kayakers undisturbed.

Sarah and Margaret both enthused so much about Greenland, that in 1998 the Club organised an official Meet to North West Greenland. From her previous visits Sarah felt that North West Greenland was partic-

ularly suited to the capabilities of the Club, and indeed had already started scouting for possible areas to visit. An additional bonus helped to make the official Meet possible. Esme Speakman, well-known for her adventurous spirit and enthusiasm for remote places had died leaving a legacy to the LSCC which was constituted as the ESMA Fund with the specific purpose of enabling exploration. Although Sarah was keen for the Club to go to Greenland, during her presidency of the Club she was so pre-occupied with the renovations to Milehouse, that it wasn't until Kate Ross's presidency in 1998 that there was sufficient energy to organise a Club expedition.

Kate herself is a keen Alpinist and well able both to take the lead on occasions and also to judge the competency of Club members. It was agreed early on in the planning that this was to be a 'members only' expedition. Margaret Graham was co-ordinator, while Sarah arranged transport and liaison with the local people. Evelyn McNicol was the expedition doctor, Pat Ransley organised insurance, while Kate Charles had the thankless task of coping with the baggage. Everyone had a role; Jean Lawrence was Base Camp co-ordinator, Edna Stewart produced a comprehensive botanical report, and Julia Banks and Marion Boyle kept the records and wrote up the report afterwards. It all sounds very well organised and even hierarchical, but in reality everyone chipped in and covered all the many tasks.

The expedition left from Glasgow Airport on 24th July 1998, destination Ilulissat, then by helicopter to Uummannaq, with excitement mounting at their first views of the Nussuaq peninsula where they were

Margaret Graham, Kate Charles and Sarah Mackay North West Greenland, 1998

Photo: Kate Ross

Jean Lawrence approaching first top, 'Point 1833', Greenland, August 1998

Photo: Julia Banks

bound. Slight panic over Kate Charles' rucksack which had somehow ended up in Kangerlussuaq, but helpful locals soon effected a reunion.

Folks couldn't wait to get started and the very next day saw seven of them trekking up a very high traverse just below the peak behind their camp, giving magnificent views over to Alfred Wegener's Land. The group was all at roughly the same level of fitness, and initially it was hoped that groups might split up and change around a bit, but owing to the difficulty of the terrain this was not possible, so that apart from at Base Camp, there were two distinct groups. The two Kates, Sarah and Margaret were keen to explore a little bit of the Greenland Ice-Cap, while the others – Evelyn, Marion, Edna, Jean, Julia and Pat – explored around the settlement at Uvkusigssat for a few days and then moved on by boat to establish Base Camp at the western end of the sledge route on the Alfred Wegener peninsula.

The Ice-Cap group were taken by boat to the head of Qaumarujuk fjord and over to the far side of a wide braided river, where they ensconced themselves in a comfortable camp-site and settled down to an evening meal around midnight, enjoying the sun lighting up the tops around. Next day they set off, each carrying packs of around 40lbs. beginning over very rough loose moraine, but then scrambling up over easily angled granite slabs. This was walking into the unknown. The ice-cap stretched ahead of them into seeming infinity, the innocent snow covering the treacherous shadows of deep crevasses, and the only features being the dark rocks of the 'nunataks' sticking up out of the snow. These peaks of rock had no names, but were simply known by their height, such as '1170' or '1320', and it was these features that were the team's objectives. Quoting from Sarah's account of the group on their way down from Nunatak '1170'.

> The ice-cap is fairly flat (gently sloping, nice for Nordic skis) and would be rather boring once there were no more nunataks.
>
> Something to eat in the sun and cold wind and we set off down again at 03.30. Back at the tents at 05.30 hrs. on a slightly different line on nicely frozen snow. The tents looked minute on the snowy waste and the views to Uvkus and down towards Kangerdluarssup glacier were marvellous.
>
> Very cold wind now. We have just had brew of tea and are going back to sleep now. The sun is still shining but with all this snow, one can't really sit out. We are having to melt water for cooking.

After seven days out from the Base, having climbed four of these rocky summits and carried out a tricky, but accurate piece of navigation off the ice-cap, they rejoined the others at Base Camp. The other group had also been very active. After exploring Uvkusigssat, they had climbed almost to the top of Uvkus Peak and also the hill immediately behind the camp, and then had a very stormy journey by boat round to the Base Camp. They were now busy reconnoitring the Sledge Route up into the hills behind the base. This turned out to be very unpleasant going over large loose boulders and very steep scree. Also the weather had turned really miserable, so all were confined to base for a few days.

On 9th August the group of four set off up the Sledge Route to make an attempt on point '1833'. Sarah tells the tale;

> Up at midnight – just at the point when I felt I might sleep.
>
> Off at 01.05. Cold. Set off straight up the moraine to the south of the camp – easier going than we had feared – and then turned left when we hit the ridge.
>
> After about two hours we met new snow and soon after we hit our first crevasse (small) so roped up. Dawn. Lovely pink light on our hill. Long snow slope, then it levelled off and got rocky. After that we put crampons on.
>
> Set off, with Kate leading up a very steep snow slope, zig-zagging. A level bit and then two steep slopes. Kate R. kept doing snow profiles and was content with what she found.
>
> At 05.30 we had got over these two bumps and were on the extreme left of the mountain. The face was impossible so all depended on being able to get round to the left. There was a bergschrund but we belayed each other across and then had fabulous views down and across to Uvkus and the lagoon area.
>
> Even then the slope looked very, very steep but Kate R. wasn't worried and we steadily gained the last 700 ft. with a big crevasse as a sting in the tail. This seemed to be the top as we were looking down on the more obvious rocky top as seen from the north......
>
> Down with no mishaps by 09.13 – just over nine hours. I feel delighted to have done '1833' – my main aim for the expedition. Now we are all drinking tea and eating oatcakes before going to sleep.

The group managed to climb another two summits, but already by mid-August the short Greenland summer was coming to an end. Their coldest morning to date was recorded on 12th August, with lumps of ice forming on the porridge plates when they tried to wash them, and steam coming off their hands even inside the tent. Time to go home,

*Marion Boyle,
Greenland, August
1998*

Photo: Julia Banks

and four days later they were all together on the plane back to Glasgow, with another store of tales and legends for the members back home.

While many Club members indulged their fascination for colder climates by heading north of the Arctic Circle, there always remained that lingering desire for the *Terra Incognita* of the South Polar regions. For decades it remained unattainable as British women were actively discouraged, and even prohibited from going to the Antarctic. The veteran explorer, Molly Porter, campaigned for many years and eventually paved the way for women to travel in the Antarctic.

1994 and 1995 were two remarkable years for the LSCC in the Antarctic. Two members of the Club were there at the same time, although, surprisingly they did not get a chance to see each other. Kate Charles was a scientist with the British Antarctic Survey based at Halley Station, and stayed for a full two and a half years, being among the first British women to over-winter in the Antarctic. Alison McLure, also a Club member and a meteorologist, was the weather forecaster at Rothera, further north on the Antarctic Peninsula, where she spent five months during the Austral summer. Alison describes the experience in her own words.

The snow hissed around my skis like snakes. The only thing I could see in the blizzard was the fuzzy shape of an oil drum marking out the snow runway. The drifting snow covered up any trace of my having been there, as if trying to show that humans were not welcome here. If it were not for the drums, I

Above: Bolivia, expedition members 2008. Back row from left: Lizzie Potts, Evelyn McNicol, Maris Buchanan, Fiona Hutchinson, Marieke Dwarshuis, Brenda Roddy, Dot Mechan, Alison Higham. Front row from left: Sarah Mackay, Margaret Graham, Kate Ross, Eve Gilmore, Mary Lothian, Karin Froebel

Below: Kate Ross, Alison Higham and Margaret Graham on Huayna Potosi (6088m), Bolivia 2008. Illimani is in the background

Hot Rock – Mary Lothian sport climbing at Kalymnos, Greece

would be lost and the nearest other shelter was one hundred miles away. I was in the Antarctic, working in the most remote, hostile and uninhabited continent on the planet.

I was based at Rothera and it was a bit daunting to be the only female among 50 men for most of the time. One or two other women came for a shorter time and it was good to have some female company. Mind you, I soon settled into a routine of work and spending time out of the base exploring. The General Assistants were all mountaineers and were keen to explore and try out their skills on willing guinea pigs. I volunteered whenever I had the chance between working. One of our early trips was to an island across the sea ice on skidoos.

This all went smoothly until we came across a break in the ice (lead) and we walked the rest of the way to the island. On the way back I jumped across one of the leads and missed. Luckily I managed to get my ice-axe in and hauled myself out, only getting wet below the waist. None of my companions had noticed my mistake, so I thought that I would keep quiet to preserve the honour of womanhood! It was only another 20 minutes back to base on the skidoos, so surely I would not freeze in that time, I thought. I did not reckon with one of the skidoos breaking down. An hour later we returned to base and I rushed off to change my clothes and check for frostbite. Luckily I was unscathed, if a tad chilly.

Other trips involved ski-ing up to mountains and then roping together to get across them. It was amazing where you would find crevasses; even at the tops of ridges you could not be sure. Once when we were ski-ing off a mountain, having successfully traversed the ridge, I heard a shout from my companions. I stopped to listen to what they had to say: 'Don't stop. There are crevasses around'. I gingerly got going again and picked up as much speed as possible to ski jump any nasty holes.

Towards the end of my time at Rothera, my work started to ease off, which meant that I could spend more time away from the base. One trip I planned deliberately with a storm coming, so that I could experience wild weather in one of the amazing pyramid tents that are used by the British Antarctic Survey. They have hardly changed since Scott's day, but they work. We made sure everything was set up properly and the storm duly got going overnight. Unfortunately, the next morning the base commander decided that we were needed back at base. This meant returning into the teeth of the storm. It doesn't take long for a jolly jaunt to turn into a survival exercise. However, we managed to return safely, although we looked pretty rough by the time we got there.

Some time later the navy ship HMS Endurance came in and some of us were invited for dinner in the Officers' Mess. We were asked to wear ties; they were obviously not used to female company! I had bought a bow tie with penguins on it for my Dad, so I wore this to dinner. There were no comments at all. They obviously did not share my warped sense of humour.

Alison says that she came back a changed person. Perhaps it is in the nature of the purity of snow and cold wind, that the Arctic and the Antarctic have a profound effect on those who are privileged to share their vastness. They are some of the most precious places on earth, and one returns humbled and inspired. Alison resolved to make the attempt to reduce her ecological footprint to as little as possible. Perhaps we can share her sentiment that one day our own 'footprints' may be erased as effectively as her ski tracks in the Antarctic.

Alison McLure spent the summer of 1995 as a meterologist at Rothera, Antarctic

Photo: Alison McLure Collection

*Picking a way
through the Jugal
Himal ice-fall, on the
first women's
expedition to the
Himalayas, 1955*

Photo: LSCC Archives

9: The Top of the World

THE ENTHUSIASM with which the LSCC congratulated and
supported their men-folk when they went on expeditions to the
Himalaya and, in the case of Harold Raeburn, to Everest, contains,
undoubtedly, some degree of envy and longing, and it wasn't long before
the women themselves were turning their hopes and dreams to the highest tops of all.

Nowadays it is a relatively easy matter to register with a qualified guide
or trekking agency and go to the mountain area of choice – even Everest itself, if one has plenty money to spare. But back in the 1950s it
was an entirely different matter. Maps were hard to obtain and highly
inaccurate, sometimes missing out entire mountains, valleys and glaciers,
as the high altitude ground between Nepal and Tibet had never been
surveyed at close quarters and large parts remained unexplored.

The idea to go to Nepal began with Monica Jackson, a small ball of
enthusiasm, who had the advantage of being born and brought up in
North India, is a speaker of Hindustani, and a highly proficient alpinist who had already climbed in the Himalaya. In Monica's own words;

> For me, the seeds of adventure lay in the day I met Esme Speakman in a climb-
> ing hut in the French Alps. Not only was this the beginning of a firm friendship
> and happy climbing partnership, but it was through Esme that I became a
> member of the Ladies Scottish Climbing Club and made the acquaintance of
> Betty Stark and Evelyn Camrass.

Evelyn was a Glasgow doctor, an all-round athlete, keen on ski-ing,
hockey, and with wide mountaineering experience in Scotland of rock
climbing and winter snow and ice climbing. She had climbed in the Pyrenees, ski mountaineered in Austria, and was a member of the first all
women party to the Lyngen Alps in Arctic Norway. The description of
Betty Stark is best left to Monica.

Before I ever met Betty, I happened to mention her name to a climbing friend – not a member of the LSCC – 'Oh, Betty Stark,' said this person in a hushed voice, 'She's very tough. She breaks into bothies.'

It makes me laugh now to think how very wide of the mark was this description of my good friend and climbing companion, Betty Stark. I don't know what gave rise to this reputation for ruthlessness, but it was quite unjustified. She is a law-abiding body.

Betty lives in Glasgow and is a speech therapist attached to Lanarkshire County Council. She also has a teacher's diploma and a Diploma in Speech and Drama…as a result she is generally the stalwart mainspring of the annual LSCC ceilidh. She is well-read, good at languages and has a literary bent. She is also highly sensitive, moody, introverted and possessed of a nice wit and keen sense of humour. She is a brave and reliable rock climber and something of an expert on snow and ice

Expedition member Betty Stark, 1997

Photo: LSCC Archives

Then there was Esme who at the last moment was prevented by illness from going on the expedition. Esme had lived and worked in Switzerland and had wide alpine experience. She was a very competent steady climber, possibly the most experienced of the group. She was also a magnificent photographer and was the only one of the four to have knowledge of surveying. Her pulling out was a sad blow, but as Monica said.

Some indication of the respect we all had for her is shown by the fact that though she did not accompany us, we always thought of her as part of the expedition.

Monica herself was already committed to joining an expedition to Nepal led by the Swiss guide, Raymond Lambert. Eventually Monica made a bold decision to resign from the Lambert expedition and throw in her lot with the women. Plans and excitement grew as the expedition blossomed.

So it was decided, and from that time on the thing seemed to grow almost of its own volition. It was discussed by Betty and Evelyn in a tent in Arctic Norway and by Esme and me in a mountain hut in Switzerland. Later, sentences beginning, 'I've just thought of something else we ought to do…' were shouted from stance to stance on rock climbs in Glencoe and on Ben Nevis, and blown away by the gale on misty Highland ridges. Plans were argued out over sodden sandwiches as we crouched shivering behind boulders in snowstorms on Scottish mountains. And agreements were reached by candle-light over cups of tea in Scottish climbing-huts.

It is interesting to note that making a 'first' for women was never really part of the plan. Although women had climbed in the Himalaya before 1955, it had always been as members of expeditions planned and led by men. This was truly a first.

To begin with, I should like to make it clear that the 'first ever' aspect was quite unpremeditated. It was not until our plans had already begun to take shape that it occurred to us that we were creating a precedent…Of course when we realised that we would be pioneering in more senses than one, we were quite pleased, since it might improve our chances of obtaining financial backing. On the other hand, we thought it would mean that we would have to contend with a good deal of prejudice first. Both these surmises proved correct.

Dwarfed by ice-cliffs and crevasses, members on their first ascent in the Himalaya in 1955, named by them Gyalgen Peak after the Head Sherpa

Photo: LSCC Archives

Being a 'first' inevitably put great pressure on the three women to be extra meticulous in their organisation, and, if possible, successful in their outcome. As they themselves were only too aware, mistakes or disasters in a mixed expedition would have gone unremarked or evoked sympathy; with a women's one the world could have said; 'Well, what did you expect?' These three spent nine months (appropriately) of meticulous planning to bring the project to birth. Their aim was to explore in the Jugal Himal, right on the border between Nepal and Tibet, an area untrodden and unmapped, and possibly the last large unexplored area of the Nepal Himalaya. They also hoped as a bonus to make a first ascent if possible – an ambitious and exciting plan.

A remarkable feature of the expedition is the modesty of the women and the modesty of their means. They said of themselves, 'We could not pretend to be brilliant climbers', and they chose to have no leader, asserting that in this way they co-operated better. They approached the Himalayan Committee for a recommendation, not really expecting to get it because of their gender, and because they were, as they themselves put it, 'nowhere near the top flight of British climbers'. Perhaps it was this very attribute of realistic modesty that won the argument for they were amazed and gratified when their obvious good sense, mountaineering competence and enthusiasm earned them the recognition they sought.

The whole expedition was carried out on a shoestring. Not for them the luxury of fixed camps all the way up the approach to the mountain. They couldn't afford extra tents, or even special high altitude tents, using the old familiar 'Palomine' that so many have used to start out their camping careers. This meant that they had to wait in the mornings until the ice thawed sufficiently to allow them to take down the tents ready for carrying up to the next camp. They did pay for porters but had only four climbing Sherpas with them on the mountain itself. When they gave the Sherpas extra gloves these were sometimes their own spare pair and not part of a budgeted expedition surplus.

April 1955 saw the expedition well under way, leaving Kathmandu and trekking up the Indrawati Valley where they had their first thrilling view of the high peaks.

> In the morning the air was sharp and clear. We came out to see the shapely hills stretching northward, their planes receding into a blue distance. Our eyes, accustomed to Scottish scenery, at first saw the faint white line above them as morning mist or cloud. It was only when we looked a second time that we realised with wonder and delight that the whole horizon from east to west was clasped by the Great Himalayan Chain. It is one thing to know from the map that there are mountains of this size in such numbers, but it is quite another to see for oneself their beauty and awesome architecture, each one retaining its individuality in a bewildering profusion of peaks.

From the accounts of the expedition it is clear that the route in to these high mountains, through deep gorges and high passes was by no means obvious. The maps made by the Indian surveyors were only quarter inch to the mile, and although reasonably accurate for the foothills, the high peaks had been surveyed from a distance by triangulation, so progress depended very much on guesswork and local knowledge. Trying to find a way onto the glaciers, 'they set off upstream by a path which was here and there indistinct, into a country where no white person had preceded us.'

Often the most difficult and dangerous part of a Himalayan expedition is not found on the ridges or faces of the peaks themselves, but on the treacherous approach through the icefall – those parts of a glacier where the frozen river of ice splits and cracks into a jumbled mass of fissures and towers as the ice grinds over a steeper part of the valley floor. The ice is constantly changing, groaning and moving and can be moulded into huge towers or seracs, which can topple and crash, or be rent by the great gashes of crevasses. Somehow a way must be picked through this maze, often under a barrage of stones falling from above as thawing releases them from the grip of the ice. A place to be treated with caution and a healthy respect, and best tackled in the morning before delicate snow bridges melt or collapse or avalanches begin to thunder down. Betty Stark gives us a vivid account;

> At one place we had to cross a slender bridge of ice. At another we climbed an ice-wall terminating in a sharp knife-edge, and leapt across an unexpected crevasse beyond. We were too pre-occupied to realise that the clouds were coming up, until we found ourselves engulfed.
>
> When we came out on the flat of the glacier above, still harassed by the criss-cross of crevasses, we could see the knobs of a long snow-covered central moraine leading up into the mist – the glacier's vertebrae. We took a compass bearing on this before the mist settled and marched on it for over an hour. But first, having reached easier ground, we could stop and change places on the rope. Monica took over the lead from Mingma, for we wanted to do our own route-finding. In any case, as she pointed out to him, if she fell into an unsuspected crevasse, she was easily hauled out again. Shortly afterwards this was proved when she did slip into a hidden crevasse – to waist level only. She said it was like crashing through a skylight window, the ice tinkling like glass far below.

However such trials brought their reward next morning as they emerged from their tents.

> Next morning the walls of the tent were bellied inward with the weight of newly fallen snow. A thump or two from inside cleared this away, and the sun shone through. I struggled out, half-asleep, having no idea of what I should see. The impact of the scene and the cold air outside woke me up at once into startled awareness. A peak stood at the head of the glacier which I had not seen before, shapely and beautifully buttressed, glowing with great intensity in the rich yellow light of the early sun. It seemed to leap from a sky of darkest blue. I felt as though a sudden splendid chord of music had rung out across the sky and I wanted to shout aloud.

As they progressed up the mountain, camps were established until eventually they reached Camp IV high up on the glacier where they were faced with a seemingly insurmountable obstacle

> Betty led up and down with vigour the swelling waves and sharp crests of snow-covered ice. Some of the crevasses we encountered were immense, their walls striated in layers of different colours – pastel pinks, blues, greens, and creams – like slices of some exotic Neapolitan cake. We managed to skirt or cross them all until Betty climbed a last steep serac and stopped short at the top. At her feet was the biggest crevasse any of us had ever seen. It seemed to stretch from end to end of the glacier and her heart sank. But our blood was up, and we were not going to be beaten now if we could help it...After about half an hour of hard and hair-raising battle the crevasse suddenly surrendered and the first party scrambled with relief onto solid ice again.

By now the party was well above 18,000 feet and suffering the effects of altitude. Altitude affects people in different ways, none of them pleasant. Blinding headaches, sleeplessness, nausea, loss of appetite and concentration, and sometimes the more serious effects of cerebral or pulmonary oedema. Evelyn suffered so badly that she was finally too ill to go with them to the summit. Monica seems to have suffered less than the others, perhaps because of her previous experience of high altitude climbing. At any rate everyone inevitably experienced the breathlessness that comes from lack of oxygen and each laborious step upwards becomes a painful struggle. Betty's diary reflects this pain;

> Long, long slopes went up and up, mostly soft snow with ice showing through unexpectedly. Monica took her turn at leading and step -cutting, but I was feeling the altitude and it was all I could do to follow. I tried every system I could think of to keep going; breathing more quickly than I need; taking two breaths to every step; then three, then four, but all were exhausting. I wanted to cry, but no-one would give me time!

Indeed Betty was so demoralised by what she perceived as her lack of fitness that she offered to turn back. To her surprise the suggestion elicited an outpouring of praise from Mingma, the Sherpa, who proceeded to compare the performance of various 'sahibs' he had climbed with most unfavourably with that of the 'memsahibs'. Suitably encouraged, Betty continued.

In addition to all these pains, the ultra-violet reflection of sun at this altitude off the glittering surface of the glacier can cause snow blindness and severe burning. Any part of the skin left unprotected by layers of cream would erupt in painful blisters, and as one gasps for air, even the roof of the mouth and the tongue can become blistered as well so that drinking orange juice or tea can become torture.

One might be forgiven for wondering if it is all worth it, but the final reward of the summit which they called Gyalgen Peak, named after their head Sherpa, is graphically described by Monica.

> Mingma and I set off up the ice, our crampons gripping well. I had hoped to lead all the way, because I felt fit and energetic, but the sight of clouds coming up on the horizon made me abandon the idea in the interests of the expedition. If Mingma led in his present exalted mood, I should have to follow at his pace and we should get up much quicker than if I led at my own slower pace. This turned out to be a wise decision, though at times I thought I was going to die.
>
> Mingma went up that ice very nearly at a run with me tearing after him. We had never before moved so fast in the mountains, and I was now higher than I had ever been before – we must have been well over 21,000 feet. I could not get my breath fast enough at the pace at which we were climbing, and once stopped, gasping that I must halt. Mingma said anxiously, 'The clouds, memsahib.' They were very near and the sight of them spurred me on to greater efforts. Suddenly Mingma stopped, and, with a beaming smile pointed and said, 'Look, the summit.' We saw the ice slope easing off ahead to end suddenly in a little apex of snow. The sight of it was like a dose of oxygen. I took an enormous breath, said, 'All right, come on,' and we went up side by side to the summit.

About half an hour later, just as they were thinking rather anxiously of leaving, Betty and Ang Temba arrived at the summit, and all were able to enjoy the amazing view of countless peaks in one direction and a sheer drop to the Tibetan plain on the other. Somehow summits always

Evelyn McNicol on the first ascent of an 18,500ft peak named Bidean nan Nighean (Hill of the Maiden), and climbed with a Sherpa in 1955

Photo: Evelyn McNicol Collection

seem a little awkward and they celebrated together with mint cake and chocolate before beating a hasty retreat.

Of course this was by no means the end of the story. On the descent they were hit by a mighty storm of thunder and lightning and blizzard which confined them to their cramped tents for two days. Even getting into the tent was a struggle;

> By the time I reached my tent my right hand had lost all sensation and was useless. The zip on my tent door was very stiff (a zip opening to a mountain tent is never a good idea) and I struggled to open it with my left hand for what seemed an age. It yielded at last, but my left hand was now going the way of the right and I could not close the zip again. Meantime gusts of wind blew more and more snow into the tent. At last I got the door closed and sat there, breathless, covered from head to foot with a film of snow, like everything else in the tent. Then my hands began to come back to life, and I rolled over on my sleeping bag in agony. The pain was so great that I thought I was going to be sick. However, it passed off after a bit and I began to feel better.

Two of the Sherpas had removed their goggles for a short time and become snow blind, and so they had to be led step by faltering step across a knife-edge snow bridge over a vast crevasse. A thaw had set in, a precursor to the monsoon, making the ice-fall doubly treacherous

> It was not until we reached the top of the ice-fall that this fact was truly brought home to us. The ice-fall was no longer a familiar friend but a potential enemy. It was especially dangerous near the top. Where all had been firm snow before was now a wilderness of twisting crevasses covered with a layer of rotten snow. Once embarked on this sinister passage we began to sweat freely. We would jump crevasses to find the surface upon which we landed beginning to disintegrate under our feet. We would plunge our ice-axes in to give a belay to the next on the rope, only to feel the ice-axe go through into empty air. There did not seem to be a moment when one or several of us was not conscious of being perched on a tenuous crust of melting snow over yet another apparently bottomless well.

At last Camp I was reached and they began the long reluctant walk out to Kathmandu. Some days were spent carrying out important reconnaissance work, discovering new passes and sorting out the muddled record of glaciers. The new glacier they had discovered on their way up Gyalgen Peak they appropriately named 'Ladies Glacier'. Evelyn also made an ascent of an 18,500 foot peak named Bidean nan Nighean (Hill of the Maiden). All the time they kept glancing backwards for a last glimpse of the wonderful mountains they had come to love.

The women greeted their accomplishments with typical modesty, saying,

> We had not accomplished anything spectacular, but then we had never hoped to do so with such a small party. We had succeeded in doing what we had set out to do, which was to explore the Jugal Himal, the last large unexplored area of Nepal Himalaya. That we had managed to climb an unknown peak of over 21,000 feet was really beside the point – a kind of bonus.

It is perhaps a closer measure of their achievement to quote the flyleaf of their book *Tents in the Clouds*.

Recently three women – a London housewife, a Lanarkshire speech therapist and a doctor from Glasgow – pooled their resources, sailed to India, flew to Kathmandu, capital of Nepal, and investigated this remote, romantic region. Their modest expedition made headline news, for not only was the work they undertook of considerable scientific value, but their expedition was the first composed only of women to venture into the Himalayas.

A remarkable feature of the whole expedition was the good will with which it was carried out. Not only did three very independent-minded women work really well together under severe stress and very hard conditions, it is obvious that they became good friends with their Sherpa climbing companions, winning their close trust and respect, and having a great deal of fun and merriment, parting from them at the end with tears of affection on both sides.

It is an interesting footnote, perhaps due to the modest approach of the three Scotswomen, that a full seven years later *The Times* inaccurately attributed a first all-women's ascent in Nepal to an expedition to the Kanjiroba Range, where a 22,000 foot peak was climbed. However, even on this expedition, Dorothea Gravina was an LSCC member.

It was to be a another ten years before Nepal was re-visited by a Club member. Eleanor Lloyd played the bassoon in the BBC Scottish Orchestra. A tall, stately woman, she joined the Club in 1948, and the manner of her joining is indicative of Eleanor's intrepid spirit. Following a lively Hogmanay party which lasted until 3.30am, she rushed off on the spur of the moment and caught the 4.30am train north and booked herself in to the Clachaig Inn in Glencoe for a weekend's climbing.

The LSCC was also in Glencoe that year, based at the Kingshouse, and Esme Speakman, spotting a lone climber, invited Eleanor to join them. So began many years of companionship on the hills. Eleanor spent some time doing social work in the United Mission Hospital in Kathmandu in 1964, and she gives a delightful account of several weeks trekking in the Annapurna Sanctuary and also in the Helambu Valley accompanied only by two porters. This was still the era before commercial trekking companies opened up these areas to tourists, and Eleanor gives a vivid impression of the warm and generous hospitality offered by local families. This was not an expedition to the high tops, but more of a gentle, intimate journey full of appreciation for the local people and culture as is shown in this extract from the Journal;

> The next night I was happy enough to find a place for my tent beside the Indrawati River. I was surrounded by an intrigued audience, who watched every movement and every mouthful with deep interest, till darkness drove them back to their own homes and I was left in peace – only disturbed by frogs. One plopped right onto my chest just as I was falling asleep!
>
> The third night was spent in the porch of a gyang or Buddhist temple – just outside the locked door of the main shrine, where the carved images sit, but we slept surrounded by wall paintings of terrifying deities, threatening and grasping the Wheel of Life with teeth and claws.
>
> The fourth day we were soon over the ridge into Helambu (the Sherpa country). Here, though I had expected to use my tent, hospitality was so generously offered, and in such comparative comfort and cleanliness, that the tent was not necessary for the rest of this trek.

Kate Ross abseiling on Khan Tengri in the Tien Shan

Photo: Kate Ross
Collection

With some foresight she concluded.

> As I left Nepal a week later, it seemed to me that I had been just in time to know the country in all its primitive simplicity before it is taken over by 'progress' and industrialisation.

Sadly Eleanor was seriously injured in an accident getting off a bus and never recovered full use of her leg, suffering a great deal of pain and having to walk with crutches. However, this did not deter her from going out with the Club, and Eleanor attended Meets faithfully, taking slow, often painful walks, and returning with fascinating accounts of interesting birds and plants – as well as superb photographs.

Of course Nepal did indeed change and open up to tourists, and over the years a growing number of LSCC members took advantage of easier access and visited many parts of the Himalaya. They travelled in the Karakoram, Ladakh, Tibet and Nepal, some trekking over high passes, some, like June Ross, finding rare botanical specimens, some heading for the high tops.

A feature article in the *Glasgow Herald* of 1975 begins with this intriguing sentence;

> Time, we felt, was running out. Our united ages already amounted to 256, and if we wished to trek or climb in the Himalayas, obviously we could wait no longer."

The title of the article – *Pensioners in Paradise* – explains all. Christina Macnair, Grizel Paterson, Margaret Darvall, and Esme Speakman were all over 60 years old, and typical of most older LSCC members, they were all fit and keen enough to go on yet another adventure, this time to the area of the Himalaya around Manali in North India. As Christina put it, they were keen enough just to be in the Himalaya, and for Christina and Grizel it would be a first time, but they might even be fortunate enough to add a modest peak as well.

It is one of the given rigours of almost all expeditions to the high tops that they have to start with hair-raising epic approach journeys in rickety old jeeps, and this expedition was no exception. Christina's diary describes the drive through the Beas Gorge;

> Stopped for tea and photos – on to Pandala where we were told that the road ahead through the Beas Gorge was blocked – several hours delay – landslides and mud – though it turned out the real cause was a lorry with a broken axle. We stopped – then went on a bit. Go back? walk on? We did both! Finally our driver decided to have a go – magnificent driving, through mud ruts and debris, end to end lorries both ways, trying to pass. Magnificent gorge, if you could bear to look. On – stop – on – stop. Many abandoned lorries – families cooking at the roadside. Eventually got through to Manali where the road was a stream bed.

Unfortunately after all the excitement of the drive and the hard slog of the walk in, it rained so hard that on their first approach they never saw the promised panorama of peaks, and they had to go back down. However the weather brightened eventually and they set off again, this time establishing a magnificent camp-site at Beas Kund, and on July 22nd, Esme and Margaret set off to attempt to climb Ladakhi Peak

Crossing a typically swift glacier torrent on the Millennium Expedition to Ladakh, 2000

Photo: Alison Higham

(18,300 feet). Both were experienced climbers and managed it without too much of a struggle, although racing for time against bad weather. However, one aspect that is often overlooked is the suspense of those who wait for them back at Base Camp. Again Christina describes how she and Grizel felt during their long wait;

> Back to camp, watching for climbers. As it got later, began to worry as we knew Kranti (one of the Sherpas) had no torch, so we gave Grizel's torch to a porter and suggested he went up to meet them. Soup – but no sign of them. Now dark, though starry – the moon was not yet up. Constantly peering into the dark – saw a light, but not sure whether it was just the porter. Finally, about 7.30pm we realised that Chamba and another porter were down, and we learned they were all coming down. At last, after 8.30pm, they struggled in, one torch between the lot – but they had got their peak! Great jubilation and relief.

In 1996 Kate Ross joined an expedition to climb Khan Tengri in Tien Shan. Kate is an experienced all-round climber as well as having been a highly regarded President of the LSCC and Chair of the Mountaineering Council for Scotland. But always Kate is first and foremost a mountaineer and explorer and never allows pressing committee duties to crowd out challenging mountain adventures. However as Kate herself commented, 'You don't get fun at high altitude', and undoubtedly over a certain height, there is a lot of sheer determination and physical stamina required to overcome the pain barrier. Hence the necessary acclimatisation approach to the high tops, which can often be sheer delight.

In preparation Kate undertook two back-packing treks on her own to over a height of 5000 metres. She recalls camping amid glorious flowers with a spectacular mountain backdrop; villages where no women were seen in public, but where the men were always courteously helpful to unusual mountain travellers, even to the extent of offering to re-sole her boots! She remembers the colour, clamour, scents and sounds of buying spices in the local market, and venturing up a glacier on her own without rope or crampons.

*Karin Froebel, left,
and Marion Boyle on
the summit ridge of
Stok Kangri, Ladakh,
2000*

Photo: Alison Higham

At the end of what Kate describes as her best-ever personal trip, she had to give up splendid isolation and take a helicopter to the Base Camp for Khan Tengri at a height of over 4000 metres. The contrast between the pleasant unspoilt isolation enjoyed by Eleanor Lloyd in Nepal in 1964 and Kate Ross's experience in Tien Shan in the Karakoram 32 years later could not have been greater. As Kate wrote in the Club Journal:

> The helicopter swooped over the ridges and glaciers and deposited me at the North Luchilik Glacier Camp at 4000m. It looked like a misplaced Mediterranean campsite with rows of frame tents, cooking and restaurant tents and a sauna!

All the time there were men sitting around drinking vodka and a constant coming and going of Japanese tourists, expeditions from Korea and Iran – even a goat! Here she met up with the team leader and her male companions for the expedition. She was the only woman in the party and soon found that it was a highly demanding trip.

> 'Why am I doing this?' My legs felt like lead, my sac was too heavy, breathing was an effort, hauling up fixed ropes for 1000m between Camp 1 and Camp 2 seemed like purgatory. The Greek islands seemed very appealing. We had set up Camp 1 at 4600m on a shale platform. Camp 2 at 5600m required digging and flattening snow or sometimes sitting on sacs thinking about digging. After four days establishing and stocking these camps we retired to base for a rest. While it snowed we had snowball fights with a Korean expedition, relaxed in the sauna and ate. The daily excitement was when the helicopter arrived. What would it be today – Japanese tourists, a French trekking group, fresh bread, a live sheep (but not for long!) and always vodka.
>
> Three days in base and we were off on our summit bid. Above Camp 1 there are fixed ropes over much of the route, put up by Russian guides. Close your mind to frayed strands, knots with no ends visible. In the Alps I wouldn't contemplate using gear in this state, but it speeds up the rock sections. I take consolation in the fact that everyone else is heavier than I am. Camp 2 still seemed a long way, but it was reached with less pain this time around.
>
> Camp 3 at 5900m is a permanent snowcave which can sleep about eight people. Above us you are left with a choice of establishing a Camp 4 (approx 6400m) on an exposed ridge or trying for the summit in a single 1100m push.

After setting off in an attempt to do the summit in one go, they were forced to turn back and spend another night of discomfort in an overcrowded dripping snow cave. Storms blew up and discomfort grew. At last...

> 'It's 4am and clear. Graham and I melt snow and brew up and at 5am set off – still dark. Half-an-hour later the peaks take on a dawn glow and we progress steadily – rock steps, snow bridges, fixed ropes. At 8.30am we are at Camp 4. I shove a muesli bar and spare gloves in my pocket and secure my sac to the fixed ropes – I'll move faster without it. The couloir gets steadily nearer. The rock barrier to it is thankfully easier than described. At the top of the couloir is a steep traverse. The snow is soft and unstable and we kick steps across, moving with care. We're onto the exposed snow ridge looking down on all the peaks around us and down the complete route to base. It's awesome – have we really climbed that?
>
> Still 250m to go but *nothing* will stop us now. We take slow steady steps

up the slopes of snow and broken rock. Twenty steps and pause to get your breath back. It's OK until a step breaks and you're reduced to a gasping fish. Over a slight rise and the metal tripod appears.

Stunning views, Pobeada to the south and numerous steep, dramatic peaks all round in Kazakstan, Kirgistan and China...the Tien Shan running southwards to the Pamirs, Hindu Kush, the Karakoram...Blue skies, no wind. There's nothing to say. The world belongs to us.

Her appetite for the high places well and truly whetted, Kate was back in the High Himalaya three years later, this time on an expedition to Ama Dablam. Ama Dablam is one of the most stunning peaks of the whole Himalayan chain and its mighty bulk totally dominates the whole Khumbu Valley.

Catching the tail-end of the monsoon downpour, Kate and five companions trekked up to Namche Bazaar and on to Camp 1 at 5300 metres which marked the end of the relatively easy ground. The route led up an impressive ridge with a massive drop on either side. This soon led onto hard rock graded up to mild VS standard with dramatic towers and pinnacles. A Grade 3 rock and snow gully followed – no joke with a load of heavy gear and at an altitude above 6000 metres. They left camp for the final summit push at 8.0am, as Kate said, *'With usual throwing up'*. Front-pointing up a steep 50 degree snow face she reached a tiny ledge, crouched delicately past a serac, and there, standing proud of the huge cornices was the summit. *'All climbing – cornices – the lot – an absolutely brilliant peak'* was Kate's verdict.

As the Millennium approached, the Club began planning how to celebrate appropriately, and it was Kate herself who coined the phrase '20,000 feet in the year 2000'. The objective was to find a peak over 20,000 feet in height well within the capabilities of as many Club members as possible. Kerstin Phillips and her husband, John, had spent an enjoyable time in Ladakh in 1991, and Ladakh had the added attraction of still being a relatively isolated part of the Himalaya. Plans went ahead and the Club agreed to spend some weeks in Ladakh with the aim of culminating the trip by going up Stok Kangri.

Mary Webster (front) & Margaret Graham on the summit ridge of Stok Kangri, 2000

Photo: Kate Ross

*Alison Higham,
Marion Boyle and
Karin Froebel summit
Stok Kangri, Ladakh,
2000*

Photo: Alison Higham
Collection

Sixteen LSCC members and two of their partners made up the party, which split up into four separate expeditions, each choosing a route suitable for their abilities and to enable them to acclimatise. They would then meet up at the end for a final celebration climb of Stok Kangri – well over the required 20,000 feet.

Two of the parties opted for fully supported treks which meant that all their gear was carried by ponies, camps and meals were prepared for them, and they had the delightful experience of travelling through spectacular scenery without being bent double and sweating under huge burdens. A third party chose lightweight backpacking, crossing high passes and following deep gorges with dramatically swollen rivers. The fourth group were the most energetic undertaking a 20 day trek from Darcha in Himal Pradesh to Lamayuru in Ladakh. The crossing of the Shingo La pass at 5100 metres was really taxing involving an ascent of 3000 metres in five days – without a rest day.

Finally all met up in Leh at the beginning of August. Dragging themselves away from the temptations of the apricot pies at the 'In Style German Bakery', they had an exciting jeep drive avoiding a bridge washed away by the flooded Indus river, to arrive finally at a chaotic welter of expedition gear.

On August 7th a triumphant group climbed the exposed ridge of loose crumbling rock to the summit and gazed out over stunning views of the High Himalaya. What more fitting way for the LSCC to celebrate the Millennium?

10: Of Bothies, Ballads and Birthdays

LADIES SCOTTISH CLIMBING CLUB; Ladies Scottish Chatting Club; Ladies Scottish Ceilidh Club – one thing is sure; from its inception the LSCC has enjoyed partying almost as much as it enjoys the hills. Initially social gatherings took place in gracious Edinburgh drawing rooms, where home baking and silver teapots were the order of the day. Over the years standards may have slipped somewhat to black billycans over smoking fires, but the enjoyment remains the same.

Sometimes these early social events involved husbands, invited guests and speakers and on such occasions public assembly rooms were necessary, with between 80 to a 100 members and guests participating. It was the practice of the Club in its early days to invite someone of note to be the Club's Honorary President, and in 1914 the then incumbent, the Marchioness of Breadalbane, suggested that the Club adopt the Gaelic word *ceilidh* to describe its social gatherings. Since that date there have been many social events of such a wide variety that it is indeed doubtful whether the respected Marchioness would recognise them for her original genteel gatherings. In 1920 the practice of having evening ceilidhs was begun, with immediate success.

The programme for these events was always varied and interesting. Talks and lectures, usually illustrated with lantern slides, and sometimes featuring quiz nights, were popular. Often too there was country dancing, with vigorous Eightsome Reels, Petronella, and Dashing White Sergeant obviously familiar to all. Communal singing played its part and Club members down the years have displayed great talent at adapting popular songs and writing witty verses about the peculiarities of Club members. Indeed such literary gems were these songs that when the Junior Mountaineering Club of Scotland (JMCS) compiled a club songbook, they asked the LSCC for permission to use some of their songs.

Many of these ditties were composed on the JMCS bus, which left Glasgow at crack of dawn and regularly gave lifts to climbers heading for Crianlarich or Glencoe. One can picture the songsters, sweaty, happy, steaming up the windows of the bus, boots and socks hung around to dry, heads together, 'moothie' at the ready, laughter as the 'back-of-the-bus' bursts into song. Songs that would later be transposed to the elegance of the drawing rooms – perhaps with some genteel adaptation!

A unique feature of the LSCC annual ceilidhs was the 'dramatic production'. The record of 1920 describes the first such event, a practice which continued for over 60 years. These performances were highly creative, displaying considerable classical and literary knowledge and a great deal of inventive fun, linked in some, often abstruse way, to the exploits of the Club. It was all good light-hearted fun, full of in-jokes and much amateurish cavorting. Many enjoyed it hugely; others found it acutely embarrassing, especially when guests from other clubs were present. In 1933 the 'ceilidh' evenings were replaced by a more formal annual dinner, recorded here in the Club record with some questioning of the appropriateness of such jollifications.

> Another innovation was the Dinner which took the place of the time-honoured Ceilidh. Some members viewed such a proceeding with misgivings. Ceilidhs are unique. No other Clubs have Ceilidhs. Could we produce our usual programme of foolery at a Dinner? Does anyone but ourselves enjoy our foolery anyway? Probably not, but does that matter?

Obviously not, for the practice of amateur theatricals continued apace for many years. Here is how the record of 1952 described one such event;

> We were entertained by the Great North of Scotland Section to a drama entitled 'Crime on Ben Nevis', written by our Honorary Secretary. For three acts we were gripped by the adventures of the Caledonian Ladies Mountaineering Club. We had always thought our own adventures breath-taking enough but they were nothing compared to what was here revealed. The intrepid women of the CLMC push one another over cornices, glissade Gardyloo Gully in a one-er and are haunted in the CIC Hut – all in rhyme too. Pat Bell starred as the heroine, Annabel Alder, and Ikes excelled herself as the wicked Malvina Wyvis; they were supported by a talented cast: Mrs Jeffrey as the President, Agatha Eagach, Gill Mann as Jean Jingle, the novice; Janie Cameron as Flora Gillean, Ilse Bell as Sarah Sgumain, and Christina Macnair doubled the parts of accompanist and prompter. It was a howling success.

One early production was entitled 'Jacques the Spy' reflecting the exploits of the Scarlet Pimpernel. Somehow or other John Knox and Mary Queen of Scots featured in one, and Victoria and Albert in another. On the year of the first landing on the moon various members in heavy boots were depicted defying gravity by climbing down their routes instead of up, thus involving a re-definition of Munro's Tables. Even the names of the characters showed the degree of inventiveness of the authors, as for example, 'Bella Karabiner', 'Night-scented Stock' and the 'Common-tater'.

The annual AGM was not the only occasion on which the Club displayed its theatrical talent. New Year Meets had certain traditions that prevailed well into the 1970s and indeed, parts of which persist to the present day. Hogmanay and 'seeing in the New Year' were opportunities for more innocent entertainment. Many a new young member, on being initiated into the peculiarities of the Club, was challenged, delighted or embarrassed (depending on character) by being expected to participate in charades of an evening.

As the words chosen for acting out syllable by syllable usually referred in some way to the location of the Meet, this gave rise to some inspired performances. Take, for example, 'Killiecrankie'. Broken into its component parts it gives ample scope for a five act drama – 'kill', 'lie', 'crank', 'ee', followed by a rousing battle of Killiecrankie. Fortingal lent itself to a classical Roman theme, playing on the old legend that Pontius Pilate was born there. Sheets, togas, hand-washing, imbibing, and suitably ruffty-tuffty barbarians all featured in the programme. Such scenes inevitably encouraged high spirits, and the author somewhat shame-facedly recalls following others, who should have known better, in an attempt to do a hand traverse around the picture-rail of the lounge of the Tilt Hotel in Blair Atholl.

Such pranks are seldom seen now at New Year Meets. Maybe we have grown older and wiser and put away childish things; maybe the fact that we no longer foregather at hotels, but use our own Club huts or youth hostels, has modified our behaviour; or maybe the younger members are more dedicated climbers and commit the Hogmanay sin of Going To Bed Betimes For An Early Rise Tomorrow. It is to be hoped that some of us at least never grow up.

As early New Year Meets were always held in hotels, such as Crian-larich, Tyndrum, Inveroran or Kingshouse, a tradition was established of having a New Year dinner together on January 1st. It was to these events that the Honorary Presidents sent their renowned hampers with gifts of pheasants, turkeys and guinea-fowl. (Those were the days!) Even when younger more impoverished members stayed in youth hostels, barns, or shivered in tents, they still struggled into long skirts and party clothes to join the others in the hotel for the dinner. Although meets are no longer held in hotels, the custom of a New Year Feast persists, and whether in huts, hostels or tents, a typically gourmet meal seems to materialise out of rucksacks and food boxes.

Throughout the winter months Club members would foregather once a month in someone's house for slides and chat, and it was at these evening meetings that plans were hatched for adventures and expeditions. Initially the monthly meetings were held in Edinburgh, usually at the large doctor's house of the Inglis Clarks. Soon an active Glasgow section was flourishing. In the 1960s first mention is made of the evening meetings held in Christina Macnair's home. Christina lived with her two sisters, Barbara and Rachel in 'Benview', a large rambling stone house in the west end of Glasgow. Evening meetings at Benview became something of an institution and continued month by month for over 40 years.

Here members who had been to interesting and far-flung places would recall their exploits; trips to undiscovered corners of Scotland would be re-told; quiz nights held; navigation instruction studied, all illustrated with superb photographs and followed up by coffee and cake. Occasionally a guest speaker might be invited, but usually there was enough talent and to spare amongst the Club members. Sarah Mackay's home in Edinburgh fulfilled a similar function and, although venues have changed, winter evening meetings are still a regular feature.

Soon the Club expanded beyond the central belt and now the 'Outliers' - those living within a wide radius of Perth and Stirling – hold regular meetings in each others' houses. The Outliers' season always starts in September with a hilarious musical ceilidh. A Scott Joplin duet with two people struggling for a place on a single piano stool is a sight not to be missed. It is perhaps a reflection of the increasing mobility of society that the fastest growing group is now the Northerners, based more or less around Inverness, but extending from Skye to Assynt. (For some reason their original name of Peat Hags was rejected!)

In the summer months evening meetings take place appropriately enough on evening walks or on rocky outcrops, such as The Whangie, Traprain Law, Craig y-Barns, or Ben A' an. And nowadays of course all year round meetings on the various local climbing walls. Add to this garden parties, strawberry teas, and other social delights, and it can be seen that the Club was never short of social entertainment.

However the LSCC is indeed a climbing club and not a social club, and some of the best ceilidhs and parties take place in bothies, huts and tents. Of course in the early days of the Club it would be considered 'not quite the thing' for ladies to go sleeping in tents or roughing it in dosses. This did not in any way seem to restrict their activities, however, as the founder members regularly went on long walking trips over the length and breadth of Scotland. One has to assume that most of their accommodation was provided by those ever-welcoming wives of shepherds and keepers. And here of an evening would be ceilidhs in their original setting. Elizabeth Ranken playing her bagpipes in a crofter's kitchen must have been a star turn, and many must have been the songs and tall stories enjoyed around the fireside

Even as early as 1927 women were venturing into the wilds and sleeping in deserted cottages, although, as this account tells, not without some trepidation and anxiety. Two relatively new club members were spending a few days walking in the Cairngorms. Early on they discovered that the distance from Aviemore to the mountains is by no means short. The two were growing weary, with blistered feet, when they remembered hearing about an empty bothy in Glen Einich;

> It seems absurd to think of the fuss we made next day debating whether we should risk spending a night in it...We found the bothy at the lower end of the glen, in a corner between the Allt na Beinne Beg and the Allt na Beinne

Mor. Our hearts trembled lest the door should be locked or some other tenant be there before us, for we wished to make our first experiment alone. We were ungenerous enough to desire the peace and stillness and majesty of the hills for ourselves alone. Our fears were groundless, so we had a look around.

The bothy had two apartments – a stable containing an old pail and a rat-trap, and a living-room. The latter held a table, two benches, one short and very wobbly in one leg, an iron kettle beside the hearth, and some empty bottles (*bothies don't seem to change much with the years – Author*)

Having overcome their initial misgivings, the two soon settled in, and after a grand day out on the hills, recalled a happy experience;

Our last memory is a satisfying one. A fire burned in the bothy hearth, the kettle gurgled hopefully. The hole in the window was stopped up with brown paper. The two candles blazed away in bottles. The table, covered with a newspaper, was ready for our evening meal. An orange on the shelf looked gaudier than ever, the gay cover of a sixpenny packet of chocolate told of a land somewhere flowing with milk and honey. Rucksacks filled with heather stood ready to take up duty as pillows. Outside, old grandfather Allt na Beinne Mor growled remarks to whimpering grandmother Allt na Beinne Beg. Purring contentedly, we drew a bench closer to the fire and dozed.

By the 1950s women were bothying, dossing and camping with the best of them, so that someone commenting on the LSCC could say that they were 'nothing but a band of tinkers'. Anywhere would serve if caught out on the hills with night coming on. On one occasion Margaret Jones and a friend missed the bus back to Glasgow and spent the night in a railway signal box near Ben Cruachan. A comfortable doss apparently, its only drawback being the big glass windows all round which rendered it somewhat public for getting dressed in the morning!

A recent meeting of the Glasgow members of the Club spent some time reminiscing on how many things have changed over the years. Imagine for example: no zip fasteners; food carried in tins, nothing freeze dried or packed in plastic; sandwiches wrapped in greaseproof paper; 'delicacies' such as pemmican or dried custard; aluminium 'M & B' medicine tins for carrying camping food; heavy hemp ropes; gym shoes used for climbing rocks. How much easier it is nowadays to travel light.

The Mountain Bothies Association does a grand job of maintaining and renovating old bothies in many remote parts of Scotland and some of the best – and worst – nights out have been spent in these. On official Club Meets, bothies are not relied upon, in case others are already there, so tents are usually taken along as an alternative.

Perhaps the most miserable night out in a bothy that the author can remember was in Gelder Sheil on the way in to Lochnagar. This miserable doss was an old stable with no fireplace and nothing but a concrete floor. The snow was deep outside, the only meagre heat came from a single primus stove, and one of the party was sickening for flu. Nothing for it but an ignominious retreat to the Bank House in Braemar. Sheila Donaldson, a Club member, just happened to be married to the bank manager. Unfortunately the house was locked. However, desperate dossers were not to be deterred and access was gained via the kitchen window – not, alas, to the bank vaults themselves! Not that money had any priority over a warm bath and bed.

A ceilidh may be held anywhere. Brenda Roddy and Dot Mechan provide entertainment in Knoydart while on the Great Stravaig

Photo: Marion Boyle

This is Margaret Graham's description of some of the vagaries of actually finding a bothy in Glen Dessary.

As it was pouring with rain and plans to camp had to be changed at the last minute, we set off at about 9.45pm on the Friday evening in the gathering gloom towards Kinbreack Bothy. As there was a path I calculated it would take about an hour and a half.

The path vanished into the bog fairly soon. Despite being the end of June it was pitch dark and it continued to pour with rain! We carried on, staggering and squelching through the bog in the dark. There was a communal whoop of joy when we saw faint lights in the distance.

Our problems were not over yet; the burn beside the bothy was in spate and it was impossible to cross over at the stepping stones. It was agreed that the only way forward was to wade the burn. So at about midnight, we linked arms then launched into the raging torrent – which was up to the top of our legs.

You can imagine our relief at arriving at the warm dry bothy. Never let it be said that the LSCC are wimps! I have always said that to really appreciate a bothy you have to find it in failing light and pouring rain.

Frequent use is made of other clubs' huts and there are often reciprocal rights for their use. The SMC has several excellent huts; the Raeburn Hut near Laggan, the Ling Hut in Torridon; the Naismith Hut in Elphin; Lagangarbh in Glencoe; and perhaps most famous of all the CIC Hut on Ben Nevis, built in memory of Charles Inglis Clark, (the son of LSCC founder Jane, and brother of Mabel), who was killed in the First World War. The hut is well-situated in the northern corries of Ben Nevis right at the foot of all the classic climbs. It is a squat, solidly built hut, as indeed it needs to be to withstand all that severe Scottish weather can hurl at it. In a strong wind the windows have to be shuttered lest they blow in and the whole hut shudders in the gale, but once the stove is

*Heather King
addressing the haggis
at a Blackrock
Cottage Burns Supper*

glowing and the kettle boiling a convivial atmosphere can prevail over wind and storm.

There was a less than auspicious occasion when the author was organising a meet at the CIC. It was the depth of winter and snow was deep on the hills. The arrangement was to meet at the hut itself on the Friday evening and the author held the only key. Fine as far as it went, but her car broke down irrevocably and there was no way of contacting the three Club members, this being long before the days of mobile phone communication. The author conjured up grim pictures of her companions struggling up to the northern corries in the dark and snow, only to find a locked hut, and there to wander blindly calling into the blizzard. She was a wee bit worried until inspiration hit. She called up the Fort William police and a patrol car duly turned up at the car park in time to avoid an uncomfortable night (and save themselves a rescue call-out).

Much has already been said about the warmth and conviviality of our own club huts at Blackrock and Milehouse and indeed it would be hard to better the atmosphere of a good ceilidh around the fire at either of these huts. Out come the musical instruments – penny whistles, bodhran, guitar, mouth-organs, even flutes – and rousing singing is enjoyed with varying degrees of tunefulness. Even the august committee meetings have been known to hurry through the business so that music, song and laughter can begin. Woe betide the chairperson who allows the meeting to drag on too late, and may the midges pursue anyone who raises AOCB at 11pm.

Since 1993 a tradition of Burns Suppers has been maintained with the celebrations alternating between Blackrock and Milehouse. In some ways the primitive nature of Blackrock lends itself to such festivities. The kitchen windows soon steam over with the simmering of haggis, neeps and tatties. Whistles and flutes pipe in the haggis in the absence of bagpipes; the haggis is duly addressed and cut up with implements ranging from ice-hammers to pitons. The table groans under food, the fire burns up brightly. Sage advice is given from the auld hags to the lassies anent the laddies, and then the music, songs and poetry take over. At some point Tam O'Shanter will be read with suitable dramatic effect. And how appropriate the Bard's words can be;

> The storm without might rair and rustle
> Tam did na mind the storm a whistle

Surprisingly enough it is often easier to get warm and snug in a tent than in a bothy or hut. When buying a tent most people's first consideration is its weight and its reliability in wild weather. Modern tents can be amazingly light and also amazingly small, so that a one-person bivvy tent is more like a cocoon encasing the body with little room for anything else. However, some public-spirited souls also consider the party-potential of their tents. Mary Lothian's tent, veteran of many an Alpine trip, became known affectionately as 'the Pleasure Dome'. The author's own tent, recently back from a trip to North Rona, was the only one big enough for partying. It became more and more noisome as bodies packed in and ate their meals and left their cans, so that eventually it became known as the 'Shag's Nest Restaurant' (anyone familiar with this bird's nesting habits will know just how disgusting it is). At any rate a tent with a sizeable porch is a boon to party-goers.

By now the reader should have a pretty good idea of the LSCC as a practised party animal. However, all these events are surpassed when the Club really puts its mind to celebrating Significant Birthdays. The Club's 21st Birthday was comparatively low-key in its celebrations, being marked by a larger than usual turn-out at the annual dinner. However, 'a delightfully refreshing atmosphere pervaded the whole evening, as though the Club, in reaching its majority, had started on a new and joyous lease of life.'

The 50th anniversary of the Club in 1958 was celebrated in fine style.

Mrs Jeffrey backed by the Lix Toll Boulder at the LSCC 50th Anniversary in 1958

Photo: Riona Barclay (LSCC Archives)

The club record described it as *'A memorable year. Comradeship, a spirit of achievement and co-operation between young and old was the keynote of its success.'* A Jubilee Dinner and Ceilidh was held after the AGM on January 25th.

> The Jubilee Dinner has come and gone – and what a good evening it was! As one recent member wrote to me: 'I only wish we had an excuse to have a similar celebration next year. Fifty years is an awfully long time to wait!'

As usual the dinner was followed by a dramatic presentation, which suitably enough took the form of an 'Anthology of the Club's doings' over the preceding 50 years. This involved narration and mime and was even accompanied on the bassoon and the piano. It must have been quite an extravaganza. Earlier in the year well-known photographer and climber, Ben Humble, had made a short film to celebrate the Jubilee. It was entitled 'Early Days' and showed three women climbing a mountain in long skirts, which were conveniently discarded on reaching the rocks.

No birthday celebration of the Club would be complete without returning to our origins – the famous Boulder at Lix Toll. Grizel Paterson composed an 'Incantation' for the event which was duly read out through a megaphone by the President, Mabel Jeffrey. Here follows an extract, fairly typical of the couthy style of parodying Scottish songs;

Ye veterans and ye youngsters
Ye gentle and ye tough
Pour now a glad libation
We can never thank enough
Never thank enough the Founders
O' the best Climbing Club of all
And the bonnie, bonnie Boulder
She's the Queen abune them all.

Be bolder now and bolder
Ye climbers of the Bens
What though you're getting older
Ye maun scorn the sodden glens
To the Boulder we owe being
And life and friends and soul
So we bless the bonnie Boulder
The Boulder at Lix Toll

Founder member Lucy Smith was then living in the Lake District and was unable to travel north, so 15 Club members went to visit her, bearing goodies to hold a Hut Dinner in her honour at Rawhead Cottage in Langdale. The weather was not in celebratory mood, as the following day one group climbed Pavey Ark in deluges of rain, while the others traversed Bowfell in a howling gale.

> At four o'clock most of the company drove through the spring verdure of Langdale to the Vale of Winster where Lucy Smith now lives in the old vicarage, a charming pink-harl house, part of which dates back to the 16th century. A most sumptuous tea awaited us. There were all kinds of cakes baked from Lakeland recipes and tea was served in the old oak-beamed dining room and drunk from Lucy's grandmother's Rockingham china. It was another delightful and poignant celebration.

Lest one is beginning to think that all the Club can do is eat, drink, and be merry (one might be forgiven), mention must be made of the Jubilee Meet at Fafleralp in the Lotschental in Switzerland. Eighteen members and guests attended and the highlight was the ascent of the Aletschhorn. The expedition involved carrying all their supplies for three days over the Beitch Pass at a height of 10,269 feet, thence descending to the Oberaletsch Hut. Next day the party traversed the Aletschhorn by the south and west aretes, one rope led by a guide, the other by Esme Speakman. It was by no means an easy undertaking with the descent of the west ridge involving some difficult ice-work.

The Jubilee year was then rounded off with a New Year Meet at Crianlarich Hotel; a return to the venue of 1909. Slides ancient and modern, club songs and stories, a white and silver star cake welcomed in the next 50 years of Club history.

Inevitably perhaps suitable libations at the Boulder featured in the celebration of the 75th anniversary of the Club in 1983. This time some of the more observant participants might have noticed an abundance of sitka spruce grown to just about shoulder height. This was to have future significance! The 75th celebrations were appropriately energetic

A Centenary demonstration of mountaineering clothing through the ages outside the Kingshouse Inn, Glencoe 2008. From left: Kathie Murgatroyd, Evelyn McNicol, Alison Higham, Helen Steven, Eilidh Nisbet, Kate Ross, Marion Boyle, Sarah Mackay and Margaret Graham

Photo: Rik Higham

for a climbing club. The fitness programme may even have commenced at the dinner in Killin on April 16th when the Club joined in dancing the 'Reel of the 75th Anniversary' arranged specially for the occasion by Katrina Dawson. (Instructions are available for those interested in Scottish Country Dancing)

However the real challenge came on June 25th when the Club planned to have members on 75 Munros in one day. The day dawned bright and early with Kate starting off procedures by reaching the summit of Cairngorm at 2.10am. By mid-morning 40 parties, made up of 60 members and 34 guests were bagging summits thick and fast. Sue Ross did six of the Ben Lawers range, transported to start and finish by Charles Jeffrey, grandson of founder, Mabel; Sarah Mackay and her daughters did the classic South Cluanie Ridge; even in New Zealand Tish Knutsen was climbing Mount Herbert in solidarity. So keen were they to succeed that the 75th Munro was reached by 1.21pm by Avril Walkinshaw accompanied by her seven year old daughter, for whom this was her first Munro. Of course they didn't stop at number 75 and actually a total of 119 were completed, the last one being Ben Starav ascended at 6pm by Lindsay Urquhart. All in all the total was impressive.

Events were being co-ordinated from Ann Winning's house in Aberfeldy and excitement and rejoicing grew as reports kept coming in all day long. Celebrations were in order. Katrina Dawson was shepherding a reporter from *The Scotsman* up Ben Vorlich and this is how he recalled the event:

> When you've spent your day tottering up and down only one 'Munro' before collapsing in a heap, the achievement of the Ladies Scottish Climbing Club looks as inexplicable as it is awesome. On Saturday, to celebrate their 75th anniversary, they aimed to scale 75 hills over 3,000 feet but instead managed 120 – with one member not only reaching her goal of 11, but throwing in four extra.

And his article goes on to describe very sympathetically the ethos which has been the Club tradition over all the years:

> Spend any time with the club and you find any images of masochists or viragos are quite misplaced: though their stamina and skill are not in doubt and though you need all-round ability on the Scottish hills to become a full member, there's nothing crazy or reckless about this group. Indeed there's an ethos that is unusual, if not unique, among prestigious climbing clubs.
>
> The 'spirit of rivalry' is actually outlawed in their constitution and caution is put forward as a virtue…Making 'love of the hills' rather than amazing feats a priority enables them to accommodate active members aged from 20 to the late 70s…It also means they don't look down – like many climbers – on walking in the Moorfoots or Pentlands.

And now we are 100. 2008 was the grand Centenary year and the Club was determined to celebrate in style. Festivities began appropriately enough at Hogmanay with a huge bonfire in the back garden of Milehouse. Margaret Graham dragging more and more bundles of combustible material was counter-balanced by Jeff Banks and John Higham prowling anxiously around the perimeter with buckets of water.

Of course the Boulder had to be re-visited. This posed rather a problem, as those little shoulder-high spruce trees had by now grown to a mighty and impenetrable forest. The search for the Boulder began in 2005 and everyone thought it would be an easy task to find such a mighty boulder even in the middle of a thick dark wood. As the due date grew ever nearer, the Boulder had still not been found and this began to look somewhat embarrassing for a Club of experienced navigators. Many hours were spent hacking through dense undergrowth and many dishevelled seekers began to despair, but at last in the autumn of 2007 by dint of some creative lateral thinking and much burrowing, the heroic Marion Boyle DISCOVERED the Boulder. Immediately trees were marked, map references noted and GPS positions fixed. All was well; the party could proceed.

And proceed it did. April 19th dawned sunny and breezy. From around noon cars began shuttling back and forth from Killin to the end of the excellent boardwalk specially built for the occasion by Jeff and Julia. A piper led the way through the trees and there in front, green, mossy, and massive stood the Boulder. Suitable drams were poured, toasts drunk, and then seven Club Presidents, past and present clambered up to line up for a photo. Pam, aged 92, was seated at the foot observing the ungainly antics. Someone suggested that a gap be left in the photo so that Pam, who was also a past President, could be digitised in. 'Nonsense', said Pam, 'Give me a hand. I'm going up there to join them.' Which with plenty of encouragement she duly did. Previous boulder songs were sung and new poems recited.

In suitably jolly frame of mind, all then repaired to a grand dinner at the Atholl Palace Hotel in Pitlochry where all danced the night away to the music of Freeland Barbour and the Occasionals. Indeed, observing the behaviour of some members on the dance floor, one wonders if the appellation 'ladies' is still appropriate.

May 17th saw a motley collection of women gathered at the foot of the Buachaille in Glencoe dressed in a varied assortment of period gear. Some sported long skirts, wide hats and elegant blouses; Alison Higham

Curved Ridge, Buachaille Etive Mòr, climbed in 'Old Style' with long skirts and hats in May, 2008

Photo: Rik Higham

was resplendent in tweed jacket, knickerbockers and genuine nailed boots; Evelyn McNicol sported the same cotton anorak that she had worn to the summit of a Himalayan peak in 1955; yet others were in the latest multicoloured lycra, hung about with racks of climbing aids. Some even had hawser-laid ropes slung over their shoulders.

The aim was to climb the Buachaille by a variety of rock routes clad in the clothes of the past century, and then to hold a party at the summit. Twenty-nine members and guests set off, and none went up the tourist route, all choosing rock routes of varying degrees of difficulty. Needless to say those hampered by long skirts chose Curved Ridge as being one of the easiest routes, and, as skirts awkwardly billowed around their ankles, hats slipped down at inopportune moments, and nails fell out of elderly boots, they came to appreciate some of the difficulties encountered by the founder members. Added to this were constant demands to 'Just pose there for a moment' – always at the trickiest spot. Altogether many routes were accomplished that day – D Gully Buttress, North Buttress, Curved Ridge and Agag's Groove to name but a few, and eventually all foregathered at the top, although a cold wind discouraged lingering. By tea-time a crowd of Club members had gathered at the Kingshouse to pose for group photos and enjoy the excellent photographic exhibition of the Club history.

For its main event of the centenary year, an expedition to Bolivia to climb high peaks was planned, and this highlight of the year will be described later in this chapter. However, the author, as President of the Club that year, felt really strongly that some kind of adventure in the Scottish hills should be part of the celebrations of a Scottish club. Following the example already set by other members, she planned a Great Stravaig. The idea was to begin from Glencoe the day after the mass assault on the Buachaille and spend the next three weeks back-packing through the hills, finishing up at a Club meet in Dundonnell. They would carry tents but would have the option of sleeping in bothies, and there would be occasional luxury stops at hostels or bunk-houses. It was designed to be as inclusive as possible so that folk could join the Stravaig for a day, a weekend, even a few hours.

After much poring over maps and consultation with others, a plan was agreed. The route began on the West Highland Way, going over the Devil's Staircase to Kinlochleven; then through to Fort William with a camp on the way. A lift to Glenfinnan took them to the real start of the wilderness. Glenfinnan, via Corryhully bothy, over Sgùrr nan Coireachan to Oban bothy at the head of Loch Morar; then over a high pass to Sourlies bothy at the head of Loch Nevis. From there into The Rough Bounds of Knoydart, with a night in the hostel at Inverie, over the pass to Barrisdale, out to the road at Kinlochhourn, then over into Kintail with a night at Ratagan Youth Hostel. Back into wilderness again with a camp near Iron Lodge, Bendronaig Lodge and out to Strathcarron.

Through the Coulin Pass to Torridon, along the side of Loch Maree to Letterewe, and so into the wilds of Fisherfield, finishing up at Shenavall bothy and out to the main road at Dundonnell, with a grand finale on top of An Teallach. Looking at the route it might be fair to say that it covered some of the best mountain scenery in Scotland and included everyone's favourites. The total distance was 222.5 kilometres and by the time a few essential Munro tops had been included, the total height was 11,055 metres. A truly epic trip.

In the end only two people completed the whole trip; the author herself and Marion Boyle, who, having just retired from 40 years of a really hard teaching job, was de-mob. happy. However, a total of 17 other Club members and guests joined in at various points over the course of the three weeks. Most vital of all was the back-up provided. Kathie Murgatroyd drove countless miles to link up at the various rendezvous points always with an uncanny sixth sense of exactly the right food and drink needed. Undoubtedly this knowledge of what was needed came from her own amazing achievement in 1982 of doing all the Munros consecutively using only a bike and her feet. Others too would meet

Marion Boyle at an idyllic camping pitch above Letterewe while on The Great Stravaig in 2008

Photo: Helen Steven

The high point of The Great Stravaig. Looking west from the summit of A' Mhaidhean, Fisherfield Forest, 2008

Photo: Marion Boyle

up with the 'stravaigers' en route and, oh, how wonderful these luscious strawberries and millionaire's shortbread and that welcome bottle of wine, or that bumper pack of 'compeed' for juicy blisters. In fact when the author's boots had practically disintegrated, Brenda Roddy exceeded the call of duty by actually swapping boots and thus saving the Presidential Feet.

Every expedition of this sort has its moments of heaven and of sheer hell, and this one was no different. A low point was probably the long pull over Bealach nan Daoine from Loch Morar to Loch Nevis. There was no track, the going was very rough, the rucksacks seemed to have a will of their own, becoming heavier and heavier, and the day was hot and very, very humid. Enough said!

The moments of sheer joy far outnumbered the hard times and will remain in the memory. The vivid blues and spring greens of the path along the shoreline from Barrisdale to Kinlochhourn; meeting a lone badger bumbling purposefully along a ridge on An Socach; camping between two lochs – one with a red-throated diver, the other with a black-throated diver; the canoeists who left money for us to have a drink at Inverie; the spectacular cliffs and views out west from the summit of A' Mhaidhean – these are just a few of the memories that will stay.

Scotland is indeed a land to treasure.

A Centenary Meet had to be something really special, so planning began as far back as 2005. Members were invited to submit their ideas to Sarah Mackay, and Bolivia, East Greenland, Patagonia and the Pyrenees were all put forward. Bolivia won the day and the next discussion centred around which area to go to. This proved very hard to decide with suggestions coming thick and fast and all passionately argued. Eventually it was agreed to have the main meet in the Cordillera Real from July 16th to 23rd. In keeping with the general ethos of the Club the area had to be reasonably accessible, with day walks, short treks, and peaks of varying degrees of difficulty so that all ages and abilities from the fearfully fit to the 'not as fit as I used to be' were catered for. Eventually Condoriri was chosen for base camp with Carlos Escobar from a local trekking company providing transport and camp supervision. There was even a mess tent on site and breakfast could be served at any time from 3am to 9am – luxury indeed! In the end 19 people committed themselves to the expedition; 13 members and six husbands or partners.

Then there was the business of acclimatisation. Even La Paz itself is the highest capital city in the world, so everyone planned to spend two or three weeks beforehand in a variety of exciting locations ranging from the Galapagos Islands, Lake Titicaca, Cuzco, trekking near Sorata or Illimani, and, of course, Machu Picchu.

Evelyn McNicol, at the age of 81, was delighted to be included and, with her husband Alan, they certainly made the most of their time in Bolivia. Starting with eight days cruising around the Galapagos Islands, they then joined Karin Froebel and Maris Buchanan for a week in Peru, including a visit to Machu Picchu, then crossing Lake Titicaca on a hydrofoil, before joining up with the main group at La Paz to travel up to base camp.

Mary and Jim Lothian, Sarah Mackay, Brenda Roddy, Dot Mechan, Eve and Chris Gilmore decided that actually following the Inca Trail and walking up to Machu Picchu would be a good way to get fit. Eve describes the journey.

> The 'flat' sections of the Inca Trail were 'Inca Flat', which is undulating! The most challenging section for me was a long persistent slope up to Dead Woman's Pass at 4,200m altitude. We were well laden, trying to get fitter for our Bolivian week. With our backpacks on I was amused to hear a group of young fellow trekkers describe us as 'obviously experienced mountain walkers'. Did that make us 'old' or merely 'experienced'?...A highlight for me were the views of Machu Picchu from the Sun Gate just as the sun reached the rocks and ruins. It is truly a World Wonder and to see it all in such a way is something I feel privileged to have experienced.

Later Alison and John Higham, Eve and Chris, and Fiona and John Hutchinson enjoyed some excellent days climbing in the Khara Khota Valley. After some days on easier peaks, the highlight came on their last day, on Cerro Jankho Huyo, as Alison Higham recalls.

> The big day! Breakfast at 5.00 and away soon after. Eve decided not to come and John Hutchinson and Chris would see how they went. In an hour we were at the col and after a short rest continued up to our gear dump. We picked up the gear and abandoned headlamps and anything else we could and continued

*Dot Mechan, Maris
Buchanan and
Brenda Roddy.
Summit of Tarija
(5320m), Centenary
Expedition to Bolivia,
2008*

Photo: Alison Higham

up to the snowline. The snow was rock hard as usual, so on with the crampons and ropes. Everyone going well, albeit slowly. In places the snow was
very uneven and it was difficult to get a rhythm but we continued following
the ridge wherever possible. There were two steeper sections, the second of
which gave me great breathing problems trying to front-point up, but suddenly
there was the top and there were Chris, Fiona and John waiting for us. We
had done it! 5512m!

Not so fortunate were Lizzie Potts and Marieke Dwarshuis who had
their climbing boots stolen from under the fly-sheet of their tent. A
painful two and a half hour hobble in stocking soles and they were able
at last to borrow one pair of trainers, but it was hardly an auspicious
start to their expedition.

Kate Ross and Margaret Graham also had their share of adventures.
They had decided to hire a guide and go trekking in the Illimani area.
All began well with an idyllic campsite at the foot of Illimani itself. The
first hint of trouble was when instead of the expected man with a burro,
two porters arrived. Not to worry; this was meant to be an easy day on
a good track. It soon became apparent that the guide had other ideas
and headed in the opposite direction, following a faint suggestion of
a track over boulder fields and stream washouts, and eventually crawling up steep scree and mine spoilings to reach a col at 5000 metres.

Over the next few days it became obvious that the guide was new to
the job and didn't really know the way and Kate and Margaret had to
take matters into their own hands. The climax came near the end of
their trip as they attempted a 'shortcut' through an abandoned mine.
With one head torch between them, they lowered themselves down wet
slippery rock through a hole which seemed to lead into the bowels of
the earth. The 'shortcut' was meant to take ten minutes. After one and
a half hours of slithering over wet mud, squeezing through slits in the
rock and inching down narrow ledges, they wisely retreated back to

Karin Froebel and Marieke Dwarsuis en route to Pequena Alpamayo (5370m), Bolivia 2008

Photo: Margaret Graham

welcome daylight. Altogether a nerve-jangling experience.

At last the Club and its guests all foregathered in Condoriri at a camp-site north of Laguna Chiar Khota. It was certainly a beautiful site, with fine mountains all around and plenty of walking and climbing to suit all tastes. Beautiful maybe, but being at a height of 4600 metres it was also very cold indeed, especially as the sun disappeared behind the mountains at 5.30pm and didn't reappear until 8 in the morning. Added to that constant wind and dust made it a rather uncomfortable place.

However this did not keep them from climbing. For Dot and Brenda this was their first experience of alpine climbing, and Maris had not done any for a long time. This account by Brenda of the ascent of Tarija

Fiona Hutchinson (front) and Sarah Mackay ascending Pyramid Blanca, Bolivia, 2008

Photo: Alison Higham

reflects some of their doubts and triumphs.

> We found base camp pretty tough. We were actually miserable at times thanks to tummy bugs and the cold. This combined with poor weather at times meant that we were quite limited in what we could build up to achieve. We'd been training for ages to get our fitness levels up to manage a big snowy peak but with the impact of altitude, sickness, etc. at one stage we wondered if we'd actually manage to do one.

> On the last full day Alison Higham led Maris, Dot and myself on a rope to do a mountain called Tarija. Dot and Maris were feeling a bit wobbly the day before, worried that it might be too tough. But you know what Alison's like – incredibly patient and supportive as was Jim, so we all gave it our best shot. It was flipping freezing – at the foot of the glacier it was -7.5°C at 7.15am and it was really cold until about 11 when the sun made it over the hill to where we were walking. It was a long plod, but we managed it. When we made it to the summit it was a brilliant feeling...Given that the day before we didn't know if we'd make it, it was brilliant that all of us managed and nobody cried! We were as high as kites for the rest of the day.

For many the highlight was climbing Pyramid Blanca (5230m). Leaving the campsite at 6am they reached the foot of the glacier by dawn and made up two ropes of three with Kate, Margaret and Alison in the lead, followed by Fiona, Sarah and Eve. Eve commented that with an average age of 60, they might be considered 'mature', but age notwithstanding they overtook a team of young Chilean men, who commented, *'If this is the older Scottish women, I can't wait to see the younger Scottish women in action on a mountain'*! Much encouraged they pressed on, with Alison leading up a band of loose rock and a last steep snow pitch to the summit, which only had room for one rope at a time.

The culmination of their time in Bolivia and Condoriri and their main objective was Pequeno Alpamayo, 5370 metres, a truly beautiful and impressive peak. Mary Lothian writes;

> The grade was about AD- with an impressively steep ice/snow ridge. Two ropes of 3 and 4 members made their way via the west-south-west ridge to the summit where we enjoyed stupendous views of Huayna Potosi, Pyramid Blanca and Cabeeza de Condor. The sun shone, everyone felt elated, the crack was good, the company great, and we had achieved our goal, What more can you ask of a day on the hill? What a day!

For most of them this was the end of the trip and they were heading home. However Alison, John, Jim, Mary, Margaret and Kate stayed on a little longer and had a magnificent two day expedition up Huayna Potosi, 6088 metres. Altogether it seemed a suitable climax for our Club centenary.

Perhaps Fiona's comments on reaching the top of Pyramid Blanca provide a suitable comment on why climbing with the LSCC is so special:

> All the elements that made it one of my most memorable days on a mountain were present – great companions, mutual support, beautiful mountains, reaching the summit, fantastic views and a safe return.

Thanks ladies!

11. Beyond the Next Horizon

SO WHAT OF THE NEXT 100 years? So much has changed in the climbing world and so much is still changing, sometimes almost imperceptibly over the years, sometimes with alarming rapidity, so that the old-timers are literally left standing.

Take transport for instance. It is a far cry now from the days when a chauffeur-driven car (complete with hamper of goodies) would arrive to collect weary climbers, although it sounds somewhat akin to the modern practice of using a mobile phone to order a taxi to the foot of a Munro. From being a rarity, the presence of cars at crowded car-parks often betrays an approach to a popular Munro.

Nowadays it is almost inconceivable to think of reaching the mountains without 'wheels', and yet 100 years ago the ways of approaching the hills somehow seemed more varied and exciting. Our founders used dog-carts, charabancs, steam trains on little long-forgotten branch lines, even paddle steamers on the lochs, and, of course, their own feet over many long approach marches. It is interesting to note that, whereas during World War I access to the hills was not unduly curtailed, World War II saw petrol rationing and a greater dependence on cars. These comments from the Club Record of 1940 could be prophetic for our present oil-hungry world.

> The motor is now such an adjunct to mountaineering and the plight of the petrol-less climber so sad, that one wonders if a catastrophe were needed to bring climbers back to the joys of walking, and to an appreciation of those who, in former days, attained the most remote peaks afoot.

The next 100 years may see some fairly drastic changes in our pattern of access to the hills if petrol-fuelled car use becomes increasingly prohibitive. Already some experimental Public Transport meets have been organised in the Club, and car-sharing has become a much more conscious norm. Along with this has come a growing feeling of responsibility towards the environment, and part of our centenary celebrations recognised this by organising two conservation work weekends with the National Trust for Scotland in Glencoe.

Cheap air fares too may become a thing of the past. In recent years the world has indeed shrunk and it has become possible and affordable to go to the Alps at least once a year; to plan wonderful trekking in the Himalaya, South America or even the Poles; to go ski-touring in Norway or Canada or the US. Rock climbing in Corsica, Spain, Cyprus or Jordan is increasingly popular, free from the curse of midges, and blessed with sun-warmed rock. Will such trips become expensive treats in the future, and may this bring the Club back full circle to re-discovering Scotland as an exciting playground? In some ways this kind of exploration of Scottish possibilities was part of the inspiration behind the Centenary Stravaig.

So many unknowns. Will climate change mean that we can no longer enjoy ice-climbing in Scotland? Will competition climbing in leisure centres and crags overtake long classic mountain routes? Will exploration become so commercialised that the far-flung corners of the earth

*Meall Mheadhonach
of Suilven from the
flanks of Caisteal
Liath*

Photo: Tom Prentice

can only be explored with trekking companies and guides? Will health
and safety regulations and a litigious culture make climbing a prohibited sport? Will the LSCC remain a women-only Club?

Who knows the answers to such questions? And indeed, do we really
want to know?

From my sitting room window I can see the whole panoply of the
Assynt hills, from Canisp, Suilven and Stac Pollaidh all the way south
to An Teallach and the Torridon giants. These amazing mountains are
reckoned to be some 3000 million years old, dwarfing a mere centenary
into insignificance. What a comfort to feel the strength and stability
of these ancient rocks, and how small and trivial are our doubts and
questioning in the face of such grandeur.

The mountains remain. How good it is to feel the buffeting of an
Atlantic gale, to explore the wrinkles on the rocks with the fingertips,
to feel the January frost catch in the lungs, to lie back in the pollen
heavy heather, and to feel the firm tread of bootfall on the homeward
track. The Scottish mountains are past, present and future joy.

And what of the Club? Who knows. All I can say is that I owe a huge
debt of gratitude to the LSCC for their companionship over the years.
What a strong, vivid, amusing, challenging, capable bunch of women.
My hope would be that this glad companionship of mountains and good
friends continues well into the next century.

Club Chronology

1907	Founding of the Ladies Alpine Club
1908	Founding of LSCC at Lix Toll Boulder
1908	First Club Meet at Crianlarich
1921	Founding of Pinnacle Club
1924	The first Glasgow members join the Club
1928	First Alpine Meet in Arolla
1929	21st Birthday celebrations and publication of first Club Journal
1947	Annie Hirst, first woman to compleat the Munros
1947	Blackrock leased for the Club
1954	Expedition to the Lyngen Alps, Arctic Norway
	Cynthia Marr, Evelyn Canrass, Betty Stark, Elma Wrench and Angela Hood
1955	First women's expedition to the Himalaya
	Monica Jackson, Evelyn McNicol (Camrass), Betty Stark
1957	Esme Speakman makes a first ascent of the south face of the Grand Cornier
1958	Jubilee Year celebrations
1963	Milehouse bought by the Club
1964	Anne Littlejohn first woman to compleat all the Munros and Corbetts
1964	Anne Littlejohn establishes a record time for the Greater Traverse of the Cuillin Ridge
1964	Betty Stark and Evelyn McNicol (Camrass) invited to join the Scottish Peruvian Expedition
1968	Eilidh Nisbet and Esme Speakman join the Women's East Greenland Expedition
1970	Ladies Scottish East Greenland Expedition (12 club members took part)
1973	Illicit ascent of Edinburgh Castle Rock
1980	Tuesday Walks start
1982	Kathie Murgatroyd first woman to do all the Munros on foot and by bike
1983	75th Anniversary – 75 Munros in one day (actually 119 Munros)
1987	Cynthia Grindley and Angela Soper make the first women's ascent of Old Man of Hoy
1994/5	Kate Charles and Alison McLure in Antarctic
1995	Revival of regular Alpine Meets
1996	Kate Ross climbs Ama Dablam
1998	North West Greenland Expedition
2000	Millennium Meet in Ladakh
2008	Centenary Year: Bolivia Meet; Centenary Stravaig; mass ascent of Buachaille Etive Mòr

Alpine Meets

1928; 2003	Arolla
1930; 1965	Chamonix
1931; 1960	Zermatt
1949; 2009	Pontresina
1958	Fafleralp
1962	Saas Fee
1985; 2002; 2001	Austria
1995	Lauterbrunnen
1996	Dauphinee
1997	Randa
2001; 2006	Saas Grund
2007	Pyrenees and Grindelwald

SCOTTISH MOUNTAINEERING CLUB
SCOTTISH MOUNTAINEERING TRUST
Prices were correct at time of publication, but are subject to change

HILLWALKERS' GUIDES

The Munros	£22.00
Munros GPS data sets – from SMC website	£10.50
The Corbetts and Other Scottish Hills	£22.00
The Cairngorms	£18.00
Central Highlands	£18.00
Islands of Scotland Including Skye	£20.00
North-West Highlands	£22.00
Southern Highlands	£17.00

SCRAMBLERS' GUIDES

Skye Scrambles	£18.00
Highland Scrambles North	£18.00

CLIMBERS' GUIDES

Scottish Winter Climbs	£24.00
Scottish Rock Climbs	£24.00
Ben Nevis	£21.00
Glen Coe	£21.00
North-East Outcrops	£21.00
Arran, Arrochar and Southern Highlands	£15.00
The Cairngorms	£24.00
Highland Outcrops	£17.50
Lowland Outcrops	£21.00
Northern Highlands North	£21.00
Northern Highlands Central	£24.00
Northern Highlands South	£24.00
Skye	£24.00
The Islands	£24.00

OTHER PUBLICATIONS

Ben Nevis – Britain's Highest Mountain	£27.50
The Cairngorms – 100 Years of Mountaineering	£27.50
Hostile Habitats – Scotland's Mountain Environment	£16.00
Scottish Hill Names – Their origin and meaning	£15.00
A Chance in a Million? Avalanches in Scotland	£15.00
The Munroist's Companion	£16.00

Visit our website for more details and to purchase on line:
www.smc.org.uk

Distributed by:
Cordee Ltd, (t) 01455 611185 (w) www.cordee.co.uk